Cædmon's Hymn

and

Material Culture

in the World of Bede

Medieval European Studies VII
Patrick W. Conner, Series Editor

Other Titles in the Series:

Volume I
Via Crucis: Essays on Early Medieval Sources and Ideas
Thomas N. Hall, Editor
with assistance from Thomas D. Hill and Charles D. Wright

Volume II
Hêliand: Text and Commentary
Edited by James E. Cathey

Volume III
*Naked Before God:
Uncovering the Body in Anglo-Saxon England*
Edited by Benjamin C. Withers and Jonathan Wilcox

Volume IV
Theorizing Anglo-Saxon Stone Sculpture
Edited by Catherine E. Karkov and Fred Orton

Volume V
Old English Literature in its Manuscript Context
Edited by Joyce Tally Lionarons

Volume VI
*Ancient Privileges:
Beowulf, Law, and the Making of Germanic Antiquity*
Stefan Jurasinski

Volume VII
Innovation and Tradition in the Writings of the Venerable Bede
Edited by Scott DeGregorio

Volume VIII
The Power of Words
Edited by Hugh Magennis and Jonathan Wilcox

Volume IX
Cross and Culture in Anglo-Saxon England
Edited by Karen L. Jolly, Catherine E. Karkov, and Sarah L. Keefer

Cædmon's Hymn and Material Culture in the World of Bede

Six essays edited by

Allen J. Frantzen

and

John Hines

West Virginia University Press
Morgantown 2007

West Virginia University Press, Morgantown 26506
© 2007 by West Virginia University Press

All rights reserved

First edition published 2007 by West Virginia University Press

15 14 13 12 11 10 09 08 07   9 8 7 6 5 4 3 2 1

ISBN-10 1-933202-22-X
ISBN-13 978-1-933202-22-8
(alk. paper)

Library of Congress Cataloguing-in-Publication Data

Cædmon's hymn and material culture in the world of Bede. / [edited] by Allen J. Frantzen and John Hines.
    p.   cm.   – (Medieval European Studies; 10)

1. Cædmon. Hymn. 2. Cædmon. 3. Bede, the Venerable, Saint, 673-735. 4. English literature–Old English, ca. 450-1100–History and criticism. 5. Latin literature, Medieval and modern–England–History and criticism. 6. Civilization, Anglo-Saxon. 7. Art, Medieval—England. 8. Christian literature, English (Old)–History and criticism. 9. England—Civilization—To 1066. I. Title. II. Frantzen, Allen J. III. Hines, John. IV. Series.
IN PROCESS

Library of Congress Control Number: 2007938838

Contents

Preface 1

Abbreviations 13

Material Differences: The Place of Cædmon's Hymn
in the History of Anglo-Saxon Vernacular Poetry
Daniel P. O'Donnell, University of Lethbridge 15

Literary Contexts: Cædmon's Hymn
as a Center of Bede's World
Scott DeGregorio, University of Michigan Dearborn 51

Cædmon's Created World and the Monastic Encyclopedia
Faith Wallis, McGill University 80

All Created Things: Material Contexts
for Bede's Story of Cædmon
Allen J. Frantzen, Loyola University Chicago 111

Cædmon's World: Secular and Monastic Lifestyles and
Estate Organization in Northern England, A.D. 650–900
Christopher Loveluck, University of Nottingham 150

Changes and Exchanges in Bede's and Cædmon's World
John Hines, University of Cardiff 191

Bibliography 221
Index 255

Preface

THE ESSAYS IN THIS BOOK use the nine-line poem known as Cædmon's hymn as a lens on the world of Bede's *Ecclesiastical History of the English People*. Cædmon, a cowherd who is given a divine gift, retells the great narratives of Christian history in the traditional form of Anglo-Saxon verse. An immense amount has been written about this episode, much of it concentrating on the hymn's significance in the history of English literature. Relatively little attention has been paid to what the story of Cædmon and his hymn might tell us about the material as well as the textual culture of Bede's world. The essays in this collection seek to connect Cædmon's hymn to Bede's material world in various ways. Each chapter begins with the hymn and moves from the text to the worlds of scientific thought, settlements and social hierarchy, monastic reform, ordinary things, and others. The connections we explore are not comprehensive, but should instead be regarded as a sampling of the material concerns Cædmon's hymn raises.

Bede, as all readers of the *Ecclesiastical History* know, presents Cædmon's hymn as a miraculous intervention into literary tradition. While making ambitious claims for the literary significance of the hymn itself, Anglo-Saxonists have generally kept their distance from the episode's miraculous elements. An exception is C. L. Wrenn, who wrote that Cædmon "had achieved the revolutionary miracle of applying to the new Biblical material the traditional aristocratic heroic metrical technique and the traditional heroic diction of pre-Christian times, with its formulaic vocabulary, which had been developed for the description of heroism in war." The wonder was not that "a herdsman would suddenly make poetry (since that would have been quite natural in the Northumbria of those days), but rather that an ignorant peasant should in a single night acquire the power and poetic diction which only years of absorption of inherited tradition and training could be supposed to have rendered possible."[1] Setting to one side the difficulty of how anyone might have "achieved" a "miracle," revolutionary or otherwise, we can see that Wrenn understood Cædmon first and foremost as a working poet, not as a figurehead. So squarely was Cædmon positioned in the technical tradition of Anglo-Saxon verse that Wrenn could move from the hymn and the miracle to an explanation of the Old English poetic half-line and its meter.[2]

Cædmon worked on the estates of Hild's monastery at Whitby. In the fourth book of the *Ecclesiastical History*, finished in 731 A.D., Bede describes how the cowherd, who had "lived in the secular habit until he was well advanced in years and had never learned any songs," would withdraw from feasts when the harp was passed and each guest was expected to sing. On one such evening, Cædmon retired to the cattle shed, where it was "his turn to take charge" of the animals. He slept and dreamed that "someone stood by him" who commanded him to sing. Cædmon replied that he could not sing and had for that reason left the feast. But the figure insisted, "Nevertheless, you must sing to me." When Cædmon refused, he was again commanded to sing, and this time he "began to sing verses which he had never heard before in praise of God and the Creator."

Bede supplied the text in Latin rather than Old English, and in a curious comment that has borne much scrutiny, went on to note, "This is the sense but not the order of the words which he sang as he slept. For it is not possible to translate verse, however well composed, literally from one language to another without some loss of beauty and dignity."[3] Cædmon reported his gift to

---

1   C. L. Wrenn, *A Study of Old English Literature* (New York, 1967), p. 37.
2   Wrenn, *A Study of Old English Literature*, pp. 37–40.
3   Quoted from *Bede's Ecclesiastical History of the English People*, 4.24, ed. and trans. Bertram Colgrave and R. A. B. Mynors (Oxford, 1969), pp. 416–17.

his supervisor, who in turn took him to see Hild, the abbess of the monastery. As a test, Hild's learned men read stories from Scripture to Cædmon; he returned the next day and recited them in verse. Soon thereafter Hild "instructed [Cædmon] to renounce his secular habit and to take monastic vows." He joined the monastery and spent the rest of his life composing poems for the edification of the faithful.

The hymn survives in a number of forms presumably written down after Bede recorded his Latin version. The Anglo-Saxon Poetic Records wrest the poem out of its narrative context (a fate visited on many other Old English poems, it has been noted) and give two versions.[4] The Northumbrian text is as follows:

> Nu scylun hergan   hefaenricaes uard,
> metudæs maecti   end his modgidanc,
> uerc uuldurfadur,   sue he uundra gihuaes,
> eci dryctin,   or astelidæ.
> He aerist scop   aelda barnum
> heben til hrofe,   haleg scepen;
> tha middungeard   monncynnæs uard,
> eci dryctin,   æfter tiadæ,
> firum foldu,   frea allmectig.[5]

This is the more familiar West-Saxon version:

> Nu sculon herigean   heofonrices weard,

---

4 See Fred C. Robinson, "'Bede's' Envoi to the Old English *History*: An Experiment in Editing," *Studies in Philology* 78 (1981), 4–19, also published as *Anglo-Saxon Studies*, ed. Joseph S. Wittig (Chapel Hill, 1981); and "Old English Literature in its Most Immediate Context," in *Old English Literature in Context*, ed. John D. Niles (Totowa, NJ, 1980), pp. 11–29.

5 Quoted Elliott Van Kirk Dobbie, ed., *The Anglo-Saxon Minor Poems*, *The Anglo-Saxon Poetic Records*. 6 vols. (New York, 1931–1953), 6: 105.

> meotodes meahte   and his modgeþanc,
> weorc wuldorfæder,   swa he wundra gehwæs,
> ece drihten,   or onstealde.
> He ærest sceop   eorðan bearnum
> heofon to hrofe,   halig scyppend;
> þa middangeard   monncynnes weard,
> ece drihten,   æfter teode
> firum foldan,   frea ælmihtig.[6]

This translation by Stanley B. Greenfield and Daniel G. Calder accounts for some of the variations in the two texts:

> Now let us praise the Keeper of heavenly kingdom, the might of the Creator and His thought, the works of the glorious Father, how He of each of wonders, eternal lord, established the beginning. He first created for the sons of men [Nthn.] / for the children of earth [WS] heaven as a roof, the holy Shaper; then middle-earth, the Keeper of mankind, eternal Lord, afterwards made for men, [made] the earth, the Lord almighty.[7]

Assessments of the poem's significance as a revolutionary force in the poetic tradition must rest on the hymn's language, meter, and its literal meaning. Greenfield and Calder discuss a number of gaps and ambiguities in the text. They suggest, for example, that a missing but understood *we*, the subject of

---

6   Quoted Dobbie, ed., *The Anglo-Saxon Minor Poems*, 106. On the printing tradition surrounding the text, see Kevin S. Kiernan, "Reading Cædmon's Hymn with Someone Else's Glosses." *Representations* 32 (1990), 157–74, reprinted in *Old English Literature: Critical Essays*, ed. Roy M. Liuzza (New Haven and London, 2002), 102–24.

7   Stanley B. Greenfield and Daniel. G. Calder, *A New Critical History of Old English Literature* (New York, 1986), p. 229. The last lines would be better translated without the duplicated predicate, "afterwards made, the earth for men, the Lord almighty."

the verb "sculon herigean" in the first line, might be in apposition with *weorc wuldorfæder* in the third line: "Now ought we, the works of the glorious Father, praise the keeper."[8] Questions about language are also questions about the created world to which the hymn refers. Are "we" indeed "works of the glorious Father," or are the Father's "glorious works" there for us to praise? Does *teode* (third person singular preterit, *teon*) mean "to make" or, as it is translated elsewhere, "to adorn"?[9] What is the significance of formulaic variants, especially between *aelda barnum* ("the sons of men" in the Northumbrian version) and *eorðan bearnum* ("the sons of earth," West-Saxon version)? How do we inclusively regender both of these male terms? Is earth "made" for humanity or rather decorated for us ("adorned")?[10] Inquiries into the episode have ranged much more widely. It is not clear what the exact nature of the miracle of the cowherd actually was or whether, as P. A. Orton suggested, it represented a "clean break with the heathen past."[11] Some think the poet adapted existing formulas to new content, others that he merely attached a new vocabulary to them. We can understand why a poem of praise should be the first recorded religious verse in a given Christian vernacular, but we must also wonder how the poet's attention to divine creation is meant to focus the mind on human creativity, poetic and otherwise. Might, thought, and the ability to inspire wonder might be seen as shared by the Creator and his created alike.

Bede's portrayal of Cædmon's miraculous inspiration has been used to foreground many questions about the Old English

---

8   Greenfield and Calder, *A New Critical History*, pp. 229–30.
9   *Teon* is translated as "to adorn" (without comment) in Bruce Mitchell and Fred C. Robinson, *A Guide to Old English*, 6th ed. (Oxford, 2001), p. 377.
10   These and similar questions are outlined by Greenfield and Calder, *A New Critical History*, pp. 229–31.
11   P. R. Orton, "Cædmon and Christian Poetry," *NM* 84 (1983), 163–70.

language and its history. The episode also points to questions that few readers of the text have asked. Bede's account forces us to ask how different realms of experience and hitherto separate, even contrastive, forms of cultural life could be conjoined in an exemplary tale whose point is not cultural life itself but rather the productive and virtuous progress of Christianity. This is a material concern on several counts. The story of the hymn's composition begins in a humble context, realistically sketched and framed by a recognition of the agricultural and social bases on which early Anglo-Saxon monasticism rested. As the essays gathered here seek to show, Bede then situates the narrative within broader historical, scientific, and theological schemes belonging to the world of Latin and ecclesiastical scholarship and to the cultural practices and traditions that surround them. These essays examine models of cultural change in which Bede and his work participated; these models, which underlie the miraculous transformation on which Bede concentrates, do not concern themselves primarily with theological (much less literary) questions. What was Cædmon's status and that of other workers in the monastery? How was their status changed (if it was) by this episode? What were the practices of animal husbandry in which the monastic estates were involved, and how were they connected to those of other settlements and to trading settlements? Within the monastery, what kind of school was run by the learned figures who became Cædmon's pupils, as Bede calls them? What was the cosmological framework within which these scholars would have understood Cædmon's account of creation? Faith Wallis sees Hild's insistence that Cædmon join the monastery as the most important fact of the episode.[12] What was the nature of Hild's authority as abbess over these men and the others? The story of Cædmon was designed to fit into the

---

12 For an especially influential discussion, see Clare A. Lees and Gillian R. Overing, "Birthing Bishops and Fathering Poets: Bede, Hild, and the Relations of Cultural Production," *Exemplaria* 6 (1994), 35–65.

larger purposes of Bede's writing. The new poetic tradition inaugurated by Cædmon presumably heralded change in the social, as well as the intellectual, life at Whitby.

In assessing these developments, the following essays pursue a variety of distinct but integrated disciplinary perspectives.[13] Indeed, it would seem that almost from the time that the disciplines of medieval studies came to be differentiated and to assert their distinctiveness—and, very often, the distinctive national character of their subject materials—scholars have been seeking to bring these disciplines into some kind of alignment.[14] This collection claims to break no new theoretical ground concerning interdisciplinary or cross-disciplinary work, although we believe that it does further this endeavor.

Existing interdisciplinary collections seek to identify the insights shared by various theoretical models of medieval studies and take what can be called the "complementary" approach. But recent thinking on interdisciplinarity has shifted from complementarity to difference, with scholars now identifying gaps between and among the perspectives and insights of various disciplines. An example within Anglo-Saxon studies is the debate on the function and form of the Ruthwell and Bewcastle crosses

---

13 Recent examples include *The Anglo-Saxons: From the Migration Period to the Eighth Century, an Ethnographic Perspective*, ed. John Hines (Woodbridge, Suffolk, 1997), and *The Construction of Social Identity in Anglo-Saxon England*, ed. Allen J. Frantzen and John D. Niles (Gainesville, 1997). Most such collections are long on literary investigations. Among attempts to theorize the problem of interdisciplinary work is *Speaking Two Languages: Traditional Disciplines and Contemporary Theory in Medieval Studies*, ed. Frantzen, a collection focused on Old and Middle English literary theory and criticism.

14 For observations on the relationship of medievalism to nationalism, see the introduction to R. Howard Bloch and Stephen G. Nichols, ed., *Medievalism and the Modernist Temper* (Baltimore, 1996), pp. 1–22.

between Fred Orton and Richard N. Bailey, which extends beyond the meanings of crosses to scholarly methods for classifying and recovering those meanings. Orton argues against scholarly methods that are committed to similarity; Bailey insists that those same methods can produce meaningful differences.[15] A lengthy review of this volume by Colin Ireland shows how even sharp debates over methodological differences can reproduce historical paradigms that simplify the character of the early English Church.[16] Another gap is emerging as archaeologists have moved away from the text-centered, and often text-confirming, models of a half-century ago and concentrated on "independent archaeological criteria for defining settlement character and status," a view that some see as alienating "historical insight from current archaeological studies."[17]

Either interdisciplinary approach, complementary or differential, has its limitations. The former tends to emphasize that distinct disciplines can reach similar conclusions and thus rein-

15   Fred Orton, "Rethinking the Ruthwell and Bewcastle Monuments: Some Strictures on Similarity; Some Questions of History," in *Theorizing Anglo-Saxon Stone Sculpture*, ed. Catherine E. Karkov and Fred Orton (Morgantown, 2003), pp. 65–92, and Richard Bailey, "'Innocent from the Great Offence,'" in the same volume, pp. 93–103.
16   Ireland's review of *Theorizing Anglo-Saxon Stone Sculpture*, ed. Karkov and Orton, is found in *Peritia* 19 (2005), 339–50.
17   The quotation is from C. P. Loveluck, "A High-status Anglo-Saxon Settlement at Flixborough, Lincolnshire," *Antiquity* 72 (1998), 146–81. The response is from a review of *Image and Power in the Archaeology of Early Medieval Britain: Essays in Honour of Rosemary Cramp*, ed. Helena Hamerow and Arthur MacGregor (Oxford, 2001), and specifically to Loveluck's contribution there, "Wealth, Waste and Conspicuous Consumption: Flixborough and its Importance for Middle and Late Saxon Rural Settlement Studies" (pp. 78–130). For Patrick Wormald's review, see *English Historical Review* 119 (2004), 160.

force rather than alter existing insights. The latter sometimes leads to another kind of conformity that juxtaposes canonical literary and artistic works to works from marginalized, non-elite cultures and groups. Neither approach, in the end, necessarily produces new insights into primary material. Interdisciplinary work has been promoted by a variety of theoretical approaches, including gender studies and cultural studies. [18]Rather than experiment with recent interdisciplinary theory, in its many varieties, contributors to this volume seek to advance cross-disciplinary dialogue by using a single text as a focus on Bede's world and the operations of material culture within it. These essays show how multiple, integrated insights into the signs and operations of the people and culture of Bede's time and place can emerge from close analysis of a single, familiar, textual core. The volume is designed to help Anglo-Saxonists compare methods and claims made within the disciplines of archaeology, literary and textual criticism, medieval science, history, and theology. The studies seek to produce new views of the hymn and its period and to explore the consequences of the differences these views produce.

Daniel P. O'Donnell's essay on the sources and analogues of the hymn shows the wide variety of narratives and myths in which the story of Cædmon is embedded. His analysis casts doubt on

---

18   Among other work, see Julie Thompson Klein, *Crossing Boundaries: Knowledge, Disciplinarities, and Interdisciplinarities* (Charlottesville, 1996), and Klein, *Mapping Interdisciplinary Studies* (New York, 1999), both offer helpful discussions of the history and concept of interdisciplinary work. *American Academic Culture in Transformation: Fifty Years, Four Disciplines*, edited by Thomas Bender and Carl E. Schorske (Princeton, 1997), examines disciplinary practices, with case studies, in economics, political science, philosophy, and English since World War II. Applications of interdisciplinarity are discussed by Lisa Lattuca, *Creating Interdisciplinarity: Interdisciplinary Research and Teaching Among College and University Faculty* (Nashville, 2001).

the long-standing assumption that Bede himself saw the episode as a radical transformation. Scott DeGregorio seeks to broaden understanding of the hymn paradoxically by confining his frame of reference to Bede's exegetical writing (as opposed to the context of vernacular poetry almost always chosen for the hymn). Placing Bede's *Ecclesiastical History* within the context of Bede's commentaries, DeGregorio emphasizes Bede's concern with monastic reform. Faith Wallis uses the building metaphors of the hymn to move outward from textual and literary-historical concerns to Bede's cosmography. Her essay demonstrates Bede's indebtedness to architectural metaphors and connects the hall metaphor of the hymn not only to Anglo-Saxon halls but to the encyclopedia of monastic scriptural allusions.

Turning to wider contexts for the hymn, Allen J. Frantzen studies the relationship of Bede's famous miracles to the material contexts of Book 4 of the *History*, showing how the everyday and the material are integrated into Christian subject-object relations and demonstrating how Cædmon's hymn comments on the partnership between sacred and secular things. Chris Loveluck situates the social spaces of Bede's narrative within the archaeological world of Anglo-Saxon England. He connects Bede's narrative to new views of Middle Anglo-Saxon England and shows how difficult it is to distinguish secular and monastic contexts—these being the very differences, it would seem, Bede took pains to disguise. John Hines concentrates on the role of change and exchange in Book 4. He underscores Bede's careful control of the vocabulary used to describe the cowherd's achievement and explains how the language of the episode points to the social structure of Anglo-Saxon monasteries at the heart of an expanding world of trade, exchange, production, and distribution.

This volume began as a panel involving several of the contributors joined at the International Congress at Kalamazoo in May 2005, a session suggested by the work and example of Elizabeth Ashman Rowe. The editors are grateful to Hoyt N. Duggan and

Preface

the editors of the Society for the Electronic Edition of Norse and English Texts for permission to reprint sections of Daniel P. O'Donnell's work. We also thank the anonymous readers from the West Virginia University Press for useful criticism and express special gratitude to Press director Patrick W. Conner for his guidance.

Abbreviations

BAR: *British Archaeological Reports*
CBA: *Council for British Archaeology*
CCSL: *Corpus christianorum, series latina*
CSEL: *Corpus Scriptorum Ecclesiasticorum Latinorum*
MGH: *Monumenta germaniae historica*
PL: *Patrologiae cursus completus*, series latina
TTH: *Translated Texts for Historians*

Material Differences:
The Place of Cædmon's Hymn in the History of Anglo-Saxon Vernacular Poetry

Daniel Paul O'Donnell

CÆDMON'S HYMN IS A SEMINAL POEM. Its text is among the earliest attested examples of sustained poetry in any Germanic language.[1] Its author is one of only three Anglo-Saxon vernacular poets for whom we have both contemporary biographical information and an identifiable example of his surviving work.[2] In Bede's account of the poem's genesis, we have the single most sustained discussion of vernacular poetic production and performance to survive the Anglo-Saxon period.[3] It is also the only account of a historical Anglo-Saxon poet whose life is known to us primarily because he could sing.[4]

In this essay, I examine Cædmon and his hymn in the context of its scholarly reception. First, I discuss a number of analogues to Bede's account of the poet and conclude that their differences are far more important than their similarities in understanding Cædmon's significance to his biographer. Second, I reevaluate modern arguments concerning Cædmon's place in Anglo Saxon literary history. Although he is often described as

---

1   See W. P. Lehman, *The Development of Germanic Verse Form* (New York, 1971).
2   See Daniel Paul O'Donnell, *Cædmon's Hymn: A Multi-Media Study, Edition, and Archive* (Woodbridge, Suffolk, 2005), pp. 14–19. The other poets are Bede and Alfred.
3   O'Donnell, *Cædmon's Hymn*, p. 3.
4   O'Donnell, *Cædmon's Hymn*, pp. 16–17.

daringly innovative, particularly in his use of epithets, I argue that both the poem and Bede's chapter suggest that he was in fact a very traditional poet who was valued primarily for his formal skill.

The Analogues

Perhaps because of a traditional sense of the poem's uniqueness, scholars have devoted an immense amount of energy to tracking down analogues to Bede's chapter. Approximately forty-five so-called analogues to the Cædmon story, and, with some overlap, perhaps fifteen to the hymn itself have been discovered since 1832, when Palgrave first pointed out similarities between Bede's chapter on Cædmon and the *Prefatio* and *Versus de poeta* associated with the Old Saxon *Heliand*.[5] While the initial grounds for the hunt were, as these examples suggest, classical and medieval Europe, twentieth-century researchers have ranged far more widely, finding parallels among the aboriginal cultures of Australia and North America, the Fiji Islanders, the Xhosa of Southern Africa, the lives of the English romantic poets, and Hindu and Muslim tradition. Not the least of the benefits to be reaped from a study of these analogues is the glimpse

---

5   Francis Palgrave, *History of England: Anglo-Saxon Period* (London, 1831), p. 341. The relevant texts from the *Heliand* are known only from printed sources, though they are usually assumed to be older than the *Heliand*. A comprehensive count is impossible, since the term "analogue" is used flexibly in the secondary literature and since scholars frequently propose analogues in passing in books and articles on topics otherwise seemingly unrelated to seventh- and eighth-century Anglo-Saxon England. Most known analogues are indexed in the work from which this essay has been drawn, O'Donnell, *Cædmon's Hymn*, pp. 191–202 . One exception is an analogue recently noticed by John D. Niles, "Bede's Cædmon, 'The Man Who Had No Story' (Irish Tale-Type 2412B)," *Folklore* 117 (2006), 141–55.

they offer into the material possibilities suggested by creation accounts and myths of innovation and transformation. These analogues, like Bede's story of Cædmon, range far beyond the literary in their significance.

The search for analogues often has been conducted with more enthusiasm than rigor. The idea that stories paralleling the Cædmon story might be found in cultures far removed from medieval Europe was first argued in a brief note by Aurner[6] and, more analytically, in a subsequent essay by Pound. Pound's observation that "[i]llustrative material" paralleling Cædmon's life and work "might be multiplied almost indefinitely" appears to have been understood as a challenge by subsequent generations of scholars.[7] In addition to discovering closer or more distant parallels to the Cædmon story in numerous and unexpected quarters, researchers have also managed to produce a variety of partial analogues to individual elements and motifs.

The exhaustive hunt for analogues to Bede's story was begun by scholars who were impressed by the mythic quality of Bede's account and who sought to demonstrate its lack of authenticity, either by finding its source or by demonstrating that its details were so commonplace as hardly to merit consideration as legitimate historiography. Rather than using the analogues to test Bede's accuracy, subsequent studies have tended to see the proposed parallels as opportunities for establishing the folkloric, psychological, anthropological, or cultural contexts within which Bede (or in some cases subsequent generations) understood his subject's experience and significance.[8] These studies

---

6 Nellie S. Aurner, "Bede and Pausanias," *Modern Language Notes* 41 (1926), 535–36.

7 Louise Pound, "Cædmon's Dream Song," *Studies in English Philology: A Miscellany in Honor of Frederick Klaeber*, ed. Kempe Malone and M. B. Ruud (Minneapolis, 1929), p. 239.

8 Among numerous studies that accept the possibility of a historical Cædmon, see E. G. Stanley, "New Formulas for Old: Cædmon's Hymn," *Pagans and Christians: The Interplay between Christian Latin*

Daniel P. O'Donnell

focus on the originality of the episode and ask how Bede might have transformed the materials he inherited. By uncovering and publishing many similar stories from around the world, scholars have established a substantial body of comparative material that can then be used to assess the cultural and archetypal influences within which Cædmon and Bede composed their respective works.

One result of this assembly of material has been the perhaps surprising discovery that very few of the supposed parallel narratives closely mirror Bede's account.[9] After a search spanning

> *and Traditional Germanic Cultures in Early Medieval Europe*, ed. T. Hofstra, L. A. R. J. Houwen, and A. A. McDonald (Groningen, 1995), pp. 131–48; Roberta Frank, "The Search for the Anglo-Saxon Oral Poet," *Bulletin of the John Rylands University Library* 75 (1993), 11–36; Allen J. Frantzen, *Desire for Origins: New Language, Old English and Teaching the Tradition* (New Brunswick, 1990); Jeff Opland, *Anglo-Saxon Oral Poetry: A Study of the Traditions* (New Haven, 1980); Francis P. Magoun, "Bede's story of Cædman: the Case History of an Anglo-Saxon Singer," *Speculum* 30 (1955), 49–63. Modern exceptions to this agnosticism concerning Cædmon's historicity include G. R. Isaac, "The Date and Origin of Cædmon's Hymn," *NM* 98 (1997), 217–28 and Klaus von See, "Cædmon und Muhammed," *Zeitschrift für deutsches Altertum und deutsche Literatur* 112 (1983), 225–33. See also Paul Cavill, "Bede and Cædmon's Hymn," *"Lastworda betst": Essays in Memory of Christine E. Fell, with her Unpublished Writings*, ed. C. Hough and K. A. Lowe (Donington, England, 2002), pp. 1–17.

9 The approach taken here has been criticized for its emphasis on literal and textual detail over more structuralist approaches to Bede's story (see Niles). The defense, however, lies in the nature of the scholarship under discussion: the great bulk of "analogue" scholarship has concentrated on finding and reporting specific and concrete parallels between elements in Bede's account of Cædmon and stories drawn from historical sources on the assumption that these similarities of detail are significant in

nearly two centuries, no sign of the many similar traditions, so often and so confidently predicted in early analogue studies, has yet to appear. The gift of poetic utterance by a dream visitor, the key feature of the story in most modern readings,[10] does have numerous parallels in other cultures. Beyond this central feature, however, the analogues tend to show more differences from than similarities to Bede's account.

The extent to which the so-called analogues fail to parallel Cædmon's story in any great detail was demonstrated most convincingly by Lester. Setting out to "test the supposition that the Cædmon story is paralleled widely elsewhere," Lester broke Bede's account of the poet into twenty-four "essential" features against which most of the then-known analogues could be compared:[11]

> (*a*) there is a religious environment, (*b*) the subject is an old man, (*c*) he tends animals, (*d*) he is previously untrained in poetry, (*e*) his social awkwardness sets him apart from others, (*f*) he sleeps, (*g*) a certain person (*quidam*) appears, (*h*) the subject is greeted by name, (*i*) he is instructed to sing or recite, (*j*) he replies that he cannot, (*k*) the instruction is repeated, (*l*) the subject requests guidance as to what to sing, (*m*) he is told to celebrate God's works, (*n*) he sings God's praise in his sleep in verses he has never heard, (*o*) he adds more on awakening, (*p*) he immediately recognizes his gift as divine, (*q*) his gift is tested by others, (*r*) others recognize his gift as divine, (*s*) he

understanding Bede's chapter. Given the immense effort involved, it is not unreasonable to ask how close (or useful) this approach and the proposed parallels actually are. As I demonstrate below, the research, taken on its own terms, is useful, though not perhaps in the way originally intended.

10 See Kevin S. Kiernan, "Reading Cædmon's Hymn with Someone Else's Glosses," *Representations* 32 (1990), 158.

11 G. A. Lester, "The Cædmon Story and its Analogues," *Neophilologus* 58 (1974), 225.

is supplied with new subject matter, (*t*) he produces pious and religious verse, (*u*) he produces his work after an overnight period of thought, (*v*) the verse is in the poet's own language, (*w*) it is of great excellence, (*x*) the subject becomes a great poet.

The results of Lester's comparison were surprising. Of the fourteen analogues Lester examined, only one, the story of Mohammed's Call, agreed with Bede's account in more than half these features—and even then only for a total of fifteen out of the possible twenty-four (63 percent). No other analogue agreed with the Cædmon story so closely, with the four next-closest stories duplicating nine points each (38 percent congruence) and most of the remainder only five (21 percent).

Nor are the differences between these supposed analogues and Bede's account trivial. A majority agree with Cædmon's story on four main points—that the subject was asleep immediately before receiving his gift (67 percent), that the gift itself involved the appearance of one or more visitors (83 percent), that he is instructed to sing or recite (83 percent), and that the verse is in the poet's own language (83 percent).

But other significant aspects are found in few if any of the parallels Lester examined. Cædmon's great age and low status, for example, are combined in no other story. While Valmiki, the sage to whom the Sanskrit *Ramayana* epic is traditionally ascribed, is old, he does not have low status: his great age is presented instead as a means of indicating, along with his wealth, high social position, and reputation for wisdom, the reason why he was found to be particularly suited for the task.[12]

Parallels to Cædmon's initial refusal to sing, likewise, are found in only two of the proposed analogues: St. Dunstan and Mohammed's Call. Only in the latter does the protagonist request guidance in choosing his subject matter or recite an explicitly religious text about creation. In only five stories does the

---

12 Lester, "The Cædmon Story," p. 229.

inspiration come to a subject who is said explicitly to lack any skill in traditional poetic genres.[13]

In contrast to Bede's account of Cædmon, a large number of other analogues portray their subject as a younger man who actively seeks out inspiration from his visitor, engaging in deliberate consciousness-altering exercises or otherwise encouraging the development of already-existing poetic abilities. The subjects about which these protagonists ask or are asked to sing likewise differ greatly. In one case (Abīd ben al-Abras), it is for inspiration in composing a revenge poem; in other examples, it is to compose tragedies (Aeschylus), Latin hymns (St. Dunstan, Godric of Finchale), or praise poems in honour of a great poetic predecessor (Hallbjörn). Moreover, Bede's account of Cædmon's inspiration appears to be unique in the nature of the test Cædmon is asked to undergo in order to prove his legitimacy. I am aware of no other analogue in which the protagonist is asked to demonstrate his skill by composing a new song to a text of his examiners' choosing without reconsulting his muse.

The failure of the analogue-hunters in their search for close parallels to Bede's chapter on Cædmon is doubly significant. As Ward has shown in relation to Bede's miracle stories, differences between Bede's work and broadly similar stories in other sources can be as revealing as the similarities.[14] On one hand, the absence of direct or even very close parallels to Bede's story of Cædmon suggests that he was not simply adapting a tale he heard elsewhere or cutting his account out of folkloric wholecloth. On the other hand, that so many stories agree with his chapter at one or more points provides us with a basis for sepa-

---

13   These are: *Hallbjörn, Heliand Poet, Melrose Monk, Mohammed,* and *Abīd ben al-Abras*. For details, see O'Donnell, *Cædmon's Hymn*, Note E, pp. 191-202.

14   Benedicta Ward, "Miracles and History: A Reconsideration of the Miracle Stories used by Bede," *Famulus Christi: Essays in Commemoration of the Thirteenth Centenary of the Birth of the Venerable Bede,* ed. G. Bonner. (London, 1976), pp. 70–76.

Daniel P. O'Donnell

rating what is common in Cædmon's story from what is unique or unusual. These material differences allow us to appreciate what Bede considered to be important in the story, and, just as significantly, to demonstrate what Bede *could* have done with his tale had he wanted to bring it more closely into line with other stories of similar types of inspiration known to him or current elsewhere in world literature.

Mohammed's Call

The most instructive place to begin such a comparison is with the story that, perhaps surprisingly, shows the closest similarities to Bede's account of Cædmon's inspiration: that of Mohammed's Call as told in the *Qur'ān* and associated Islamic tradition:

> One night near the end of Ramadan, when he was in his fortieth year, Mohammed was meditating alone in a cave. An angel in the form of a man appeared and commanded him to "Recite"! Mohammed answered, "I am not a reciter," whereupon the angel crushed him in an embrace, released him, and commanded him again to recite. Mohammed once more replied that he was not a reciter, whereupon the angel again crushed him an embrace. Releasing, him again the angel commanded:
>
> Recite in the name of thy Lord who created!
> He createth man from a clot of blood.
> Recite; and thy Lord is the Most Bountiful,
> He who hath taught by the pen,
> Taught man what he knew not.
>
> Mohammed recited these words, and, after the angel vanished, fled the cave. But as he was running away an angel filled the sky and reassured him, saying, "O Mohammed, thou are the Messenger of God, and I am Gabriel." Mohammed ran to

his wife and told her what had happened. She in turn went to her cousin Waraqah. "Holy! Holy!," said the blind old man. "By Him in whose hand is the soul of Waraqah, there hath come unto Mohammed the greatest Nāmūs, even he that would come unto Moses. Verily Mohammed is the Prophet of this people. Bid him rest assured."

When Mohammed returned to the cave, he had a second revelation: "Nūn. By the pen, and by that which they write, no madman art thou, through the grace of thy Lord unto thee, and thine shall be a meed unfailing, and verily of an immense magnitude is thy nature." After a period of silence extending over many years, Mohammed's mission began in earnest with his third revelation, later recorded as the 93rd Sura:

> By the morning brightness, and by the night when it is still, thy Lord hath not forsaken thee nor doth He hate thee, and the last shall be better for thee than the first, and thy Lord shall give and give unto thee, and thou shalt be satisfied. Hath He not found thee an orphan and sheltered thee, and found thee astray and guided thee, and found thee needy and enriched thee? So for the orphan, oppress him not, and for the beggar, repel him not, and for the bountiful grace of thy Lord, proclaim it![15]

The similarities between this story and Bede's account of Cædmon have been noted by a number of scholars.[16] The stories' narratives follow almost identical patterns until after the protagonists' first performances. Their subject is an apparently illiterate man who is asked to perform in some way by an un-

15 This account has been paraphrased and shortened from that found in Martin Lings, *Muhammad: His Life Based on the Earliest Sources* (New York, 1983, rev. ed. 2006).

16 Zacharias P. Thundy, "The *Qur'ān*: Source or Analogue of Bede's Cædmon Story?" *Islamic Culture* 63 (1989), 105–10; see also von See, "Cædmon und Muhammed."

announced and (initially at least) unrecognized interlocutor.[17] Both men are approached by their visitor while they are in a particularly receptive state: while dreaming in the case of Cædmon; during a meditative retreat in that of Mohammed. The interlocutor repeats his request several times in both stories, and is rebuffed at least once by each man—although Mohammed, who refuses to recite three times, is far more steadfast than Cædmon, who asks for advice on what he should sing immediately after his interlocutor's second request. In both cases the conversation ends with the interlocutor indicating the material that is to be performed. In the story of Cædmon's Inspiration, the interlocutor provides the subject about which the herdsman is to sing; in that of Mohammed's Call, Gabriel provides both the subject and the text Mohammed is to recite. Both protagonists conclude their performances by committing this first text to memory. Finally, both men tell the story of their vision to a close associate as soon as they are able (Cædmon tells his reeve; Mohammed tells his wife), who then passes the story on to a person of higher authority for authentication (the Abbess Hild and her counsellors in the case of Cædmon; the wise old Waraqah in that of Mohammed).

The differences between the stories, however, are as significant as their similarities. Where in Bede's account Cædmon is certain almost immediately that his vision represents a true and exceptional gift from God, Mohammed is, initially at least, far less sure and requires frequent reassurance: first from the archangel Gabriel on the slopes of Ḥirā', later from his wife Khadījah and her cousin Waraqah (both indirectly via Khadījah

---

17 Bede makes no mention of Cædmon's literacy, though the poet is usually assumed, on historical grounds, to be illiterate. In the *Qur'ān*, Mohammed is frequently described as the *ummî*, "unlettered," prophet though there is debate as to the precise implications of the term in context and the extent of the Prophet's literacy; see Karen Armstrong, *Muhammad: A Biography of the Prophet* (San Francisco, 1992), p. 88.

Material Differences

and later in person), and finally from God himself via the next two revelations.

The reception the subjects receive after their initial revelation is also quite different. As Bede notes, Cædmon is accepted into Hild's monastery and set to work composing sacred songs and scriptural translations after a brief test of his abilities (4.24, pp. 418–19). His success as a propagandist, moreover, is equally immediate. Bede reports twice that Cædmon's singing excites his audience to turn from sin and toward good works, and notes how even the monks assigned to teach him the sacred books were enchanted by the beauty of his song.

Mohammed, in contrast, while initially able to gather a small group of disciples, and, of course, ultimately become the leader of a significant religious, political, and military force, nevertheless both keeps his gift relatively quiet in the first few years of his revelation and suffers ill-treatment, exile, and war, as Waraqah predicted.

The most important difference between the two tales, for our purposes, lies in the precise nature of the gift each man receives in his vision. In Cædmon's case, the gift is that of poetic inspiration: his visitor commissions him to compose a song about creation rather than to perform a pre-existing text. Nothing about Cædmon's subsequent career suggests he ever needs to consult with his interlocutor again. He adds more material of his own invention to his original song the morning after his vision, and, without additional help, he is able for the rest of his life to translate "whatever he learned from the holy Scriptures by means of interpreters, . . . quickly . . . into extremely delightful and moving poetry, in English, which was his own tongue" ("quicquid ex diuinis litteris per interpretes disceret, . . . post pusillum uerbis poeticis maxima suauitate et conpunctione conpositis in sua, id est Anglorum, lingua," 4.24, pp. 414–15). This emphasis on Cædmon's ability to compose is reflected in the test set by Hild and her counsellors; while they question him about his dream and visitor, they accept him into the monastery only after he proves himself able to compose a new poem on a subject of his examiners' own choosing.

In Mohammed's case, the gift received is that of revelation. While Mohammed's work does require considerable effort and interpretative skill, he is himself not responsible for the content of the messages he recites. It is indeed a tenet of Islam that the Prophet does not invent his texts. Mohammed is told what he must say; his gift is the ability to understand what these (sometimes very hard to decipher) messages mean. Mohammed, in contrast to Cædmon, is not required by his closest associates to perform or produce additional revelations after he reveals the content of the first.[18] Waraqah's initial comments on the divine origin of Mohammed's first revelation come immediately after he hears of it—second hand—from Khadījah. And unlike Cædmon, Mohammed must endure an initial dry spell. Although a second reassuring message comes to him almost immediately (Sura 68), he is forced to suffer through several years of silence before the revelations begin again in earnest with Sura 93.

Although the story of Mohammed is, in many ways, the closest analogue to Bede's account of Cædmon, many differences underscore the extent to which Bede's interest in Cædmon lies in the poet's ability to compose rather than in the miracle of his gift. Cædmon is not only a poet to Bede but is also a Christian poet and, in Bede's eyes, the best ever to attempt the composition of religious verse in Old English. Although, as George Kane first pointed out in 1948, Bede does not actually claim that Cædmon was the first to compose Old English religious verse;[19] the origins of vernacular Christian verse have been the subject of a number of other proposed analogues. None of these agrees

18 My thanks to Krista Hopkins for this point.
19 George Kane, "The Poetry of Cædmon," *Modern Language Review* 43 (1948), 250–52. The point has been revived influentially by David N. Dumville, "'Beowulf' and the Celtic World: The Uses of Evidence," *Traditio* 37 (1981), 109–60; see further O'Donnell, *Cædmon's Hymn*, p. 13, n. 8.

with Cædmon's story on as many points as that of Mohammed's Call, although one, the story of Ntsikana, an early nineteenth-century Xhosa religious leader and poet, comes close; a second, concerning Aldhelm, the Anglo-Saxon scholar and Cædmon's near contemporary, offers other useful points of comparison. Once again, the differences these tales show to the Cædmon story are as revealing as the similarities. In particular, Bede's account uniquely emphasizes the lack of continuity between Cædmon and contemporary vernacular poets. In contrast, the stories of Aldhelm and Ntsikana depend on the reader recognizing an essential connection between their subjects and the vernacular traditions they adapt. Although Cædmon's hymn is a very traditional Germanic poem in the formal sense, Bede presents it as owing little if anything to the techniques and habits of earlier poets. Aldhelm and Ntsikana, by contrast, are invariably portrayed as adapting existing techniques and forms for new Christian ends.

Aldhelm and Ntsikana

Aldhelm has been described as "the first English man of letters"[20] and "perhaps the most important figure in the history of Anglo-Latin, indeed of Anglo-Saxon, literature."[21] He knew most of the leading political and ecclesiastical figures of his day and had a profound effect on the development of English Latin literary life. He is the first Englishman known to have turned his hand to Latin poetry, and he remained an important influence on Anglo-Latin prose and verse style almost to the Conquest.

His importance to us, however, lies in his claim as a potential rival to Cædmon for the title of the first recorded English vernacular religious poet. Aldhelm, an approximate contemporary

---

20 Michael Lapidge and James L. Rosier, eds., *Aldhelm, the Poetic Works* (Cambridge, 1985), p. 1.
21 Andy Orchard, *The Poetic Art of Aldhelm*, Cambridge Studies in Anglo-Saxon England, 8 (Cambridge, 1994), p. 1.

of the Whitby herdsman, is reputed to have composed a significant and well-loved body of vernacular verse. According to William of Malmesbury's early twelfth-century *Gesta Pontificum Anglorum*, Aldhelm was a favorite poet of Alfred the Great, a king whose interest in and taste for vernacular poetry is well documented in contemporary sources. Unfortunately, and in contrast to Cædmon, no contemporary accounts or identifiable examples of this vernacular poetic production survive. One incident, however, is recorded both in William's history and, in a slightly different and less detailed form, by Faricius of Arezzo in his late tenth-century *Vita S. Aldhelmi*. In this story, Aldhelm is said to have used his abilities as a vernacular poet to compose Old English songs or poems in order to entice the laity back into church for his sermon. (Faricius leaves the genre and language of text unspecified in his *vita*, referring instead simply to Aldhelm's *eloquia*.) Given the dates involved, the tale, if true, must have occurred at approximately the same time Cædmon received his vision.

> The people at that time, being semi-barbarous and too little interested in divine sermons, used to run home immediately after the mass had been sung. And so the holy man positioned himself in the way of those who were leaving by standing on a bridge that connected the town and the country as if he were someone professing the art of singing. After doing this multiple times he earned the sympathy and the attention of the people. Once he had gained this, by gradually inserting scriptural phrases between the more light-hearted phrases, he led the people back to sanity; if he had considered acting strictly and with excommunication, he would assuredly have accomplished nothing.[22]

---

22 "Populum eo tempore semibarbarum, parum divinis sermonibus intentum, statim, cantatis missis, domos cursitare solitum. Ideo sanctum virum, super pontem qui rura et urbem continuat, abeuntibus se opposuisse obicem, quasi artem cantitandi

Material Differences

A second, and in many details, closer analogue to the Cædmon story comes from nineteenth-century southern Africa. Ntsikana was a member of the Cira clan in the late eighteenth and early nineteenth centuries and was famous among his people for his social accomplishments, which included composing, singing, dancing, and divining. In the early years of the nineteenth century, he underwent a visionary experience that left him with the gift of prophecy and an ability to compose Christian religious hymns in the style of traditional Xhosa eulogistic verse. He became the leader of a small Christian congregation that became known for its use of his hymns in their services. One of these, *Ulo Thixo Omkulu, ngosezulwini* or "Ntsikana's Great Hymn," was reported by Opland in 1977 to be still "perhaps the most popular hymn among Christian Xhosas today."[23]

Our knowledge of the relevant aspects of Ntsikana's life come from two main sources. The moment of his actual inspiration is narrated by his son and disciple, William Kobe Ntsikana:

> On the day that he was called by the Spirit, he had risen early and was leaning leisurely against the poles of his cattle-fold. When the sun rose, one of its rays smote him. Then he was heard calling to a boy who was attending the calves, "Do you see what I see?" The boy said, "No." Three times he asked him, and still the boy said "No.". . . Then he went to a *mdudo* (dance),

---

professum. Eo plusquam semel facto, plebis favorem et concursum emeritum. Hoc commento sensim inter ludicra verbis Scripturarum insertis, cives ad sanitatem reduxisse; qui si severe et cum excommunicatione agendum putasset, profecto profecisset nichil." See N. E. S. A. Hamilton, ed., *Willelmi Malmesbiriensis monachi de gestis pontificum Anglorum libri quinque.* Rerum britannicarum medii ævi scriptores (London, 1870), 5, 190.

23 For the translation, see Opland, *Anglo-Saxon Oral Poetry,* p. 118. The quotation is from Opland, "Cædmon and Ntsikana: Anglo-Saxon and Xhosa Traditional Poets," *Annals of the Grahamstown Historical Society* 2 (1977), 63.

together with other people. But on this day, when he stood up to dance, the wind arose. At last he sat down. Then later on he stood up again to dance, and again the wind rose. Thereupon he ordered all those of his household to accompany him home. And when he came to the river, he washed off the red ochre. And they wondered what had befallen him. . . .

On reaching home, he told them what had befallen him, and also that they must not listen to Nxele, who was misleading the people, but listen to this Thing that had entered him. "This Thing that has entered me enjoins that we pray, and that all must kneel!" Thereafter he held divine service at all times, and he was wont to put on his kaross of leopard-skins, and read therefrom.[24]

The story of Ntsikana's death comes from another source, the report to the Glasgow Mission Society for 1823 by John Brownlee. Brownlee reported that Ntsikana, "the chief person of the Kraal," had died just two years earlier. According to Brownlee,

> He composed a hymn in their language, which they still sing in the worship of God. On the day of his death (of which he appeared to be fully aware), although he was able to conduct the worship, he spake as one on the brink of eternity, expressing a calm resignation to the will, and an humble confidence in the mercy of God. He appeared deeply interested in the salvation of his countrymen, and earnestly entreated those around him, to meet death in its most terrific form, rather than to give up the profession of religion.[25]

---

24 Given here as translated by A. C. Jordan, *Towards an African Literature: The Emergence of Literary Form in Xhosa*, Perspectives on Southern Africa 6 (Berkeley, 1973), pp. 44–45. By "read" in this passage, we are to understand "perform." Ntsikana was illiterate and the leopard-skin *kaross* is a type of clothing worn by poets.

25 As quoted in Opland, "Cædmon and Ntsikana," p. 62.

Cædmon, Aldhelm, and Ntsikana

The similarities of these stories to Bede's account of Cædmon's inspiration are obvious. In the case of Aldhelm, the parallels are all to the middle part of Cædmon's story, in which Bede discusses the result of the poet's dream vision. While there is no suggestion that Aldhelm's poetic gifts are the result of any unexpected visitation—indeed, in the prologue to his *Enigmata* Aldhelm specifically rejects the idea that his works are dream-inspired[26]—his religious verse and performance as recounted by William and (more indirectly) Faricius does resemble Cædmon's post-inspiration poetry in a number of important aspects: it is of high quality; it has a strong effect on the behavior of those who hear it; and, in its combination of vernacular and Christian elements, it is portrayed, at least implicitly, as having been responsible for the production of a new and unexpected vernacular genre.

The story of Ntsikana shows more thorough parallels to Bede's account. Like Cædmon, Ntsikana is a herdsman who develops his gifts as a Christian vernacular poet in response to a vision, and whose poetry proves to be extremely popular. Also like Cædmon, Ntsikana dies like a saint: he is zealous in the performance of his religious duties and the defense of the faith, shows a concern for his own spiritual health and that of his co-religionists, and is said to have had a premonition of his death.

For students of Old English, the most important aspects of Ntsikana's story lie in his obvious value as propagandistic icon and source of inspiration for those responsible for spreading the tale. Ntsikana's first biographers see their poet as both an example of the success of the initial Christian missionary activity in the Eastern Cape and a sign of the likely future success of their own efforts. Just as the association of Cædmon with Hild presumably served as a further sign of her success and significance, Brownlee introduces Ntsikana's story as evidence of the

---

26 Quoted by Orchard, *The Poetic Art of Aldhelm*, p. 136.

on-going significance of the missionary work begun by himself and his predecessors in the Eastern Cape region. As Wieland has suggested, Bede's account of Cædmon's death is modeled consciously or unconsciously on the traditional saint's life.[27] In reporting Ntsikana's life and art, the European missionaries and their followers show themselves to be similarly influenced by hagiographic style and their conscious or unconscious recognition of Cædmonian elements in Ntsikana's story. The description of his death in the biographies of Kobe Ntsikana and Makaphela emphasize the poet's saint-like willingness to die in God's service. Brownlee's report to the Glasgow Mission Society presents Ntsikana, at least generically, as a new saint for a new mission. In the course of the twentieth century, the connection between the two became explicit. In his partisan biography of Joseph Williams, the founder of the Bantu mission, Holt describes Ntsikana's great hymn as "the first hymn in the Xhosa language, and [one that] will stand in relation to all subsequent literature in that tongue like Cædmon's Paraphrase to English."[28]

Despite these superficial similarities with Bede's account, the stories of Aldhelm and Ntsikana remain very different from that of Cædmon. Perhaps the most significant of these differences lies in the relationship they establish between the new Christian vernacular poetry and the culture from which it emanates. In his account of Cædmon's hymn, Bede goes to considerable lengths to establish what he sees as the lack of any direct cultural continuity between Cædmon and the more traditional, presumably secular, poets at the *conuiuium*. Although formal

---

27 Gernot Wieland, "Cædmon, the Clean Animal," *American Benedictine Review* 35 (1984), 198. But see E. G. Stanley, "St Cædmon," *Notes & Queries* 243 (1998), 4–5, and O'Donnell, *Cædmon's Hymn*, pp. 27–28. Although Cædmon in Bede's account is clearly saint-like, there is no evidence to support Wieland's claim that Cædmon was "venerated as a saint" anywhere before the Renaissance.

28 B. F. Holt, *Joseph Williams and the Pioneer Mission to the South-Eastern Bantu* (Lovedale, Cape Province, South Africa, 1954), p. 114.

criteria show that Cædmon's hymn is profoundly Germanic, Bede's discussion of the poet's methods of performance and composition establish the herdsman poet as what we might describe as an "anti-guslar." That is, Cædmon seems to be a poet whose training, performance, and career contrast at almost every point with those of the presumably traditional and secular singers he abandons at the *conuiuium*. The opening lines of Bede's chapter establish both that Cædmon had never learned any songs before his dream vision and that he could not sing songs of pure entertainment even after his encounter with his dream visitor. Cædmon's subsequent career, likewise, is implicitly contrasted with that of traditional singers at almost every stage.[29] While modern scholarship in oral and traditional verse performance suggests that poets learn their craft while young men by listening to more experienced and accomplished singers,[30] Cædmon is said to have been an old man who habitually left festivities when singing began in order to avoid being called upon to perform. For Cædmon's fellows, the singing of songs is a pleasant social event: they perform inside on joyful occasions, accompanied by the harp, and take turns singing to an audience made up of their peers. For Cædmon, however, poetry is a solitary obligation: he receives his inspiration outside, after he leaves the hall in which his colleagues are feasting. He is commanded to sing by an apparently otherworldly visitor who neither accepts his first refusal nor asks for a song after first singing something himself. Cædmon performs without instrumental accompaniment to an audience consisting solely of his interlocutor and, presumably, the animals he was watching over that night. Cædmon's training, as Fritz and others have pointed out, resembles not so much that accorded to a traditional ver-

29 Frantzen, *Desire for Origins*, pp. 139–144; Yu Kleiner, "The Singer and the Interpreter: Cædmon and Bede," *Germanic Notes* 19 (1988), 2–6.
30 See A. B. Lord, *The Singer of Tales*, ed. S. A. Mitchell and G. Nagy, 2nd ed. (Cambridge, Mass., 2000).

nacular poet as that which is given to a monk destined to become a scriptural exegete.[31] Instead of being given additional practice in the art of his native tradition, Cædmon is instead taught scripture, patristics, and church history, a training which, as Fritz and Day have demonstrated, produces a corpus of verse almost exactly in keeping with that prescribed by Augustine for religious scholars and Latin poets.[32] In suggesting that Cædmon was a better poet than his contemporaries, Bede emphasizes the differences between his and their careers, training, methods of composition, and performance.

In the stories of Ntsikana and Aldhelm, the connection between the new Christian verse and the secular culture that preceded it is essential to establishing the poets' appeal and legitimacy. Bede is careful in his account to distinguish between Cædmon's training and skill and the mechanics of his performance from that of contemporary (and presumably traditional) Anglo-Saxon performers. By contrast, William of Malmesbury's account of Aldhelm at the bridge, and accounts of nineteenth- and twentieth-century historians and missionaries responsible for preserving the story of Ntsikana, consistently portray their subjects as accomplished traditional artists who turn their already-acquired skills to the composition of Christian vernacular poetry in traditional styles.

31 D. W. Fritz, "Cædmon: A Monastic Exegete," *American Benedictine Review* 25 (1974), 351–63; Martin Irvine, *The Making of Textual Culture: "Grammatica" and Literary Theory, 350–1100*, Cambridge Studies in Medieval Literature 19 (Cambridge, 1994), esp. p. 433; R. J. Schrader, "Cædmon and the Monks: The Beowulf-Poet and Literary Continuity in the Early Middle Ages," *American Benedictine Review* 31 (1980), 39–69, esp. 66–68; Seth Lerer, *Literacy and Power in Anglo-Saxon Literature* (Lincoln, Nebraska, 1991), p. 33.

32 Fritz, "Cædmon: A Traditional Christian Poet," *Mediaeval Studies* 31 (1969), 335–36; V. Day, "The Influence of the Catechetical Narratio on Old English and Some Other Medieval Literature," *Anglo-Saxon England* 3 (1975), 54–55.

Material Differences

This is most clearly seen in the case of Aldhelm, who is understood by his biographers to be an accomplished vernacular performer before he turns his hand to Christian material. William reports that Aldhelm's secular songs were still current in his own day, and, as Opland notes, presents the story of Aldhem's performance on the bridge as a way, in part, of mitigating this apparently damning skill by showing it being put to good use.[33] Aldhelm's actual performance of this new Christian verse, differs from Cædmon's in that it embraces, rather than eschews, the pre-Christian traditions. Where Cædmon distinguishes himself in Bede's account by performing in a different location, to a different audience, and in a different style from his contemporaries in the beer-hall, Aldhelm is said by William to adopt the traditional garb, location, and, in the beginning at least, repertoire, of the professional minstrel in his attempts to lure his parishioners back to church.

Ntsikana, for his part, lies somewhere between Aldhelm and Cædmon. On the one hand, the story of Ntsikana involves a rejection of traditional culture. Having had his vision, Ntsikana finds himself unable to dance that night at the *mdudo*. In contrast to Cædmon, who was accustomed to rise from the *conuiuium* whenever the harp approached, Ntsikana clearly expected to be able to participate in the dance and indeed tries twice before giving up. Unlike Cædmon, Ntsikana allies his Christian verse with previous pagan tradition by adopting the garb and style of the traditional poet for its performance. Opland describes Ntsikana's great hymn as being "indistinguishable in style and technique from the imbongi's eulogies in praise of a chief" and notes that the leopard-skin *kaross* in which he sang is "a manner of dress characteristic of the Xhosa imbongi or poet."[34] There are no parallels to these details in Bede's account of Cædmon.

Taken together, these differences between Bede's story of Cædmon and the analogous accounts of other pioneering ver-

---

33 Opland, *Anglo-Saxon Oral Poetry*, p. 121.
34 Opland, "Cædmon and Ntsikana," p. 64.

Daniel P. O'Donnell

nacular Christian poets suggest that Bede did not see an essential connection between Cædmon and the traditional Germanic verse that preceded him. Cædmon, Aldhelm, and Ntsikana were all significant poets whose work appears both to have appealed to their contemporaries and served a propaganda function in the development of their respective branches of the church. But these poets differ in how their relationship to the preceding vernacular tradition is portrayed. For the biographers of Aldhelm and Ntsikana, the poets' significance seems to be that they represent an appropriation—either of traditional poetic forms by the new Christian faith or of the new Christian faith as a subject matter for traditional poetic forms. For Bede, however, Cædmon's significance appears to be far more revolutionary. Rather than seeing him as a new model for poets trained in the old ways, Bede seems to have understood Cædmon as a replacement—as somebody who does not so much appropriate as obliterate the old ways of doing things.

Cædmon's Hymn and Germanic Convention

The preceding examination of analogues suggests that Bede was impressed by Cædmon's skill as a poet and was interested in demonstrating how unusual Cædmon was as a composer and performer. Few modern scholars have shared Bede's enthusiasm for the intrinsic aesthetic quality of Cædmon's work.[35] Some

---

35 For a discussion of modern opinion of the hymn's aesthetic qualities, see L. Morland, "Cædmon and the Germanic Tradition," *De Gustibus: Essays for Alain Renoir*, eds. J. M. Foley, J. C. Womack, and W. A. Womack, Garland Reference Library of the Humanities, 1482 (New York, 1992), p. 347, n. 18; Morland reports that she "cannot find any printed praise of Cædmon's Hymn before that of Wrenn [in 1946], who may have shocked the audience of his Israel Gollancz Memorial Lecture when he declared that 'the more one reads it and allows it to become assimilated in one's mind, the more one feels it has qualities of balanced and rhythmic grandeur

have shown an interest in the question of Cædmon's distinctiveness, arguing either that his poetry developed primarily out of (non-native) Christian traditions, or, more commonly, that his "bold adaptation" of pagan Germanic conventions to Christian ends marks the beginning of a new vernacular tradition in Old English and the other Germanic languages.[36] But as we shall see, there is little evidence to support either claim. Structurally speaking, Cædmon's hymn is a very Germanic poem. It shows a deep debt to the same major metrical, stylistic, and formulaic conventions found in other, mostly later, verse texts in Old English and other Germanic languages. Stylistically, there is little evidence to suggest that Cædmon's verse played the innovative role commonly assigned to it in modern literary histories. Nowhere does Bede suggest that Cædmon was known for his formulaic innovation, and Cædmon's use of traditional Germanic epithets to describe the Christian God betrays no self-consciousness about his own supposedly seminal role in the development of native Christian poetry.

Perhaps the most significant aspect of Cædmon's adherence to tradition lies in his use of so-called poetic diction and poetic formulas. At least six of the poem's forty-two words belong to the Anglo-Saxon "poetic vocabulary" (the precise number varies according to the recension examined and criteria used for establishing this vocabulary): *metudæs,* "of the creator," 2a; *uul-*

---

which still have some poetic appeal.'"
36 Cædmon's significance to the development of (Christian) Old English vernacular poetry is a critical commonplace; the wider importance of his "school" among the Germanic speaking peoples is discussed in D. H. Green, *The Carolingian Lord: Semantic Studies on Four Old High German Words: Balder, Frô, Trahtin, Hêrro* (Cambridge, 1965), pp. 286–300. For the suggestion that the poet's primary debt is to non-Germanic poetic or compositional traditions see, among others, N.F. Blake, "Cædmon's Hymn," *Notes & Queries* 207 (1962), esp. 245, and D.R. Howlett, "The Theology of Cædmon's Hymn," *Leeds Studies in English* 7 (1974), 10.

Daniel P. O'Donnell

durfadur, "of the father of glory," 3a; *or,* "point, origin," 4b; *firum,* "for men," 9a; *foldu,* "(of) earth," 9a; and *frea,* "lord," 9b.[37] A number of other forms, *uard* and *dryctin* among them, are very common elements in poetic formulas, although they are also found frequently in prose. Depending on the specific recension chosen and definition used, between nine and fifteen of the poem's eighteen half-lines can be paralleled closely elsewhere in the Old English poetic corpus: verbatim in eleven half-lines: 1b, 2a, 2b, 4a, 4b, 5a, 5b (Northumbrian *aelda* and West-Saxon *ylda* recensions), 7b, 8a, 9a (Northumbrian *eordu* and West-Saxon *ylda* recensions), and 9b; and as representative of a clear formulaic system in another three: 3b, 5b (Northumbrian *eordu* and West-Saxon *eordu*), and 6b.[38] In some, more controversial formulaic analyses, the entire poem is said to be paralleled by

---

37 This list is based on the critical text of the poem in O'Donnell, *Cædmon's Hymn* and, with the exception of *uuldurfadur,* the vocabulary printed in M. S. Griffith, "Poetic Language and the Paris Psalter: The Decay of the Old English Tradition," *Anglo-Saxon England* 20 (1991), 167–86. C. L. Wrenn claims a total of "at least nine words which must have then belonged to the aristocratic heroic-poetic tradition—words of a diction which would not be in use among the peasants": he cites five of the six listed here (omitting *or*) and *eordu, tiadæ, modgidanc,* and *middungeard*; see "The Poetry of Cædmon," *PBA* 32 (1946), 287. Neither Griffith nor J. R. Clark Hall and H. D. Merritt, *A Concise Anglo-Saxon Dictionary,* 4th ed. (Toronto, 1984), identifies any of these last four words as belonging to the poetic vocabulary, and, indeed, all four are common in prose.

38 All figures drawn from Donald K. Fry, "Cædmon as Formulaic Poet," *Forum for Modern Language Studies* 10 (1974), 227–47, reprinted in *Oral Literature: Seven Essays,* ed. J. J. Duggan (Edinburgh, 1975), pp. 41–61. Fry claims to have found parallels for "every line" in the hymn (50), but some of his "systems" seem more strained than others. See O'Donnell, *Cædmon's Hymn,* p. 68 and note 10, for further discussion.

poetic formulas or systems found elsewhere in the Old English corpus.[39] This highly formulaic structure and use of poetic language go together: many formulas make use of poetic words, and participation in common formulas is no doubt responsible for the preservation of otherwise archaic terminology in poetry long after such words fell out of colloquial use in prose.[40]

The heavy use of poetic and formulaic diction in Cædmon's hymn is significant for two reasons. In the first place, the poem is among the earliest recorded examples of sustained vernacular verse in any Germanic language.[41] While the evidence of etymology and later poetic texts suggests that much of the poem's language belongs to a traditional poetic register, this traditional register is, in the case of several words and most, if not all, formulas, first attested in the hymn itself.[42] Thus, while most scholars assume that Cædmon is drawing on and adapting a pre-existing Anglo-Saxon poetic tradition in his work, his poem is, in many, cases our earliest evidence of this tradition.[43]

---

39 See Fry, "Cædmon as Formulaic Poet," and "Old English Formula Statistics," *In Geardagum* 3 (1979), 1–6, but note the objections in John S. Miletich, "The Quest for 'the Formula': A Comparative Reappraisal," *Modern Philology* 74 (1976–77), 111–23.

40 R. D. Fulk, *A History of Old English Meter* (Philadelphia, 1992), pp. 265–68.

41 Stanley, "New Formulas for Old," p. 139.

42 "Attested for the first time" in this context means "earliest appearance in the surviving written record." Other Old English texts showing these terms may be as old as or older than Cædmon's hymn, although they are found in later (usually much later) witnesses. Thus D.H. Green cites *Widsith* (known from the late tenth-century Exeter Book) for *frea* (*The Carolingian Lord*, p. 503).

43 A careful statement of the consensus position can be found in Fred Robinson, *Beowulf and the Appositive Style* (Knoxville, 1985), pp. 29–59, esp. 30 and n. 9. See also Stanley, "New Formulas for Old," pp. 139–40. Opland, *Anglo-Saxon Oral Poetry*, argues that Anglo-Saxon traditional poetic diction may in fact date only from

Daniel P. O'Donnell

The traditional poetic vocabulary and formulas of the hymn are significant for another reason as well. As Bede's account suggests, and as the internal evidence of its Germanic vocabulary makes clear, Cædmon's poem, while one of the earliest attested examples of traditional Germanic poetry, is not itself directly representative of the earliest Germanic tradition. As a Christian poem, Cædmon's hymn by definition transforms and adapts, rather than seamlessly continues, the pre-Christian tradition from which it presumably draws its vocabulary and formulas. This can be seen nowhere more clearly than in the poem's epithets for God. Two of the four terms for God in the last five lines of the poem, *dryctin* and *frea*, have their origins in pre-Christian Germanic lordship terminology; a third, *uard*, is commonly used in a non-religious sense to describe a "keeper" or "guardian." One of these terms, *dryctin*, is attested for the first time in any Germanic language in Cædmon's hymn; a second, *frea*, is found earlier only in cognate form in Wulfila's Gothic translation of the Bible.[44]

This means that our earliest knowledge of these terms, and hence the formulas in which they are found, is from their secondary metaphorical usage in Christian poetry. In describing God as a *uard*, *dryctin*, and *frea*, Cædmon is at best comparing the Christian deity to concepts traditionally applied to Germanic heroes and leaders. At worst, his terminology may consist of little more than dead metaphor—tags already so conventional as to be more or less drained of any symbolic force. Either way, neither the hymn nor most of the subsequent Old English poetic tradition gives us direct access to the precise connotations this pre-Christian vocabulary may have had for early Anglo-Saxon audiences. As Stanley points out, only twenty-two of the approximately 15,500 occurrences of *dryctin* in the Old English corpus—despite the word's clear pagan and secular origins—

---

the seventh and eighth centuries (pp. 95–97).
44 This is the implication of Green, *The Carolingian Lord*, pp. 287 (*dryctin*) and 503 (*frea*).

are intended in the secular sense of "lord, ruler, chief."[45] A similarly effective Christianization is also seen in the other Germanic languages. Green notes that most examples of traditional Germanic lordship and *comitatis* terms such as *dryctin* and *frea* in the cognate languages survive in Christian contexts—in most cases, in contexts that can be traced to centers of Anglo-Saxon missionary work or influence.[46]

Traditionally, this Christianization of traditional Germanic poetic language and formulas has been attributed directly to Cædmon and his "school."[47] Most accounts of the poem's composition and reception assume, therefore, that Cædmon's initial audiences would have found his use of pre-Christian terms, such as *frea*, *dryctin*, and *uard*, daringly novel. Smith writes that, in Cædmon's time, "phrases belonging to Christian poetry could scarcely have become conventional, as they certainly were in later Old English; on the contrary, the poem represents the beginnings of such a diction and its freshness and originality must have been felt a generation or more after its composition; no mere assembling of clichés would have called for inspiration, divine or otherwise."[48]

Whether Cædmon's verse really had this effect on contemporary audiences is open to doubt. While the poem does contain some of the first recorded examples of presumably traditional Germanic terminology in the new, non-traditional Christian sense, nothing in the use of this terminology in the poem itself, or in Bede's account of its initial reception, suggests that Cædmon's text was valued primarily for the novelty of its diction. As we shall see below, for all his emphasis on Cædmon's distinctiveness as a *poet*, Bede's praise of the hymn as a *poem*

---

45 Stanley, "New Formulas for Old," p. 138.
46 Green, *The Carolingian Lord*, pp. 286–87.
47 See Stanley, "New Formulas for Old," pp. 139–40, and Robinson, *Beowulf and the Appositive Style*, esp. p. 30 n. 9.
48 A. H. Smith, ed., *Three Northumbrian Poems: Cædmon's Hymn, Bede's Death Song, and the Leiden Riddle*, rev. ed. (Exeter, 1978), p. 15.

concentrates on its sweetness, order, and propagandistic value. The praise he puts indirectly in the mouths of Hild and her counsellors is primarily concerned with its smoothness, propriety, and faithfulness to its sources. No one in his chapter comments on Cædmon's role in the Christianization of previously pagan poetic diction. The hymn applies its supposedly novel vocabulary without any obvious recognition of the freshness of its invocation of God as a traditional Germanic lord. This lack of attention to Cædmon's role in the supposed conversion of Germanic tradition is all the more surprising given Bede's accounts elsewhere in the *Ecclesiastical History* on the process by which pagan monuments, rituals, and feasts could be adapted to Christian use. Opland has suggested that Cædmon's hymn is important because it demonstrates how an Anglo-Saxon scop can be not "the praise-poet of a lord, but . . . a praise-poet of the Lord."[49] It is difficult, to imagine a less vehement vehicle for such a message.

The strongest evidence against the traditional reading of Cædmon's poem as a bold Christianization of an earlier pagan Germanic tradition lies in the hymn itself, which seems to show no recognition of its supposedly transformative function. Cædmon's hymn is not the poem to turn to in order to discover what it is like to mourn the loss of a recent pagan heritage, or exult in the recognition that the new religion can provide its adherents with heroes more significant and dynamic than those celebrated in the old songs. If Cædmon is responsible for introducing terms like *dryctin* and *frea* in a religious sense, then he manages to rededicate this vocabulary with remarkable ease and lack of self-consciousness. He may describe God in terms appropriate to the Germanic hero, but nothing in his poem suggests that he is using these words in anything other than the stereotypical sense they acquire in later Old English Christian translations and prayers. His use of *uard* in 1b and 7b does contain some sense of "protector" or "guardian." His description of God the

---

49 Opland, *Anglo-Saxon Oral Poetry*, p. 116.

Father as *dryctin* and *frea* in 4a, 8a, and 9b, however, shows no evidence that Cædmon actually saw Him in terms of a traditional Germanic leader.

The Hymn and Other Old English Poems

Just how little emphasis Cædmon places on the pre-Christian and Germanic connotations of the epithets he chooses can be seen when the poem is compared to two works that explicitly explore tensions between pre-Christian and Christian world views. The song of Creation in *Beowulf* (a passage with many lexical similarities to Cædmon's poem)[50] uses the ambiguity inherent in Old English poetic diction and formulas to emphasize the distance between the full Christian knowledge of world history shared by the poet and his audience and the far more limited world view available to the pagan characters of his poem. This is particularly true of the song's double ending: after the relatively orthodox account of creation in 92–98 discussed above, Hroðgar's scop goes on in 99–101 to supply what a Christian audience would initially understand as a brief resume of prelapsarian life and the introduction of the *feond* responsible for bringing death into the world:

> Swa ða drihtguman   dreamum lifdon
> eadiglice,   oð ðæt an ongan
> fyrene fre[m]man,   feond on helle.

> So the men of that community lived happily, blessedly, until one being, a fiend in torment, began to perpetrate outrages.

As the next line of the poem ("*Wæs se grimma gæst Grendel haten,*" "That savage visitor was called Grendel") indicates, however, this Christian view of the song's conclusion is, in the context of the poem's narrative at least, incorrect. The identifica-

---

50 See O'Donnell, *Cædmon's Hymn*, pp. 48-49.

tion of Grendel as the *grimma gæst* makes it clear that the scop's song actually ended in 98, not 101, and that the happy retainers and the *feond on helle* of 99–101 are in fact part of the framing narrative of Hroðgar and Heorot. In forcing his audience to re-evaluate its understanding of the precise moment at which the song of Hroðgar's scop ends, the *Beowulf* poet emphasizes the distance between contemporary Christian understanding of world history, in which the significance of the underlying biblical history is recognized, and that of his pagan characters, who are doomed to repeat the original error unknowingly. As Robinson has argued in relation to other passages of the poem, this dual vision is part of a calculated effect whereby the poet allows his "devoutly Christian audience" to admire his pre-Christian heroes "while remaining fully aware of their [i.e. the heroes'] hopeless paganism."[51]

A second example of the possibilities inherent in the pre-Christian tradition but ignored by Cædmon can be seen in the well-known passage in the *Dream of the Rood* that describes Christ's ascension to the cross:

                Geseah ic þa Frean mancynnes
efstan elne mycle   þæt he me wolde on gestigan.
Þær ic þa ne dorste   ofer Dryhtnes word
bugan oððe berstan,   þa ic bifian geseah
eorðan sceatas.   Ealle ic mihte
feondas gefyllan,   hwæðre ic fæste stod.
Ongyrede hine þa geong hæleð,   (þæt wæs God ælmihtig),
strang ond stiðmod;   gestah he on gealgan heanne,
modig on manigra gesyhðe,   þa he wolde mancyn lysan.
Bifode ic þa me se beorn ymbclypte;   ne dorste ic hwæðre
                      bugan to eorðan,
feallan to foldan sceatum.   Ac ic sceolde fæste standan.
Rod wæs ic aræred.   Ahof ic ricne Cyning,
heofona Hlaford;   hyldan me ne dorste.

---

51 Robinson, *Beowulf and the Appositive Style*, p. 11.

Material Differences

> Then I saw the Lord of mankind hasten with much fortitude, for he meant to climb upon me. I did not dare then, against the word of the Lord, to give way there or to break when I saw the earth's surfaces quake. All the enemies I could have felled; nonetheless I stood firm. The young man, who was almighty God, stripped himself, strong and unflinching. He climbed upon the despised gallows, courageous under the scrutiny of many, since he willed to redeem mankind. I quaked then, when the man embraced me; nonetheless I did not dare to collapse to the ground and fall to the surfaces of the earth, but I had to stand fast. I was reared up as a cross; I raised up the powerful King, Lord of the heavens. I did not dare to topple over.[52]

In this passage, Christ is portrayed in terms strongly reminiscent of those used by Cædmon for God the Father: he is described as the *frean mancynnes*, "Lord of mankind," 33b; *dryhten*, "Lord," 35b; *geong hæleð*, "young man/hero," 39a; *ricne cyning*, "powerful King," 44b; and *heofona Hlaford*, "Lord of the heavens," 45a. But while the terminology is similar, the force of the language is completely different. The power of the passage in the *Dream of the Rood* depends on our recognition of the double meanings inherent in the traditional poetic terms. Where Cædmon's *frea, dryctin*, and *uard* have little more metaphoric force than the relatively bland equivalents for *dominus* used by the Old English Psalter poet, the God worshipped by the poet of *Dream of the Rood* is at once both *dominus* and *miles*, a new Christian type of hero whose triumph lies in his ability to conquer by embracing apparent defeat.[53]

The seeming lack of interest in the metaphorical force of the Cædmon's vocabulary is echoed in Bede's paraphrase and account of its reception in the *Ecclesiastical History*. At no point

---

52 Michael Swanton, ed., *The Dream of the Rood* (Manchester, 1970); translation from Bradley, *Anglo-Saxon Poetry*.
53 Griffith, "Poetic Language and the Paris Psalter," pp. 167–86.

in his chapter does Bede imply that Cædmon's verse was noteworthy for anything other than its metrical quality, organization, and propagandistic success.[54] The chapter's opening lines suggest that Bede saw Cædmon's poetry as praiseworthy primarily because it was well constructed, scripturally based, never frivolous or impious, and very effective in leading his auditors to turn their thoughts to heaven. His description of Hild and her counsellors likewise portrays them as being struck more than anything by the poet's musicality and ability to translate accurately into well-formed verse. When they give him their first commission, it is for a translation of scripture or religious doctrine into *modulationem carminis*, "metrical form." After they accept him into the monastery and set him on his program of translation, they appear to be most impressed by his poetry's "sweetness." The abbess and her scholars listen to the poet's "most melodious verse," and as Bede notes, "it sounded so sweet as he recited it that his teachers became in turn his audience" ("*carmen dulcissimum*," "*suauiusque resonando doctores suos uicissim auditores sui faciebat*," 4.24, pp. 418–19).

Slightly more ambiguous evidence is provided by Bede's paraphrase. As we have seen, the epithets Cædmon uses in his original Old English are all relatively common in a religious sense in subsequent vernacular poetry. They are, in the case of *dryctin* in particular, associated with stereotypical Latin translations. In Bede's paraphrase, however, the majority of these "traditional" epithets are either omitted or translated using Latin words that carry no sense of the original connotations. Thus *dryctin*, "the standing term for *dominus*" in the Germanic languages,[55] is not translated in Bede's paraphrase using the expected equivalent. Instead it is paraphrased using *Deus*, "God," on its first occurrence in 4a and omitted altogether in the translation of 8a. The pre-Christian lordship term *frea*, 9b, similarly, is omitted in

---

54 See Leonore Abraham, "Cædmon's Hymn and the *Geþwærnysse* (Fitness) of Things," *American Benedictine Review* 43 (1992), 334.
55 Green, *The Carolingian Lord*, p. 298.

Bede's translation, which nevertheless retains the second word in the half-line, *allmectig* (translated by *omnipotens*, "omnipotent")— an adjective that, as Robinson demonstrates, was common in both pagan and Christian contexts.[56] Only in the case of *uard* does Bede translate Cædmon's traditional Germanic terminology using a Latin word with equivalent connotations, albeit even then on only one of the noun's two occurrences: in 7b he translates *moncynnæs uard* with *Custos humani generis*, "guardian of human kind," a paraphrase that retains the connotations of the original vernacular text quite closely; in 1b, however, Bede's translation of *hefaenricaes uard* by *auctorem regni caelestis*, "author of the kingdom of heaven," abandons the sense of guardianship implicit in Cædmon's original formulation.

Bede's failure to translate Cædmon's supposedly most novel epithets with either their stereotypical Latin equivalents or with forms showing similarly striking connotations is open to several explanations. One is that the epithets themselves were too new, too unusual, and perhaps too daring at the time Bede set to work. In this view, Bede avoids translating *dryctin* or *frea* with a Latin term showing a similar sense of lordship either because the traditional equivalency between these words and Latin *dominus* had yet to be established, or because, like Bishop Wulfila who consistently avoids the cognate of *dryctin* (but not, interestingly, that of *frea*) in his Gothic translation of the Bible,[57] he found the comparison too extreme for his intended readership. A second possibility, however, is that Bede simply did not consider Cædmon's specific choice of diction to be very significant. In this view, Bede's failure to use what later material suggests to be the usual Latin translation for Cædmon's vocabulary comes not from any qualms about its novelty or suitability but rather from Bede's sense that Cædmon's choice of epithets was not the most remarkable aspect of his work.

---

56 Robinson, *Beowulf and the Appositive Style*, pp. 34–38.
57 On Wulfila, see Green, *The Carolingian Lord*, pp. 265–69.

Daniel P. O'Donnell

The first evidence suggesting this assessment of Bede's view lies in the poet's treatment of *uard* in 1b and 7b. The fact that Bede uses a Latin equivalent with similar connotations to Cædmon's original in one of the word's two occurrences demonstrates that Bede did not consider *this* form to be too bold for his intended audience. The fact that he does not use similar Latin terms both times, however, suggests that he did not see its repetition in Cædmon's Old English to be particularly important to the poem's form or meaning. In this light, the omission of an equivalent for *frea* and the translation of *dryctin* as *Deus* rather than *Dominus* might as easily be a sign that Bede did not find Cædmon's specific diction to be very important as evidence that he found it too bold.

Additional evidence suggesting that Bede was not overly concerned with the originality of Cædmon's diction involves the contrasting way he treats his use of poetic variation. Bede's translation, while treating Cædmon's supposedly novel diction in an inconsistent fashion, pays extremely close attention to his use of appositive variation: in paraphrasing the text, Bede removes or rephrases every single example of repetition among syntactically apposite elements in the poem.[58] This policy has its greatest effect in the last five lines, where Cædmon's vernacular shows the most ornamental repetition. The original text's two more-or-less synonymous verbs, *scop* and *tiadæ*, are collapsed into a single Latin form, *creauit*. The five syntactically apposite nominative pronouns and noun phrases, likewise, are reduced to two-and-a-half: in translating lines 5 to 9, Bede retains the first nominative reference in each clause (*he* [translated as *qui*], 5a; *uard* [translated as *Custos*], 7b), but eliminates their poetic

---

58 Cavill, "Bede and Cædmon's Hymn," argues that Bede also removes "structural alliteration" from the poem (11). As Cavill notes, however, Bede is less decided in his treatment of this aspect of Old English poetic practice: while Bede's paraphrase does not use alliteration as a structural principle, it does reproduce some alliteration for what Cavill describes as "decorative purposes" (12).

variants, *haleg sceppend*, 6b, *eci dryctin*, 8a, and *frea*, 9b. In contrast, Bede's translation of the first four lines of the poem renders Cædmon's relatively spare Old English nearly word-for-word. The only exception comes in the equivalent to 3b through 4a, where, significantly, Bede recasts the vernacular text in order to eliminate the only example of ornamental syntactic apposition in the Old English poem's opening lines, translating "*sue he uundra gihuaes, / eci dryctin, or astelidæ*" as "quomodo ille, cum sit aeternus Deus, omnium miraculorum auctor extitit" ("as that one, as the eternal God, remains the author of all miracles").

Bede's account of the poet Cædmon is by far the most detailed contemporary non-fiction account of poetic practice to survive the Anglo-Saxon period. Bede was not an eyewitness to the events he was recording, however, and the event's greatest value to modern scholars lies in what it tells us about how Cædmon was understood by his near-contemporaries. Taken together, the evidence of the contrasts between Bede's account and the analogous stories proposed by modern scholars suggests that, for Bede at least, Cædmon was a superbly accomplished vernacular poet who broke with previous vernacular verse tradition. In contrast to poets like Ntsikana and Aldhelm, who are described by their biographers as similarly prominent vernacular poets before and after they turned their attention to Christian verse, Cædmon is shown to have had no aptitude for or interest in the old ways of singing even after his initial inspiration. Where Ntsikana and Aldhelm appropriate the garb and techniques of the traditional singer for the service of the new religion, Cædmon learns to sing in a different way, in a different place, and to a different audience than the vernacular poets who preceded him.

Despite Bede's emphasis on Cædmon's uniqueness, the evidence of the surviving poetic corpus and cognate languages does not suggest that he was, in practice, particularly innovative from an aesthetic point of view. His poetry draws heavily on traditional Germanic language and forms without showing any evidence that it was Cædmon himself who first adopted this terminology to Christian ends. His verse shows very little self-consciousness about its supposedly novel formulations for God. Bede pays no special attention to Cædmon's use of formulas or poetic diction in either his translation or his account of the poem's initial reception. What Bede's account does suggest, however, is that Cædmon was a superb technician. His paraphrase of the original vernacular pays close, if negative, attention to the rendition of Cædmon's use of ornamental apposition; his description of the poem's initial composition and reception suggests that Cædmon was valued by his contemporaries for his skill as a versifier.

Literary Contexts: Cædmon's Hymn as a Center of Bede's World

Scott DeGregorio

THE STORY OF CÆDMON IS ARGUABLY the most famous single episode in all of Bede's writings, if not in all of Anglo-Saxon literature.[1] Indeed, so great is the flood of scholarship on this one purported event that we might forget that Bede wrote anything else, or that the episode constitutes only a tiny segment of a substantially larger work. Much of the commentary on Cædmon has, in fact, approached the story in isolation, devoting little space to its setting in the *Ecclesiastical History* or to integration with the rest of Bede's output. Scholars of Old English poetry, who have produced most of the research, tend to approach the episode in a reverse direction, using evidence from later centuries as an interpretative grid for it. Viewing the story as a putative origin for Old English religious verse, they have read it chiefly for the light it throws on the vernacular literary tradition.[2] In writing about Cædmon, however, Bede must

---

1 To quote one recent scholarly appraisal, "It is, assuming it is reliable, perhaps the single most important piece of contemporary literary history and criticism to survive the Anglo-Saxon period." Daniel Paul O'Donnell, *Cædmon's Hymn: A Multi-Media Study, Edition and Archive* (Cambridge, Mass., 2005), p. 3.

2 Seminal instances of this approach include C. L. Wrenn, *The Poetry of Cædmon*, Sir Israel Gollancz Memorial Lecture, *Proceedings of the British Academy* 32 (1946), 277–95; Francis P. Magoun, "Bede's Story of Cædmon: The Case History of an Anglo-Saxon Singer," *Speculum* 30 (1955), 49–63; and Donald K. Fry, "Cædmon as Formulaic Poet," *Forum for Modern Language Studies* 10 (1974),

have had rather different concerns in mind—concerns to be sought first, not in later English vernacular poetry, or in modern theories about it, but in his own Latin writings. As far as I know, the story of Cædmon has yet to be read strictly in the context of Bede's wider oeuvre. What I shall do here is attempt such a reading, and for this I have selected three closely related issues as my focus. I begin with Bede's attitude toward the vernacular, an infrequent topic in his oeuvre. Next, I take up his view of poetry. We should not forget that Bede himself was both a poet and an educator, and that, as a result of those roles, he would have certain ingrained assumptions about poetry, even if he did not always air them in his writings as overtly as we would like. As a final task, I shall attempt to connect both of these concerns to a preoccupation that Bede did wear on his sleeve, namely the alarm he felt over the deterioration of monastic institutions and the immediate effect he believed it would have on contemporary society. By placing the story of Cædmon in the wider context of Bede's treatment of these issues, we shall endeavor to see whether a different understanding of this famous episode emerges.

Bede and the Vernacular

Apart from the story of Cædmon, only two sources throw light on Bede's view of the vernacular. The first—which is, as far as we know, Bede's latest work—is the brief letter he wrote just months before his death to Egbert, who became Archbishop of York in 735.[3] Despite its brevity, Bede's letter is a supremely important

---

227–47, reprinted in *Oral Literature: Seven Essays*, ed. J. J. Duggan (Edinburgh, 1975), pp. 41–61. For a critique of this approach, see Allen J. Frantzen, *Desire for Origins: New Language, Old English, and Teaching the Tradition* (New Brunswick, 1990), pp. 135–48.

3 *Epistola ad Ecgbertum Episcopum*, ed. Charles Plummer in *Venerabilis Baedae opera historia*, 2 vols. (1896; reprinted as one volume, Oxford 1946). For an English translation, see Judith McClure

text for any approach to the larger corpus of his writings and the overall shape of his thought. Whatever else this text does, it gives us an unobstructed view of his contemporary religious and social landscape as perceived through his own eyes. The letter is a thoroughly occasional piece, prompted by the pressing dissatisfaction Bede felt over the troubled situation of the church in his native Northumbria.[4] In terms of form and purpose, it may best be described as an extended plea, a heated call in which Bede urges Egbert, his former pupil, to use his episcopal authority to resolve the problem. The extensive list of complaints that Bede goes on to deliver in the body of the letter, and the vehement rhetoric with which he expresses them, do much to put a rather different face on the conception of the saintly, detached Bede who, one sometimes hears, lived in a world of books and knew little of the world beyond the cloister walls.[5] Throughout

---

and Roger Collins, *Bede: The Ecclesiastical Historical of the English People* (Oxford, 1999), pp. 343–57, which I cite throughout. At the end of the letter, Bede states that he wrote it on 5 November 734; he died six months and twenty-one days later on 26 May 735: see Plummer's note, *Venerabilis Baedae opera historia*, p. 388.

4   Scott DeGregorio, "Bede's *In Ezram et Neemiam* and the Reform of the Northumbrian Church," *Speculum* 79.1 (2004), 6–9; and John Blair, *The Church in Anglo-Saxon Society* (Oxford, 2005), pp. 100–8.

5   See Patrick Wormald, "Bede, Beowulf and the Conversion of the Anglo-Saxon Aristocracy," in *Bede and Anglo-Saxon England: Papers in Honour of the 1300th Anniversary of the Birth of Bede*, ed. Robert T. Farrell, BAR 46 (London, 1978), pp. 32–95, who writes that "Bede's personal history cut him off from contemporary aristocratic society and its values, and buried him, from boyhood, in a world of books" (p. 62); and David Kirby, "Northumbria in the Time of Wilfrid," in *Saint Wilfrid at Hexham*, ed. D. P. Kirby (Newcastle upon Tyne, 1974), pp. 1–34, who sees Bede's life as being governed by "cloistered seclusion" (p. 3) and "his unavoidably restricted environment and limited experience" (p. 4). For a range of contrasting views, see now the essays collected in *Innovation and*

the letter, the primary target to which Bede directs Egbert's attention is the state of pastoral care in Northumbria. There are too many monasteries but too few active centers of effective pastoral administration—so few, Bede warns Egbert, that "it would take you more than the whole year on your own to go through them all and preach the word of God in every hamlet and field." Bede continues, "it is clearly essential that you appoint others to help you in your holy work; thus priests should be ordained and teachers established who may preach the word of God and consecrate the mysteries in every small village, and above all perform the rite of baptism whenever the opportunity arises."[6] Preaching, teaching, and the importance of the sacraments are staple themes in almost everything Bede wrote.[7] What is new

Tradition in the Writings of the Venerable Bede, ed. Scott DeGregorio, Medieval European Studies 7 (Morgantown, 2006).

6   "Et quia latiora sunt spatia locorum, quae ad gubernacula tuae diocesis pertinent, quam ut solus per omnia discurrere, et in singulis uiculis atque agellis uerbum Dei praedicare, etiam anni totius emenso curriculo, sufficias, necessarium satis est, ut plures tibi sacri operis adiutores a sciscas, presbyteros uidelicet ordinando, atque instituendo doctores, qui in singulis uiculis praedicando Dei uerbo, et consecrandis mysteriis caelestibus, ac maxime peragendis sacri baptismatis officiis, ubi oportunitas ingruerit, insistant." Bede, *Epistola ad Ecgbertum Episcopum* § 5, ed. Plummer, p. 408; trans. McClure and Collins, p. 345.

7   See Thomas R. Eckenrode, "The Venerable Bede and the Pastoral Affirmation of the Christian Message in Anglo-Saxon England," *The Downside Review* 99 (1981), 258–78; Sarah Foot, "Parochial Ministry in Early Anglo-Saxon England: The Role of the Monastic Communities," in *The Ministry: Clerical and Lay. Papers read at the 1988 Summer Meeting and the 1989 Winter Meeting of the Ecclesiastical History Society*, ed. W. J. Sheils and Diana Wood, Studies in Church History 26 (Oxford, 1989), pp. 43–54; and Alan Thacker, "Monks, Preaching and Pastoral Care," in *Pastoral Care Before the Parish*, ed. John Blair and Richard Sharpe (Leicester, 1992), pp. 137–70.

Literary Contexts

here is the emphasis he places on the vernacular as a necessary tool in this pastoral enterprise. The people, he insists, must be taught the *fidem catholicam*, especially as codified in the Apostles' Creed and the Lord's Prayer. In emphasizing the importance of these cardinal teachings for society's spiritual health, Bede recommends to Egbert specific linguistic directives:

> It is most certain that all those who have learned to read Latin will know these well, but the unlearned, that is to say those who only know their own language, *must learn to say them in their own tongue* and to chant them carefully. This ought to be done not only by the laity, that is those living the ordinary life of the populace, but also by the clergy and monks, who are experts in Latin. For thus the whole community of believers may learn of what their faith consists, and how they ought in the strength of that belief to arm and defend themselves against the assaults of evil spirits (my emphasis).[8]

In the sentences that follow, Bede comes back to the vernacular again. To ensure the swift fulfillment of these pastoral objectives, he reminds Egbert that he himself has

> frequently offered an English translation of the Creed and the Lord's Prayer to uneducated priests. For the holy Bishop Am-

---

8 "Et quidem omnes, qui Latinam linguam lectionis usu didicerunt, etiam haec optime didicisse certissimum est: sed idiotas, hoc est, eos qui propriae tantum linguae notitiam habent, *haec ipsa sua lingua discere*, ac sedulo decantare facito. Quod non solum de laicis, id est, in populari adhuc uita constitutis, uerum etiam de clericis sive monachis, qui Latinae sunt linguae expertes, fieri oportet. Sic enim fit, ut caetus omnis fidelium, quomodo fidelis esse, qua se firmitate credendi contra immundorum spirituum certamina munire atque armare debeat, discat." Bede, *Epistola ad Ecgbertum Episcopum* § 5, ed. Plummer, pp. 408–9; trans. McClure and Collins, pp. 345–46.

brose advises, when talking about belief, that the words of the Creed should be chanted by the faithful each morning, as a kind of spiritual antidote to the poison with which the devil tries by day and night to infect them.[9]

The second source of interest for Bede's attitude toward the vernacular comes from a text authored not by Bede but by one of his pupils, Cuthbert, a monk and later abbot of Jarrow.[10] The text, which takes the form of a letter addressed to one Cuthwin, offers a first-hand account of Bede's death and the events of the final days leading up to it. In the course of constructing his hagiographical portrait, Cuthbert mentions two points that touch on our subject. Although seriously ill, Bede, according to Cuthbert's report, remained committed to his usual pedagogic and devotional regimen, instructing the monks by day and devoting himself to prayer and meditation by night. He would recite "familiar sacred melodies from the Scriptures" (*consueta scripturarum modulamina*), as well as "many other verses from Holy Scripture" (*multa alia de sancta scriptura*), specifically to remind his pupils of the transience of earthly existence. For that explicit purpose, we are told, Bede would even chant songs "in our own language also" (*in nostra quoque lingua*); and at this juncture,

9 "Propter quod et ipse multis saepe sacerdotibus idiotis haec utraque, et symbolum uidelicet, et dominicam orationem in linguam Anglorum translatam obtuli. Nam et sanctus antistes Ambrosius hoc de fide loquens admonet, ut uerba symboli matutinis semper horis fideles quique decantent, et hoc se quasi antidoto spirituali contra diaboli uenena quae illis interdiu uel noctu astu maligno obicere posset, praemuniant." Bede, *Epistola ad Ecgbertum Episcopum* § 5, ed. Plummer, p. 409; trans. McClure and Collins, p. 346.

10 On this work, see E. V. K. Dobbie, *The Manuscripts of Cædmon's Hymn and Bede's Death Song* (New York, 1937); and William D. McCready, "Bede, Isidore, and the *Epistola Cuthberti*," *Traditio* 50 (1995), 75–94.

Literary Contexts

Cuthbert makes a point of noting that Bede was "skilled in our poems" (*doctus in nostris carminibus*) before going on to quote, in English, his supposed death-song.[11] I shall deal with the significance of this episode momentarily when I take up the issue of poetry. As for the second point about the vernacular in this letter, right after noting Bede's poetic skill, Cuthbert goes on to mention two projects that Bede was eager to finish and that preoccupied his final moments before death. Both included translation of Latin sources into the vernacular: a partial rendering of the Gospel of John, which, Cuthbert makes a point of noting, Bede had set out to translate "for the greater profit of God's Church" (*ad utilitatem ecclesiae Dei conuertit*), and extracts from Isidore of Seville's *De natura rerum*.[12] It is regrettable that

---

11 Cuthbert, *Epistola de obitu Baedae*, ed. Plummer, p. clxi.
12 "In istis autem diebus dua opuscula memoriae digna, exceptis lectionibus, quas cottidie accepimus ab eo, et cantu psalmorum, facere studuit; id est a capite sancti euangelii Iohannis usque ad eum locum in quo dicitur, 'sed haec quid sunt inter tantos?' in nostrum linguam ad utilitatem ecclesiae Dei conuertit, et de libris Isidori episcopi excerptiones quasdam, dicens: 'nolo ut pueri mei mendacium legant, et in hoc post meum obitum sine fructu laborent.'" Bede, *Epistola de obitu Baedae*, ed. Plummer, p. clxii. There has been much debate over the nature of Bede's reference to Isidore here, regarding two issues: whether the remark has positive or negative connotations, and whether the wording of the Latin indicates that portions of Isidore's text as well as John's were translated into English. For a range of opinion, see C. W. Jones, *Bedae opera de temporibus* (Cambridge, Mass., 1969), pp. 131–32; Paul Meyvaert, "Bede the Scholar," in *Famulus Christi: Essays in Commemoration of the Thirteenth Centenary of the Birth of the Venerable Bede*, ed. Gerald Bonner (London, 1976), pp. 58–60; Roger Ray, "Bede's *Vera Lex Historiae*," *Speculum* 55 (1980), 16–17; A. K. Brown, "The English Compass Points," *Medium Aevum* 47 (1978), 232–33; and McCready, "Bede and the *Epistola Cuthberti*," 77, 88–92. I side with Brown and McCready, who point out that *excerptiones quasdam*

no trace of either work has survived. But if the veracity of Cuthbert's report can be trusted, Bede's partial translation of John's Gospel would be especially noteworthy, as it would represent our oldest known example of an attempt to English Holy Writ.

Admittedly, one would like to have more to consider than these meager scraps; however, they do allow us to draw some conclusions. In the light not only of his relative silence concerning the vernacular, but more so of the thoroughgoing Latin nature of his own extant writings, there can be no doubt that Bede was no Alfred, keen to make the vernacular *the* primary tool for cultural and religious reform.[13] On the contrary, Bede's commitment to Latin is unswerving. As Roger Ray has observed, his main goal as a writer was, in fact, no less than to draw the *gens Anglorum* into the orbit of the Catholic mainstream by means of a literary program designed to establish the norms of a definitively Christian Latin culture.[14] That goal notwithstanding, these bits from the *Letter to Egbert* and Cuthbert's letter do reveal that he did envisage some role for the vernacular in transmitting Christian truth. In this connection, what is unique about

---

is the object of the verb *conuertit*, and that the construction must therefore imply that Bede had translated portions of Isidore's text into English as well.

13   See Malcolm Godden, "King Alfred's Preface and the Teaching of Latin in Anglo-Saxon England," *English Historical Review* 117 (2002), 596–604; Jennifer Morrish, "King Alfred's Letter as a Source on Learning in England in the Ninth Century," in *Studies in Earlier Old English Prose*, ed. Paul Szarmach (Albany, 1986), pp. 87–107; and Donald Bullough, "The Educational Tradition in England from Alfred to Ælfric: Teaching *utriusque linguae*," *Settimane di Studio del centro Italiano di studi sull'alto medioevo* 19 (1972), 453–93.

14   See Roger Ray, *Bede, Rhetoric, and the Creation of Christian Latin Culture,* Jarrow Lecture, 1997, and his more recent remarks on the topic in "Who Did Bede Think He Was?" in *Innovation and Tradition in the Writings of the Venerable Bede*, ed. DeGregorio, pp. 11–35.

Literary Contexts

the story of Cædmon is that it is the one and only instance in Bede's oeuvre where he goes so far as to depict *the use of the vernacular in action*, inasmuch as he presents the Whitby cowherd actually employing his native tongue to versify sacred history.[15] In the wider context of the *Ecclesiastical History*, the episode stands as a litmus for progress, a sign that Anglo-Saxon Christianity has come so far that now the mother tongue itself may serve as a vessel for Christian expression. One may think here of Pope Gregory's directive to the missionary monk Mellitus to utilize indigenous practices to fan the spread of the faith.[16] But in point of fact, Gregory says nothing at all about the vernacular, let alone vernacular verse. These emphases come from Bede.

Bede and Poetry

When we turn to the issue of poetry, it is instructive to begin not with Cædmon—still less with the later Old English poetic tradition or scholarly theories about it—but with Bede. Again, what stands out is Bede's commitment to, and competence in, a tradition that is Latin through and through.[17] His own poetical works include the following: a book of Latin epigrams in hexameters and in elegiac couplets, now lost; a book of Latin hymns; a long Latin poem on Judgment Day, the *De die iudicii*; an

---

15 The only other place I know of where something similar occurs is Bede's discussion of the Northumbrian king Oswald who, being learned in both English and Irish, acts as an interpreter for the Irish monk-bishop Aidan, "who was not completely at home in the English tongue" (*qui Anglorum linguam perfecte non nouerat*). See Bertram Colgrave and R. A. B. Mynors, ed., *Bede's Ecclesiastical History of the English People*, 3.3 (Oxford, 1969), p. 120

16 Colgrave and Mynors, *Bede's Ecclesiastical History*, 1.30, pp. 106–8.

17 Little has been written on Bede as a poet; the only major treatment I am familiar with is by Michael Lapidge, *Bede the Poet*, Jarrow Lecture, 1993, repr. in *Bede and His World: The Jarrow Lectures*, 2 vols. (Aldershot, 1994), 2: 929–56.

even longer Latin poem on St. Cuthbert of Lindisfarne, which is the best-known of his poems; and several other short Latin poems he inserted into various individual works.[18] In addition, Bede authored a handbook on the principles of Latin verse composition, the *De arte metrica*;[19] it has survived in more than 100 manuscripts, and throughout the Middle Ages has served as the standard introduction to the subject, becoming, in Calvin Kendall's words, "one of the basic textbooks of the Western world."[20] It may well be, as Cuthbert claimed, that Bede (like Aldhelm) knew something too about the native poetic tradition of his people; what has come down to us, however, is anchored firmly in the Christian-Latin stream.[21]

Bede entered the monastic life at the age of seven,[22] so poetry came to him first as one of the subjects of the monastic curriculum. For monks, the study of metrics, like the study of everything else, had but one goal—to enable them to read the

18 Hymns: ed. J. Fraipont, CCSL 122: pp. 407–38; *De die iudicii*: ed. J. Fraipont, CCSL 122: pp. 43–44; *Vita metrica S. Cuthberti*: ed. Werner Jaeger, *Bedas metrische Vita sancti Cuthberti*, Palaestra 198 (Leipzig, 1935).

19 Bede, *De arte metrica et de schematibus et tropis*, ed. Calvin B. Kendall, CCSL 123A (Turnhout, 1975), pp. 59–171.

20 Calvin B. Kendall, ed., *Bede: Libri II De arte metrica et De schematibus et tropis. The Art of Poetry and Rhetoric*, Bibliotheca Germania, Series Nova, vol. 2 (Saarbrücken, 1991), p. 15.

21 Bede's contemporary Aldhelm of Malmesbury (d. 709) also is reported to have had an interest in vernacular poetry and, unlike Bede, to have used it as a tool of evangelization. But the sources of this tradition, Faricius of Arezzo's tenth-century *Vita S. Aldhelmi* and William of Malmesbury's twelfth-century *Gesta Pontificum Anglorum*, are later rather than contemporary. See N. E. S. A. Hamilton, ed., *Willelmi Malmesbiriensis monachi de gestis pontificum Anglorum libri quinque*. Rerum britannicarum medii ævi scriptores (London, 1870).

22 Colgrave and Mynors, *Bede's Ecclesiastical History*, 5.24, p. 566.

Literary Contexts

Scriptures and participate in the Divine Office.[23] The Psalter, as the bedrock of the latter, would have been the well from which the young Bede took his first sips of a distinctly Christian poetry.[24] The result would be the formation in him of an unshakable conviction regarding the Latin Bible's pre-eminence—that it surpassed all other writings, the classics included, and not only because of its sacred contents. In the opening book of his *De schematibus et tropis*, Bede would put it this way, addressing the deacon Cuthbert to whom he dedicated the work:

> But in order that you, my beloved son, and indeed all who choose to read these words, may know that Holy Scripture is preeminent over all other writings not only in authority, in that it is divine, and in utility, in that it leads to eternal life, but also in antiquity and its very use of rhetoric, I have decided to demonstrate by means of examples gathered from its pages that there is not one of these schemes and tropes which teachers of rhetoric can boast of in any century that did not appear in it first.[25]

---

23 See Jean Leclercq, *The Love of Learning and the Desire for God*, trans. Catharine Misrahi (New York, 1961), pp. 113–15; and Michael Lapidge, "The Anglo-Latin Background," in Stanley B. Greenfield and Daniel G. Calder, *A New Critical History of Old English Literature* (New York, 1986), pp. 5–7; reprinted in *Anglo-Latin Literature: 600–899* (London, 1996), pp. 1–36.

24 See Benedicta Ward, *Bede and the Psalter*, Jarrow Lecture, 1991; also George Hardin Brown, "The Psalms as the Foundation of Anglo-Saxon Learning," in *The Place of the Psalms in the Intellectual Culture of the Middle Ages*, ed. Nancy Van Deusen (Albany, 1999), pp. 1–24.

25 "Sed ut cognoscas, dilectissime fili, cognoscant omnes qui haec legere uoluerint quia sancta Scriptura ceteris omnibus scripturis non solum auctoritate, quia diuina est, uel utilitate, quia ad uitam ducit aeternam, sed et antiquitate et ipsa praeeminet positione dicendi, placuit mihi collectis de ipsa exemplis ostendere quia

Scott DeGregorio

The imprint left by this conviction on Bede's own writings is sizeable indeed. It is perhaps most conspicuous in his own textbooks on poetry and rhetoric, which register no trace of equivocation when it comes to Bede's own preferences. In both the *De arte metrica* and the *De schematibus et tropis*, he discards the quotations from the classical-pagan authors, who had long furnished the models used by the Latin grammarians, and replaces them with selections from Scripture.[26] So exclusionist a move as this might suggest that Bede, by virtue of the monastic tradition to which he belonged, would have no truck at all with pagan literature, including, to be sure, that of his own Germanic culture. To some extent this is surely true: there was, to his mind, no contest between pagan eloquence and Christian truth.[27] The point is repeated with force in his exegetical writings. In his commentary on Luke, he states that those who willingly give ear to "idle tales or lewd songs" (*fabulis otiosis obscenisue carminibus*) succeed only in bringing death to their souls,[28] and later, in commenting on the parable of the lost son, he associates the husks

---

nihil huiusmodi schematum siue troporum ualent praetendere saecularis eloquentiae magistri, quod non illa praecesserit." Bede, *De schematibus et tropis*, ed. Kendall, pp. 142–43, lines 12–19; trans. Kendall, *Bede: Libri II De arte metrica et De schematibus et tropis. The Art of Poetry and Rhetoric*, p. 169; translation modified.

26 See Kendall, *Bede: Libri II De arte metrica et De schematibus et tropis. The Art of Poetry and Rhetoric*, p. 22.

27 See George Hardin Brown, *Bede the Educator* (Jarrow Lecture, 1996), pp. 10–14; and Pierre Riché, *Education and Culture in the Barbarian West from the Sixth through the Eighth Century*, trans. John J. Contreni (Columbia, SC, 1978), pp. 86–99.

28 "Qui fabulis otiosis obscenisue carminibus uel detractionibus aurem libenter aperit hanc animae suae portam mortis efficit caeterosque qui non seruat sensus mortis sibi ipse reddit aditus." Bede, *In Lucae euangelium expositio*, ed. David Hurst, CCSL 120 (Turnhout, 1960), p. 158, lines 2283–86. Translations are my own unless otherwise noted.

Literary Contexts

eaten by the swine with the stories (*fabula*) and songs (*carmen*) enjoyed by the pagans.[29] In his commentary on I Samuel, he castigates churchmen who prefer "secular fables" (*fabulis saecularibus*) to God's word.[30] The sentiment is echoed again in his work on the Book of Kings; explaining that the names Hiel and Bethel mean "living for God" and "house of God" respectively, Bede takes Hiel's leaving Bethel (i.e. the Church) for Jericho as an allegory of those in the religious life who "prefer false doctrines or Gentile fables to the Church's truth in which they were instructed."[31] Similar pronouncements can be found in

29 "Siliquae quibus porcos pascebat sunt doctrinae saeculares sterili suauitate resonantes de quibus laudes idolorum fabularumque ad deos gentium uario sermone atque carminibus percrepant quibus daemonia delectantur. Vnde cum iste saturari cupiebat aliquid solidum et rectum quod ad beatam uitam pertineret inuenire uolebat in talibus et non poterat." Bede, *In Lucae euangelium expositio*, ed. Hurst, p. 289, lines 2334–39.

30 "Descendunt et hodie nonnulli relicta altitudine uerbi Dei ad quod audiendum ascendere debuerant auscultantque fabulis saecularibus ac doctrinis daemoniorum et legendo dialecticos rethores poetasque gentilium ad exercendum ingenium terrestre quasi ad fabros Philisthiim pro exacuendis siluestris siue ruralis culturae ferramentis inermes, hoc est spiritali scientia priuati, conueniunt." Bede, *In primam partem Samuhelis Libri III*, ed. David Hurst, CCSL 119B (Turnhout, 1962), p. 112, lines 1853–59.

31 "Quia uero Ahiel uiuens Deo Bethel interpretatur domus Dei, Ahiel de Bethel destructa a Josue atque anathematizata Hericho moenia restaurat cum quis eorum qui in ecclesia habitum religionis assumpserat ad agenda scelera quae ei dominus Iesus in die baptismatis donauerat redit quasque ipse anathematizauerat diaboli pompas luxuriose uiuendo repetit cum errorum dogmata uel gentilium fabulas ueritati praeponit ecclesiasticae qua imbutus est quasi de Bethel egrediens, ruinas Hericho resuscitat." Bede, *In Regum XXX Quaestiones*, ed. David Hurst, CCSL 119B (Turnhout, 1962), p. 309, lines 12–21; trans. W. Trent Foley and Arthur G.

the gospel homilies, which Bede probably preached to the *fratres carissimi* of Wearmouth-Jarrow.³² A comment with particular resonance for the story of Cædmon occurs in a homily written for Holy Saturday:

> We must not in any way suppose that salvation is possible as long as one is not afraid to cling to his disordered habits, to be delighted by pointless words (*superuacuis uerbis*), or to be impaired by disturbing thoughts. But there lies in store for a person who, with God's mercy and aid, has changed the disturbed ways of his former life, who has conceived in his heart the inspiration of divine grace (*inspirationem diuinae gratiae*), who has learned from the word of heavenly teaching to confess the true faith, to secure immediately the longed-for joys of good health.³³

It is well to recall that the narrative of Cædmon's gift of poetic inspiration begins with a similar denunciation of foolish speech.

Holder, *Bede: A Biblical Miscellany*, Translated Texts for Historians 28 (Liverpool, 1999), p. 116.

32   See A. G. P. Van Der Walt, "The Homiliary of the Venerable Bede and Early Medieval Preaching," (Ph.D. thesis, University of London, 1980), pp. 52–84.

33   "Neque ullatenus saluari putandus est quamdiu quis inordinatis moribus adhaerere superuacuis uerbis delectari turbulentis cogitationibus non timet deuastari. At qui miserante et adiuuante domino turbidam priscae conuersationis uitam mutauit qui inspirationem diuinae gratiae corde concepit qui uerbo doctrinae coelestis confessionem uerae didicit fidei restat ut confestim optata sanitatis gaudia consequatur." Bede, *Homeliarum euangelii libri II*, 2.6, ed. D. Hurst, CCSL 122 (Turnhout, 1955), pp. 221–22, lines 57–64; trans. Lawrence T. Martin and David Hurst, *Bede: Homilies on the Gospels*, 2 vols., Cistercian Studies Series, 110 and 111 (Kalamazoo, 1991), 2:53. Cf. *Hom.* 1.19, ed. Hurst, p. 139, lines 167–70; and *Hom.* 2.1, ed. Hurst, p. 185, lines 43–47.

Literary Contexts

Bede explicitly states that the songs Cædmon sang were godly and religious (*carmina religioni et pietati*), and that he never sought to "compose any foolish or trivial poems (*nil umquam friuoli et superuacui poematis*) but only those that were concerned with devotion and so were fitting for his devout tongue to utter."[34] And further still, he affirms that the lowly cowherd had been specially marked out by divine grace (*diuina gratia specialiter insignis*). Such correspondences between the story of Cædmon and the Holy Saturday homily are rather hard to miss. Surely they indicate that the story of Cædmon, however unique, can and should be placed in a wider Bedan frame, and in that way be linked to concerns that can be seen to permeate his exegetical and pastoral writings.

Yet, in spite of all this, Bede's position on the relative merits of pagan literary culture is actually more nuanced than one of outright exclusion. Having read Virgil, Cicero, and others first as a young oblate and later as the schoolmaster of the monastery,[35] he no doubt accepted the educational value of the classics. But more than that, he took the additional step, echoed by St. Augustine in Book 4 of the *De doctrina christiana*,[36] of advo-

---

34 "Namque ipse non ab hominibus neque per hominem institutus canendi artem didicit, sed diuinitus adiutus gratis canendi donum accepit. Vnde nil umquam friuoli et superuacui poematis facere potuit, sed ea tantummodo, quae ad religionem pertinent, religiosam eius linguam decebant." Colgrave and Mynors, *Bede's Ecclesiastical History*, 4.24, p. 414.

35 See Neil Wright, "Bede and Vergil," *Romano barbarica* 6 (1981–2), 361–79; and Roger Ray, "Bede and Cicero," *Anglo-Saxon England* 16 (1986), 1–16.

36 See Augustine, *De doctrina christiana*, 4.2.3–5.7, ed. Joseph Martin, CCSL 32 (Turnhout, 1962), p. 117, line 1–p. 121, line 26; also the famous passage in Book 2, where the utilizing of secular wisdom is compared by Augustine to the Israelites' seizing the gold and silver of the pagan Egyptians: *De doctrina christiana*, 2.60, ed. Martin, p. 73, line 1–p. 74, line 27. For a good discussion of

cating the Christian duty of redirecting pagan writings towards spiritual ends whenever the occasion allowed. Although Bede's remarks in this regard are directed at the classical-pagan tradition, I suggest that they might also relate to the Germanic-pagan tradition and, in this way, constitute a fitting gloss on the Cædmon episode as well.

The key Bedan text in this connection is the commentary on I Samuel, specifically the exegesis of chapters 13 and 14.[37] There, we see Bede establishing a hierarchy of values that—*pace* the more rigid attitude of St. Jerome, who drove a wedge between sacred and secular learning[38]—allows room for what he terms *saecularis eloquentia*. To be sure, Bede allows no room at all for studying the latter for its own sake; but neither does he advocate total exclusion if the proper Christian ends for secular elo-

---

Augustine's position as articulated in these passages, see Frederick Van Fleteren, "St. Augustine, Neoplatonism, and the Liberal Arts: The Background to *De doctrina christiana*," in *De doctrina christiana: A Classic of Western Culture*, ed. Duane W. H. Arnold and Pamela Bright, Christianity and Judaism in Antiquity 9 (Notre Dame, 1995), pp. 14–24.

37 See Bede, *In primam partem Samuhelis Libri III*, ed. Hurst, esp. pp. 112–23.

38 The classic text is Jerome's letter to the Roman lady Eustochium, where he recounts his famous dream in which he was confronted by the charge: "You are a Ciceronian, not a Christian" (*Ciceronianus es, non Christianus*). See Jerome, *Epistola* xxii, in *Epistulae I–LXX*, ed. Isidore Hilberg, CSEL 53 (Vienna, 1910), pp. 143–211, quote at p. 190. This long letter is known also by the title *Libellus de virginitate servanda*. For a good overview of the episode and the scholarly discussion around it, see Paul Antin, "Autour du songe de S. Jérôme," in *Recueil sur saint Jérôme*, Collection Latomus 95 (Brussels, 1968), pp. 71–100, as well as the recent massive commentary by Neil Adkin, *Jerome on Virginity: A Commentary on the Libellus De Virginitate Servanda (Letter 22)*, ARCA Classical and Medieval Texts, Papers and Monographs 42 (Cambridge, 2003).

Literary Contexts

quence may be found. In interpreting the story of how King Saul imposed a fast upon his army, and Jonathan unwittingly broke it by eating the honeycomb, Bede can find an apt figure of the proper stance the Christian should take regarding the use of secular literature. Concerning Saul's edict prohibiting his army any food before battling the Philistines, Bede concludes that the king was too strict: to deprive believers of *all* forms of pagan literature might make them more vulnerable, too weak to battle against evil. What is needed, he argues, is moderation, not total abstinence.[39] Thus Bede sides with Jonathan, whose benign departure in receiving nourishment from the honeycomb served only to make him stronger for battle. Treating Jonathan's words in I Samuel 14:29, which read, "You have seen yourselves that my eyes are brightened, because I tasted a little of this honey," Bede accordingly takes them to mean the following:

> You see, he says, that I am made more efficacious and sharper and quicker in declaiming what is fitting insofar as I have tasted a little of the flower of Tullian reading. If the Christian people had learned the sects and teachings of the Gentiles, would it not so much the more confidently and certainly deride them and at the same time overcome their errors?[40]

---

39 "Turbauit quia totum interdixit; quod si ex parte interdixisset et ex parte concessisset, commodius res uideretur exacta. Verum quia in huiuscemodi rebus spiritualium patrum sit iussis obsequendum Ionathan sorte deprehensus et oraculum domini die illa consulenti Sauli subductum manifestissime declarat." Bede, *In primam partem Samuhelis Libri III*, ed. Hurst, p. 120, lines 2200–205.

40 "Videtis, inquit, quia efficacior sum factus et acutior promptiorque ad peroranda quae decent eo quod gustauerim paululum de flore Tullianae lectionis; quanto magis si didicisset populus christianus sectas et dogmata gentilium, nonne multo confidentius et certius eorum derideret simul et convinceret errores." Bede, *In primam partem Samuhelis Libri III*, ed. Hurst, p. 121, lines 2227–32.

As the reference to Cicero implies, Bede is talking mainly about matters of literary style, how it is foolish not to utilize what is best in the artistry of pagan books by redeploying it in the service of the faith.[41] Of course, no exact parallel to the Germanic vernacular tradition can be made in this regard. Classical tradition had long since secured an indispensable place as an educational tool for Christian culture. By contrast, as Patrick Wormald reminds us, there is nothing analogous to suggest "that the vernacular had any educational utility before the days of Alfred's England."[42] Yet, if Augustine could teach Bede that it is both respectable and beneficial for Christians to borrow from the classical-pagan tradition, Bede himself might well extrapolate from there a legitimacy for doing the same vis-à-vis of his own pagan background. As his exegesis of the Saul-Jonathan saga suggests, the Church must make use of *all* that it can to wage war against every manner of unbelief. And if the techniques of vernacular literature could be accommodated to that end—and the Cædmon story suggests they could—perhaps it was Bede's prerogative to show that the pagans could be trumped at their own verbal game?

Bede and Monastic Reform

Bede's concern with monastic reform offers a final set of ideas for contextualizing the story of Cædmon. In contrast to the small amount of material on which we have had to rely so far in these pages, this topic is writ large, animating much of what Bede wrote. In recent years, it has become, quite rightly, a dominant theme in Bedan scholarship. No longer portrayed as a withdrawn monk or an idealizing historian, Bede has increasingly come to be seen as a polemical author who, in his writings, called for social and religious change in the face of a decaying

---

41 See Ray, "Bede and Cicero," pp. 3–5.
42 Wormald, "Bede, Beowulf and the Conversion," p. 47.

Northumbrian present.[43] He was, this view insists, quite well attuned to the social and religious ills of his own contemporary world and did not hesitate to propose remedies for them. As part of the *Ecclesiastical History*, a work whose reformist lineaments have been well exposed,[44] the Cædmon story needs to be seen as one strand of a much larger thematic web. To excerpt it, reading it *sub specie aeternitatis* as if it were a free-standing work, may well run the risk of occluding much that the story in its wider narrative context could potentially bring into view. It makes good sense, accordingly, to approach it with an eye to the reform discourse that so dominated the post-720 period of Bede's career when, among other projects, he was busy constructing the *Ecclesiastical History*. But in order to set the stage for that discussion, it will be expedient to look elsewhere first.

The *Letter to Egbert*, which we have already touched on, offers the clearest outline of Bede's reform program. Within its brief

---

43   The seminal article is Alan Thacker, "Bede's Ideal of Reform," in *Ideal and Reality in Frankish and Anglo-Saxon Society: Studies Presented to J. M. Wallace-Hadrill*, ed. Patrick Wormald et al. (Oxford, 1983), pp. 130–53. See also my four articles: "Reform of the Northumbrian Church"; "*Nostrorum socordiam temporum*: The Reforming Impulse of Bede's Later Exegesis," *Early Medieval Europe* 11.2 (2002), 107–22; "Bede's *In Ezram et Neemiam*: A Document in Church Reform?," in *Bède le Vénérable: entre tradition et postérite*, ed. Stéphane Lebecq, Michel Perrin, and Olivier Szerwiniack (Lille, 2005), pp. 97–107; and "Footsteps of His Own: Bede's Commentary on Ezra-Nehemiah," in *Innovation and Tradition in the Writings of the Venerable Bede*, ed. DeGregorio, pp. 143–68.

44   See Walter Goffart, *The Narrators of Barbarian History* (Princeton, 1988), pp. 235–328, and his two follow-up articles, "The *Historia Ecclesiastica*: Bede's Agenda and Ours," *Haskin's Society Journal* 2 (1990), 29–45, and "Bede's History in a Harsher Climate," in *Innovation and Tradition in the Writings of the Venerable Bede*, ed. Scott DeGregorio, Medieval European Studies 7 (Morgantown, 2006), pp. 203–26.

compass it sets out, in detail, the contemporary problems that its author believed were plaguing the Northumbrian church as well as the remedies he wanted to see instituted. In this regard, the complexion of the *Letter to Egbert* has recently been summed up well by John Blair: "This is a carefully composed and literary work, but it is anything but formal in substance: it gives vent to a boiling exasperation, and to a dying man's urgency to find solutions which others would have to implement."[45] In addition to withering standards of pastoral care, a central thrust of Bede's attack is aimed at the institution charged with the task of dispensing it, namely monasticism. He describes the situation in a passage in the *Letter to Egbert* that reverberates with Bede's fury to this day:

> There are others, laymen who have no love for the monastic life nor for military service, who commit a graver crime by giving money to the kings and obtaining lands under the pretext of building monasteries, in which they can give freer reign to their libidinous tastes; these lands they have assigned to them in hereditary right through written royal edicts, and these charters, as if to make them really worthy in the sight of God, they arrange to be witnessed in writing by bishops, abbots, and the most powerful laymen. Thus they have gained unjust rights over fields and villages, free from both divine and human legal obligations; as laymen ruling over monks they serve only their own wishes. Indeed, they do not gather monks there but rather they find those vagrants who have been expelled from the monasteries in other places for the sin of disobedience, or

---

45 Blair, *Church in Anglo-Saxon Society*, p. 101. Blair's remarks offer a nice counter, with which I fully agree, to the opinion of Patrick Sims-Williams, who argues that Bede's letter should not "be taken at face value" because it "belongs to a tradition of monastic polemic that goes back at least as far as Cassian." Patrick Sims-Williams, *Religion and Literature in Western England 600–800*, Cambridge Studies in Anglo-Saxon England 3 (Cambridge, 1990), p. 126.

Literary Contexts

whom they have lured away from other monasteries, or, for sure, those of their own followers whom they can persuade to take the tonsure and promise monastic obedience to them. They fill the monastic cells they have built with these cohorts of the deformed, and as a hideous and unheard-of spectacle, those same men occupy themselves with their wives and the children they have engendered.[46]

According to this passage, monastic life in Northumbria has fallen prey to wide-scale secularization. The resulting deterioration of purpose and standards has, Bede argues, turned monasticism into nothing more than a ruse by which secular aristocrats could gain land, property, and wealth, without having to pay so much as lip-service to the rigors of monastic discipline. It is a devastating critique of the misuse of sacred and secular

---

46   "At alii grauiore adhuc flagitio, cum sint ipsi laici, et nullo uitae regularis uel usu exerciti, uel amore praediti, data regibus pecunia, emunt sibi sub praetextu construendorum monasteriorum territoria in quibus suae liberius uacent libidini, et haec insuper in ius sibi haereditarium regalibus edictis faciunt asscribi, ipsas quoque litteras priuilegiorum suorum quasi ueraciter Deo dignas, pontificum, abbatum, et potestatum seculi obtinent subscriptione confirmari. Sicque usurpatis sibi agellulis siue uicis, liberi exinde a diuino simul et humano seruitio, suis tantum inibi desideriis, laici monachis imperantes, deseruiunt; immo non monachos ibi congregant, sed quoscunque ob culpam inobaedientiae ueris expulsos monasteriis alicubi forte oberrantes inuenerint, aut euocare monasteriis ipsi ualuerint; uel certe quos ipsi de suis satellitibus ad suscipiendam tonsuram promissa sibi obaedientia monachica inuitare quiuerint. Horum distortis cohortibus, suas, quas instruxere, cellas implent, multumque informi atque inaudito spectaculo, idem ipsi uiri modo coniugis ac liberorum procreandorum curam gerunt." Bede, *Epistola ad Ecgbertum Episcopum* § 15, ed. Plummer, pp. 415–16; trans. McClure and Collins, p. 351.

power, as Bede's contempt for the collusion of kings, bishops and noblemen responsible for such fraudulence lets us know.

Nowhere else is Bede so explicit in laying out the specific acts of perversion that were eviscerating the monastic institutions of his day. Yet he did not confine his angst over the situation to the *Letter to Egbert* alone, though it seemed to preoccupy his final earthly moments. Traces of it are detectable in much of his post-720 output too. In his commentary on Ezra-Nehemiah, for example, Bede's comments on Ezra 6:18 ("And they appointed the priests in their orders and the Levites in their divisions to supervise the services of God in Jerusalem, just as is written in the Book of Moses") give way to the following telling remark on the contemporary monastic scene:

> The order of devotion required that, after the building and dedication of the Lord's house, priests and Levites be straightway ordained to serve in it: for there would be no point in having erected a splendid building if there were no priests inside to serve God. This should be impressed as often as possible on those who, though founding monasteries with brilliant workmanship, in no way appoint teachers in them to exhort the people to God's works but rather those who will serve their own pleasures and desires there.[47]

---

47 "Ordo poscebat deuotionis ut post aedificatam ac dedicatam domum domini mox sacerdotes ac leuitae qui in ea ministrarent ordinarentur ne sine causa domus erecta fulgeret si deessent qui intus Deo seruirent. Quod saepius inculcandum eis qui monasteria magnifico opere construentes nequaquam in his statuunt doctores qui ad opera Dei populum cohortentur sed suis potius inibi uoluptatibus ac desideriis seruiunt." Bede, *In Ezram et Neemiam*, ed. David Hurst, CCSL 119A (Turnhout, 1969), pp. 302–3, lines 597–604; trans. Scott DeGregorio, *Bede: On Ezra and Nehemiah*, Translated Texts for Historians 47 (Liverpool, 2006), p. 102.

Literary Contexts

In his commentary on Solomon's Temple, Bede's interpretation of the two pillars in the portico of the temple mentioned at I Kings 7:21 provides occasion to make a similar point about the demise of effective pastoral care:

> And both pillars were appositely given the same name, since one was called "firmness" and the other "in strength" to show that in all teachers there was the one staunchness of faith and practice, and to note tacitly the sluggishness of our own time when some want to have the appearance and name of being teachers, priests and pillars of the house of God though they have absolutely none of the firm faith needed to despise worldly ostentation and make invisible goods their ambition, none of the strength needed to administer correction, none of the diligence even to understand the errors of those to whom they have been preferred.[48]

Topical remarks of this kind are rare in Bede's work. Another occurs in the *Ecclesiastical History* when, in discussing the pastoral zeal of the Irish monk-bishop Aidan, Bede contends that "Aidan's life was in great contrast to our modern slothfulness."[49]

---

48 "Et apte uocabulo simili ambo censebantur columnae cum una firmitas altera in robore dicta ut una fidei et operis fortitudo cunctis inesse doctoribus monstraretur nostrique temporis inertia tacite notaretur ubi se non nulli doctores sacerdotes et columnas domus Dei uideri atque appellari uolunt cum nihil in se prorsus firmae fidei ad contemnendas saeculi pompas ac desideranda bona inuisibilia nil habeant roboris ad corrigendos nil industriae saltim ad intellegendos eorum quibus praelati sunt errores." Bede, *De templo*, ed. David Hurst, CCSL 119A (Turnhout, 1969), pp. 206–7, lines 595–603; trans. Seán Connolly, *Bede: On the Temple*, Translated Texts for Historians 21 (Liverpool, 1995), p. 84.

49 "In tantum autem uita illius a nostri temporis segnitia distabat, ut omnes qui cum eo incedebant, siue adtonsi seu laici, meditari deberent, id est aut legendis scripturis aut psalmis discendis

Scott DeGregorio

That assertion helps link the *Ecclesiastical History* to Bede's commentaries on Ezra-Nehemiah and Solomon's Temple—which are late, heavily reformist works probably written around the same time as the *Ecclesiastical History*[50]—and beyond them to the *Letter to Egbert*, whose reformist designs are patent. True, a great disparity in tone separates the *Ecclesiastical History* from the *Letter to Egbert*; the former contains none of the vituperation of the latter. No doubt the *Ecclesiastical History* is a text "distinguished by great discretion,"[51] determined as it is "to offer readers an English religious heritage in which they could take pride."[52] But that should not prevent us from connecting the two works. Indeed, the great value of the *Letter to Egbert*, and of the remarks noted above from the commentaries, is that they color in a rationale for Bede's composing *Ecclesiastical History* by bringing into view the specific local issues that, it seems evident, were preying on his mind throughout this phase of his career. Add to this the fact that the *Ecclesiastical History* is over-

---

operam dare." Colgrave and Mynors, *Bede's Ecclesiastical History*, 3.5, p. 226.

50 The *De templo* has long been assigned a date of circa 729, based on the fact that Bede mentions it in the letter he wrote to Albinus of Canterbury when sending him a copy of the *Ecclesiastical History*; for that letter, see Plummer, *Venerabilis Baedae opera historia*, p. 3. The date of *In Ezram* has recently been more contested, but I do not accept the view of Paul Meyvaert, "The Date of Bede's *In Ezram* and His Image of Ezra in the Codex Amiatinus," *Speculum* 80 (2005), pp. 1087–1133, that the commentary was composed early in Bede's career, as a "companion piece" to the Ezra image in the Codex Amiatinus. See my remarks in the introduction to *Bede: On Ezra and Nehemiah*, pp. xxxvii–xlii, where I address Meyvaert's claims and conclude that the commentary was composed sometime in the late 720s.

51 James Campbell, "Bede I," in *Essays in Anglo-Saxon History* (London, 1986), p. 19.

52 Blair, *Church in Anglo-Saxon England*, p. 101.

Literary Contexts

whelmingly concerned with Northumbria, and it becomes possible to agree with Walter Goffart that, in this work as well as the *Letter to Egbert*, Bede wrote from the consciously reformist stance of "a forceful advocate rectifying the past as a model for action in the present."[53] This stance is particularly detectable in Book 4, in which the story of Cædmon is embedded. Following the triumph of the Synod of Whitby, recounted near the end of Book 3, Book 4 "at once presents a new and positive stage in the conversion of the English."[54] The note is struck in the opening two chapters, which recount the arrival of Theodore and Hadrian, both of whom were trained in "secular" as well as sacred literature, a detail resonant for the Cædmon story.[55] Of the happy effect their prodigious learning and knowledge of church doctrine had on the island, Bede could not be more explicit: "Never had there been such happy times since the English first came to Britain."[56] The chapters that follow add breadth to this portrayal by sketching the details of a flourishing religious culture, highlighted by the missionary work of Wilfrid, the chastity of Queen Æthelthryth, the devotion of Hild, the asceticism of Cuthbert and, of course, the vernacular innovation of Cædmon.

53 Goffart, *Narrators of Barbarian History*, p. 239. On the Northumbrian dimension of the *Ecclesiastical History*, see Goffart, *Narrators*, pp. 240, 251–53.

54 Benedicta Ward, *The Venerable Bede*, Cistercian Studies Series 169 (Kalamazoo, 1998), p. 124.

55 "Et quia litteris sacris simul et saecularibus, ut diximus, abundanter ambo erant instructi, congregata discipulorum caterua scientiae salutaris cotidie flumina inrigandis eorum cordibus emanabant, ita ut etiam metricae artis, astronomiae et arithmeticae ecclesiasticae disciplinam inter sacrorum apicum uolumina suis auditoribus contraderent." Colgrave and Mynors, *Bede's Ecclesiastical History*, 4.2, pp. 332–34.

56 "Neque umquam prorsus, ex quo Brittaniam petierunt Angli, feliciora fuere tempora." Colgrave and Mynors, *Bede's Ecclesiastical History*, 4.2, p. 334.

In crafting this portrait, Bede develops a string of motifs, and here the brunt of his emphasis falls upon the state of monastic life. Beginning in Chapter 3 with Chad's instituting a monastic rule over the area of Lindsey, Bede offers his audience instance after instance of exemplary monastic behavior and discipline: Owine, who, because ungifted in scriptural study, "applied himself more earnestly to manual labor";[57] Eorcenwold, who founded two monasteries and "established an excellent form of monastic Rule and discipline in both";[58] and Torhtgyth, who sought always "to keep the discipline of the Rule by teaching or reproving the younger ones."[59] These figures only begin the list of monastic heroes who people Book 4. As a result, this section of the *Ecclesiastical History* goes far in evoking a veritable golden age of the regular life.

Read within that context, as well as with an eye to Bede's stated anxieties about the decadent state of monasticism in his day, his presentation of Cædmon can be understood as contributing to that evocation of a glorious monastic past. As in many of

---

57 "Quod ipsum etiam facto monstrauit, nam quo minus sufficiebat meditationi scripturarum, eo amplius operi manuum stadium inpendebat." Colgrave and Mynors, *Bede's Ecclesiastical History*, 4.3, p. 338.

58 "Hic sane, priusquam episcopus factus esset, duo praeclara monasteria, unum sibi alterum sorori suae Aedilburgae, construxerat, quod utrumque regularibus disciplinis optime instituerat." Colgrave and Mynors, *Bede's Ecclesiastical History*, 4.6, p. 354.

59 "Cum autem et ipsa mater pia Deo deuotae congregationis Aedilburga esset rapienda de mundo, apparuit uisio miranda cuidam de sororibus, cui nomen erat Torctgyd, quae multis iam annis in eodem monasterio commorata et ipsa semper in omni humilitate ac sinceritate Deo seruire satagebat, et adiutrix disciplinae regularis eidem matri existere minores docendo uel castigando curabat." Colgrave and Mynors, *Bede's Ecclesiastical History*, 4.9, p. 360.

Literary Contexts

the other stories recounted in the *Ecclesiastical History*, that past is functional: it serves as a stick, as it were, for beating those in the present "who have no love for the monastic life," to repeat a phrase from the Egbert letter.[60] Proportionately, after all, the focus of the story is not the miracle of Cædmon's spontaneous singing, but is rather his induction into the regular life and the impact his life as a monk has on those around him. In this connection, one detail of his portrayal is most crucial for us. Cædmon is not just a layman but a lowly peasant—indeed, he is the *only* named peasant we meet in the *Ecclesiastical History*. And yet, in Bede's treatment, the Whitby cowherd is not only made to play the role of an expert Christian poet but is also transformed into an exemplary monk. "He was," in Bede's words, "a most religious man, *humbly submitting himself to the discipline of the Rule*. He opposed all those who wished to act otherwise with a flaming and fervent zeal"[61] (my emphasis). The calculated mention in these lines of fervent commitment to monastic discipline, when other sources let us know that it was precisely the lack of such discipline in Northumbrian monasticism that had Bede incensed to the core, is vital indeed, a key to locating the episode in the overall narrative context of Book 4 and, beyond that, in the wider web of Bede's reform-based discourse as it is evidenced in his oeuvre. Other details add weight to such a reading of the story. Chapter 24 grows out of a narrative of the life of Abbess Hild, herself a model of the monastic ideal for Bede, as is the foundation of Whitby with its extraordinary productivity of bishops.[62] In place of frivolous story-telling, Bede's Cædmon is a

---

60 Bede, *Epistola ad Ecgbertum Episcopum* § 12, ed. Plummer, p. 415; trans. McClure and Collins, p. 351.

61 "Erat enim uir multum religiosus et regularibus disciplinis humiliter subditus; aduersum uero illos, qui aliter facere uolebant, zelo magni feruoris accensus." Colgrave and Mynors, *Bede's Ecclesiastical History*, 4.24, p. 418.

62 On both Hild and Whitby, see esp. Peter Hunter Blair, "Whitby in the Seventh Century," in *Learning and Literature in Anglo-*

poet who, as others have observed,[63] is a master practitioner of a decidedly monastic technique, namely *ruminatio*, that process of chewing, savoring, and ingesting a text so as to make it a part of one's very being. By merging the performance of native *scopcræft* with this traditional monastic practice, Cædmon, Bede tells us with an obvious sense of approval, was able to produce verse so sweet that "his teachers became in turn his audience."[64] Finally, all this is most resonantly borne out by the very next chapter of Book 4. For Chapter 25, which transitions to a grim note by recounting the destruction of the monastery at Coldingham, offers up for our reflection a most apt juxtaposition. Indeed, what this chapter shows us is exactly an image of the Cædmon story in reverse—the secularization of monasticism by high-born aristocrats.[65] Surely it is significant too that, among the sins leading to that monastery's destruction, we find *fabulationum*, presumably the kind of stories that Cædmon refused to sing.[66]

Saxon England: Studies Presented to Peter Clemoes on the Occasion of his Sixty-Fifth Birthday, ed. Michael Lapidge and Helmut Gneuss (Cambridge, 1985), pp. 3–32.

63 See esp. Philip J. West, "Rumination in Bede's Account of Cædmon," *Monastic Studies* 12 (1976), 217–26; and Donald W. Fritz, "Cædmon: A Monastic Exegete," *American Benedictine Review* 25:3 (1974), 351–63.

64 "At ipse cuncta, quae audiendo discere poterat, rememorando secum et quasi mundum animal ruminando, in carmen dulcissimum conuertebat, suauiusque resonando doctores suos uicissim auditores sui faciebat." Colgrave and Mynors, *Bede's Ecclesiastical History*, 4.24, p. 418.

65 Colgrave and Mynors, *Bede's Ecclesiastical History*, 4.25, pp. 420–27.

66 Colgrave and Mynors, *Bede's Ecclesiastical History*, 4.25, ed. Colgrave and Mynors, p. 424. The Latin noun *fabulatio* can mean more than "gossip," the translation used by Colgrave and Mynors. See, for example, Alexander Souter, *A Glossary of Later Latin to 600 A.D.* (Oxford, 1949), s.v. "fabulatio," which lists the meaning as "a vain tale."

Literary Contexts

Such details, then, yield a rather different reading of the famous story of Cædmon. As noted at the outset, the interests of modern scholarship have been such topics as literary tradition and innovation, vernacular poetics and techniques of oral composition, and the origins of vernacular verse and the "Christianizing" of secular traditions. But these concerns, we have seen, are not Bede's; instead, they are the allurements of later centuries that have been read back into the episode. Connecting the story of Cædmon to concerns evident in Book 4 of the *Ecclesiastical History* and elsewhere in Bede's writings confirms that what really interests him is not versification, vernacular literature, or any other literary issue, but monasticism in its ideal guise and how it can be used as a tool for reform. Indeed, whatever else the story may accomplish, Cædmon in Bede's portrayal becomes a powerful foil for exposing the corruptions of contemporary monasticism, lacking as it does the discipline and zeal he attributes to his exemplary cowherd-turned-monk. Like so many other passages elsewhere in the *Ecclesiastical History*, Cædmon's story is no different in that it is both topical and polemical in its intent. By taking a peasant, giving him a name, and using him to attack the learned, the Bede who authored this well known and cherished episode adopts a stance that is, in the end, quite recognizably the stance he takes so frequently elsewhere in his vast literary output—that of a reformer keen to expose contemporary abuses and to advocate change.

Cædmon's Created World and the Monastic Encyclopedia

FAITH WALLIS

THE CREATED WORLD of which Cædmon sang is only one world among the many in which he moved; but the other worlds explored in this volume provide this particular world with a few coordinates within the larger galaxy of Cædmon studies. Scott DeGregorio demonstrates that the world of Cædmon is fundamentally the world of Bede, who saw in Cædmon an exemplar for monastic reform; Christopher Loveluck, John Hines, and Allen Frantzen focus our attention on a material world where buildings were ubiquitous and mattered deeply. In this volume Daniel O'Donnell, and elsewhere, Kevin Kiernan, remind us that the idea of the hymn was perhaps more important to the Anglo-Saxons than was the text of the hymn itself.[1] The reflections that I present here are indebted to these observations; as one who has expertise in history, rather than in Old English philology and literature, I propose a mapping of Cædmon's world that suggests a few questions and raises some new possibilities.

Cædmon and the History of Science

The fact that the subject-matter of the hymn is, in Bede's words, *principium creaturarum* ("the origin of creation"),[2] suggests some

---

1   See Kevin S. Kiernan, "Reading Cædmon's Hymn with Someone Else's Glosses," *Representations* 32 (1990), 157–74, reprinted in *Old English Literature: Critical Essays*, ed. Liuzza, 102–24.
2   Bertram Colgrave and R. A. B. Mynors, ed., Bede, *Bede's Ecclesiastical*

questions that might interest a historian of science such as myself. Did Cædmon have a mental picture of the created world? Was it a picture he inherited from ancient Mediterranean sources (classical and patristic) and then transformed, or was it Germanic, however that might be construed? How was it connected to ideas about the world in other texts from the Anglo-Saxon milieu? These issues have been examined by comparing the hymn to accounts of Creation in *Genesis A, Beowulf,* or *The Order of the World*. I propose that they can also be illuminated by attending to what Bede says about Cædmon's first audience, the monks of Whitby and their abbess, and how they responded to the hymn.[3]

What is salient about Bede's account of the hymn, from the perspective of early medieval science, is the reaction of Abbess Hild to Cædmon's gift: she admitted him forthwith to her monastery. Indeed, the famous episode of the miraculous gift

---

History of the English People 4.24 (Oxford, 1969), pp. 416–17. The Old English text of the hymn cited in this essay is the West Saxon version edited by Elliott Van Kirk Dobbie, *The Anglo-Saxon Minor Poems*, Anglo-Saxon Poetic Records 6 (New York and London, 1942), p. 106.

3   The term "science" is used here to designate the ensemble of early medieval ideas about the nature, the physical universe, its structure and principles of order (particularly mathematical order), the properties of creatures within it, and reflections on the way it can be understood. These issues are developed in my essay, "*Si naturam quaeras*: Reframing Bede's 'Science,'" in *Innovation and Tradition in the Writings of the Venerable Bede*, ed. Scott DeGregorio (Morgantown, 2006), pp. 65–99. Apart from the literature cited in this article above, I am indebted to Michael Lapidge's 1971 University of Toronto doctoral dissertation "Ideas of Natural Order in Early Medieval Latin Poetry," and to Pierre Bühler, *Présence, sentiment et rhétorique de la nature dans la littérature latine de la France médiévale de la fin de l'antiquité au XIIe siècle* 2 v. (Paris, 1995).

Faith Wallis

of song is embedded in a longer biography of Cædmon as a monk, and Cædmon's identity as a monk is, from Bede's point of view, the most significant element of his story. Bede praises Cædmon's strenuous devotion to the rule, his composition of edifying Biblical poetry, his foreknowledge of his death, and his exemplary departure from this world. Cædmon's life as a monk is of a piece with his poetic gift. This is underscored by his last act, which was to inquire whether the brethren had assembled to sing the *laudes nocturnas*—a symbolically satisfying detail, in that it was during the night hours that he himself composed his first song *in laudem Dei Conditoris* ("in praise of God the Creator").[4] Bede calls on the word *laus* to drive home the point that Cædmon's hymn held the meaning of his life and death as a monk: "his tongue which had uttered so many good words in praise of the Creator also uttered its last words in His praise . . ." (" . . . illaque lingua, quae tot salutaria uerba in laudem Conditoris conposuerat, ultima quoque uerba in laudem ipsius . . . clauderet") (4.24, pp. 420–21). In sum, the hymn identified Cædmon as a monk.

The hymn's subject matter—*principium creaturarum*, the "beginning," "origin," "source," "foundation," or "author" of created beings—also carried a significant charge for Bede. As a Christian, monk, and Anglo-Saxon, Bede engaged with questions

---

4 Which office Bede meant by *laudes nocturnas* is not clear. In the Benedictine Rule at least, this phrase appears in the title of chapter 10 ("Qualiter aestatis tempore agatur nocturna laus," "How the nightly office of praise should be carried out during the summer") and refers to the first night office, variously called Vigils or Nocturns. Chapter 11 further specifies that the Ambrosian canticle *Te Deum laudamus* as well as the Psalm *Te decet laus* be sung during the night office on Sunday. However, it is noteworthy that the *Laudate* Psalms (Psalms 148–150) are sung at Lauds directly after Matins, the second night office (ch. 12–13): *Le Règle de Saint Benoit*, ed. Jean Neufville and trans. with comm. by Adalbert de Vogüé, Sources chrétiennes 181–84 (Paris, 1972–77), v. 2, pp. 512–21 (text) and v. 5, ch. 2–3 (commentary).

about the created world, notably in his commentary on Genesis, but also in his cosmographical and computistical writings, *De natura rerum, De temporibus,* and *De temporum ratione.* Cædmon was also a Christian, a monk, and an Anglo-Saxon who composed a text about the created world. Both the subject-matter of the hymn, and Cædmon's treatment of it, made it obvious to Bede and his readers that Cædmon was destined to become a monk.

The link between Cædmon's hymn and his career as a monk is not infrequently reduced to the fact that Cædmon was the recipient of a miracle.[5] But why celebrate this miracle with admission to a monastery? What little attention has been devoted to this question has focused largely on the way the hymn came into being, rather than its content. Philip West, André Crépin, Paul Remley, and Donald Fritz suggest that Bede regarded Cædmon as a natural monk because he knew how to meditate in the

---

5   It has been noted by many commentators that Bede does not seem especially preoccupied by the miraculous quality of Cædmon's gift. George Hardin Brown offers a sensitive reading of how Bede understood this episode in the light of his broader understanding of miracle as a manifestation of providence, not a negation of nature: "Old English Verse as a Medium for Christian Theology," in *Modes of Interpretation in Old English Literature,* ed. Phyllis Rugg Brown, Georgia Ronan Crampton and Fred C. Robinson (Toronto, 1986), pp. 15–17. More conventional views are put forward by C.L. Wrenn, "The Poetry of Cædmon," *Proceedings of the British Academy* 32 (1946), 277–95, who mused that the miracle was not merely the gift of poetry, but a revolutionary transplantation of Germanic epic poetic practice into the soil of Christian subject matter; similar views are developed by Donald K. Fry, "Cædmon as a Formulaic Poet," *Forum for Modern Language Studies* 10 (1974), 227–47, reprinted in *Oral Literature: Seven Essays,* ed. J. J. Duggan, 41–61 (Edinburgh, 1975), and "The Memory of Cædmon," *Oral Traditional Literature: A Festschrift for Albert Bates Lord,* ed. John Miles Foley (Columbus, 1981), 282–93. G. Shepherd, "The Prophetic Cædmon," *Review of English Studies* n.s. 5 (1954), 113–22, regards Cædmon's change of life is simply an intensification of piety, a suitable response to a vision.

Faith Wallis

monastic sense of the term, that is, to "chew over" the words of Scripture or the liturgy by concentrated repetition, and "digest" them into his own prayer.[6] Bede describes Cædmon's post-visionary poetic activity in exactly such terms, invoking the particularly resonant image of the clean animal ruminating:[7]

> [Cædmon] was then bidden to describe his dream in the presence of a number of the more learned men and also to recite his song so that they might all examine him and decide upon the nature and origin of the gift of which he spoke; and it seemed clear to all of them that the Lord had granted him heavenly grace. They then read to him a passage of sacred history or doctrine, bidding him make a song out of it, if he could, in metrical form. He undertook the task and went away; on returning next morning he repeated the passage he had been given, which he had put into excellent verse. The abbess [Hild], who recognized the grace of God which the man had received, instructed him to renounce his secular habit and to take monastic vows. She and all her people received [Cædmon] into the community of the brothers and ordered that he should be

---

6 I refer, respectively, to Philip J. West, "Rumination in Bede's Account of Cædmon," *Monastic Studies* 12 (1976), 217–26; André Crépin, "Bede and the Vernacular," in *Famulus Christi*, ed. Gerald Bonner (London, 1976), pp. 170–92 esp. pp. 179–82 and n. 6, pp. 187–88, on Bede's allusions to "rumination"; Paul Remley, *Old English Biblical Verse: Studies in Genesis, Exodus and Daniel*, Cambridge Studies in Anglo-Saxon England 16 (Cambridge, 1996), pp. 39–43; and Donald W. Fritz, "Cædmon: a Monastic Exegete," *American Benedictine Review* 25 (1974), 351–63.

7 The classic exposition of monastic *meditatio*—Jean Leclercq's, *The Love of Learning and the Desire for God*, trans. Catherine Misrahi, 3rd ed. (New York, 1982), pp. 15–17, 72–75—has been considerably expanded and deepened by Mary Carruthers, *The Craft of Thought. Meditation, Rhetoric, and the Making of Images, 400–1200* (Cambridge, 1998).

instructed in the whole course of sacred history. He learned all he could by listening to them, and then, memorizing it and ruminating over it, like some clean animal chewing the cud, he turned it into the most melodious verse: and it sounded so sweet as he recited it that his teachers became in turn his audience. He sang about the creation of the world, the origin of the human race, and the whole history of Genesis, of the departure of Israel from Egypt and the entry into the promised land and of many other of the stories taken from the sacred Scriptures: of the incarnation, passion, and resurrection of the Lord, of His ascension into heaven, of the coming of the Holy Spirit and the teaching of the apostles. He also made songs about the terrors of future judgement, the horrors of the pains of hell, and the joys of the heavenly kingdom. In addition he composed many other songs about the divine mercies and judgements, in all of which he sought to turn his hearers away from delight in sin and arouse in them the love and practice of good works. (*Ecclesiastical History* 4.24, pp. 416–19)[8]

8   " . . . iussus est, multis doctioribus uiris praesentibus, indicare somnium et dicere carmen, ut uniuersorum iudicio quid uel unde esset quod referebat probaretur. Visumque est omnibus caelestem ei a Domino concessam esse gratiam, exponebantque illi quendam sacrae historiae siue doctrinae sermonem, praecipientes eum, si posset, hunc in modulationem carminis transferre. At ille suscepto negotio abiit, et mane rediens optimo carmine quod iubebatur conpositum reddidit. Vnde mox abbatissa amplexata gratiam Dei in uiro, saecularem illum habitum relinquere et monachicum suscipere propositum docuit; susceptumque in monasterium cum omnibus suis fratrum cohorti adsociauit, iussitque illum seriem sacrae historiae doceri. At ipse cuncta, quae audiendo discere poterat, rememorando secum et quasi mundum animal ruminando, in carmen dulcissimum conuertebat, suauisque resonando doctores suos uicissim auditores sui faciebat. Canebat autem de creatione mundi et origine humani generis et tota Genesis historia, de egressu Israel ex Aegypto et ingressu in

Faith Wallis

Bede does not explicitly state that Cædmon, prior to his dream, had received instruction in the Scriptures or liturgy, nor does he suggest that the hymn is a paraphrase. However, West notes that the vision takes place at night, a privileged time for meditation, and amongst ruminants in a barn. Secondly, as Mary Carruthers has observed, the foundation text of a monastic meditation need not be quoted directly. Indeed, a truly superior meditation would be a new invention, an invocation of or allusion to the parent text, rather than a mere processing of received material—for example, a recitation from memory or a pastiche.[9] Hild and her counselors viewed Cædmon's gift as a miraculous acquisition of the monastic craft of *meditatio*, which is why they tested the gift by giving him a bit of *lectio divina* to meditate on. [10] *Meditatio* is not only a process, but also a product—a prayer or composition (*oratio*) made from material collected in and retrieved from the memory. What Cædmon's midnight visitor gave him was a miraculously infused treasury of material, as well as the *donum canendi* ("the gift of song"). Cædmon was commanded not merely to sing, but to "sing me something (*canta mihi aliquid*).' "'What must I sing?' said Cædmon. 'Sing,' he said, 'about the beginning of created things.' Thereupon Cædmon began to sing verses which he had never heard before in praise of God the Creator . . ." ("'Quid' inquit

> terram repromissionis, de aliis plurimis sacrae scripturae historiis, de incarnatione dominica, passione, resurrectione et ascensione in caelum, de Spiritus Sancti aduentu et apostolorum doctrina; item de terrore futuri iudicii et horrore poenae gehennalis ac dulcedine regni caelestis multa carmina faciebat. Sed et alia perplura de beneficiis et iudiciis diuinis, in quibus cunctis homines ab amore scelerum abstrahere, ad dilectionem uero et sollertiam bonae actionis excitare curabat."

9 Carruthers, *Craft of Thought*, pp. 3–5.
10 The role of Hild's monks in shaping Cædmon's subsequent career as a poet is emphasized by Uta Schwab, "The Miracles of Cædmon," *English Studies* 64 (1983), 1–17.

'debeo cantare?' Et ille 'Canta' inquit 'principium creaturarum.' Quo accepto responso, statim ipse coepit cantare in laudem Dei Conditoris uersus quos numquam audierat . . .") (*Ecclesiastical History* 4.24, pp. 416–17).

That the hymn qualified Cædmon as a monk must, then, have something to do with the heavenly command to sing specifically about the beginning of created things.[11] Setting aside the miraculous, we might speculate that Cædmon acquired this material in the form of a catechetical *narratio* which began, as Augustine advised, with *In principio creavit deus coelum et terram* ("In the beginning, God created the heavens and the earth," Gen. 1:1). We might also speculate that he consciously or unconsciously chose to inaugurate his own poetic work of creation at this same starting point.[12] But there are other candidates for the foundation text of the hymn, such as the opening words of the Creed,[13] or the *Laudate* Psalms.[14] Indeed, all these sources may have been in Cædmon's or Bede's mind, for they all cen-

---

11 This link between monastic *meditatio* and the subject matter of the hymn is briefly invoked by Ruth Wehlau, "Rumination and Re-creation: Poetic Instruction in *The Order of the World*," *Florilegium* 13 (1994), 66–67. Wehlau is primarily interested in the symbolism of the Creation as a trope for the inception of Christian vernacular poetry, but also speculates that there may have been a pre-Cædmon tradition of Old English praise-songs about the Creator.

12 Virginia Day, "The Influence of the Catechetical *Narratio* on Old English and Some Other Medieval Narrative," *Anglo-Saxon England* 3 (1974), 51–55. For a different reading of Bede's account as a statement about the genesis of poetry, see Donald Fritz, "Cædmon: a Traditional Christian Poet," *Medieval Studies* 31 (1969), 334–37.

13 D.R. Howlett, "The Theology of Cædmon's Hymn," *Leeds Studies in English* 7 (1973–1974), 1–12, esp. p. 10; Bernard Huppé, *Doctrine and Poetry: Augustine's Influence on Old English Poetry* (New York, 1959), pp. 109, 123.

14 N.F. Blake, "Cædmon's Hymn," *Notes and Queries* n.s. 9 (1962), 243–46.

ter on God as Creator of heaven and earth. If one follows the ripples from that center outwards to the periphery of praise, one might even hear echoes of the *Magnificat*: the hymn, after all, was "born" at midnight in a stable, to one who was bidden by angel to do something that seemed impossible.[15]

Critics have shown strong interest in Cædmon's sources and his treatment of the hymn, but his choice of this theme is often taken to be either obvious or without particular meaning. Even those who argue that the content of the hymn is relevant to its reception by Hild's monks pay less attention to the theme of *principia creaturarum* than to extra-thematic elements, such as embedded Trinitarian theology.[16] Yet it is unlikely that Bede, or

---

15 The concept of the "birth" of English poetry in Cædmon has critical and theoretical dimensions which fall outside the scope of this essay, but which are explored in Allen J. Frantzen, *Desire for Origins: New Language, Old English and Teaching the Tradition* (New Brunswick, 1990), ch. 5, and (in a different vein) by Clare A. Lees and Gillian R. Overing, "Birthing Bishops and Fathering Poets: Bede, Hild, and the Relations of Cultural Production," *Exemplaria* 6 (1994), 35–65, reprinted in *Old English Literature: Critical Essays*, ed. Liuzza, 124–56.

16 The hymn is occasionally treated as if it had no content at all. Judith N. Garde omits it entirely from her *Old English Poetry in Medieval Christian Perspective: a Doctrinal Approach* (Woodbridge, 1991), presumably because it conveys no doctrine. The Creation theme in the hymn can also be reduced to a generically Christian message, encompassing the whole of salvation history: see Ruth Wehlau, *"The Riddle of Creation": Metaphor Structures in Old English Poetry* (New York, 1997), p. 9. Mark Atherton suggests that the choice of theme reflects "an early medieval emphasis on creation, on the divine inspiration of poetry and the suggested parallels between the creativity of the divine artisan and the creativity of the human poet or artist": "Saxon or Celt? Cædmon, 'The Seafarer' and the Irish Tradition," in *Celts and Christians: New Approaches to the Religious Traditions of Britain and Ireland*, ed. Mark Atherton

Cædmon's Created World and the Monastic Encyclopedia

Cædmon's patrons and fellow-monks, would have thought that the theme presented to him by the celestial visitor was chosen for no special reason, or was irrelevant to his monastic destiny. If the miracle was the gift of monastic *meditatio*, what would it mean to Hild or Bede to meditate on *principium creaturarum?*

This is a question which admits no simple or univocal answer. Nonetheless, something useful might be discovered by looking at how Bede himself contemplated the *principium creaturarum* in the opening sections of his commentary on Genesis.

> (Cardiff, 2002), p. 85. Karen Jolly argues that Cædmon's hymn is about nature because it was the consequence of a mystical experience, and mystical and natural experience were synonymous in Germanic-Christian spirituality: "Father God and Mother Earth: Nature Mysticism in the Anglo-Saxon World," in *The Medieval World of Nature: a Book of Essays,* ed. Joyce E. Salisbury (New York and London, 1993), p. 243. On the embedded Trinitarian theology, see Howlett, "Theology of Cædmon's Hymn." The question of the role of the creation story in the conversion of Germanic peoples merits deeper study. Bishop Daniel of Winchester advised Boniface that the story of Creation was a suitable starting point in the conversion of pagans, and particularly in demonstrating the absurdity of polytheism; but Cædmon's poems, while apparently didactic, were not apologetic. Daniel's letter (no. 23) is edited by M. Tangl, *Bonifatii et Lullii Epistolae,* Monumenta Germaniae Historica Epistolae Selectae 1 (1916; reprinted Berlin, 1955), pp. 38–41, and *Councils and Ecclesiastical Documents,* ed. A. W. Haddan and W. Stubbs (Oxford, 1871), v. 3 pp. 304–6; trans. Dorothy Whitelock, *English Historical Documents. Volume 1, c. 500–1042* (London: Eyre and Spottiswoode, 1955), pp. 731–33, and Ephraim Emerton, *The Letters of Saint Boniface* (New York, 1940), pp. 48–50. The creation theme, in itself or in connection with Cædmon, is not discussed in recent historical scholarship on conversion, e.g. James C. Russell, *The Germanization of Early Medieval Christianity* (New York and Oxford, 1994), Richard Fletcher, *The Barbarian Conversion* (Berkeley and Los Angeles, 1999).

In the beginning (in principio), God created the heaven and the earth. In introducing the creation of the universe, Holy Scripture fittingly, in its very first words, shows the eternity and omnipotence of God the Creator. In representing Him as having created the world at the beginning of time, it indicates without doubt that He himself existed eternally, before time. And in recounting that he created heaven and earth at the very beginning of his creative act, it declares Him omnipotent to make what He willed. For when human frailty makes anything, when for example we build a house, in the beginning we prepare the material of the structure, and after this beginning we dig into the depths; then we set stones into the foundation, then place the walls in increasing rows of stones; thus we arrive gradually at the completion of the work we began by progressing gradually. God, however, whose hand is omnipotent for the fulfilment of his task, did not need the delay of time, of whom it is written, *He made all that he wished.* (Psalm 113/115:3)[17]

17 "*In principio creauit Deus caelum et terram.* Creationem mundi insinuans scriptura diuina apte primo statim uerbo eternitatem atque omnipotentiam Dei creatoris ostendit, quem enim in principio temporum mundum creasse perhibet, ipsum profecto ante tempora eternaliter extitisse designat. Et quem in ipso conditionis initio caelum et terram creasse narrat, tanta celeritate operationis omnipotentem esse declarat cui uoluisse fecisse est. Nam humana fragilitas cum aliquid operatur, uerbi gratia cum domum aedificamus, in principio operis materiam preparamus et post hoc principium fodimus in altum; deinde immittimus lapides in fundamentum, deinde parietes augescentibus lapidum ordinibus apponimus; sicque paulatim ad perfectionem operis propositi proficiendo peruenimus. Deus autem cuius omnipotens manus est ad explendum onus suum, non eguit mora temporum qui, sicut scriptum est, *Omnia quaecumque uoluit fecit.*" Bede, *In Genesim* I,i,1, ed. C. W. Jones, Corpus christianorum series latina 118A (Turnhout, 1967), p. 3, lines 1–16 (my translation).

Cædmon's Created World and the Monastic Encyclopedia

Both the form and the content of this text illustrate the dynamic of *meditatio*. *Meditatio* begins with rumination, but its end is to make thoughts, and in monastic literature, this process was represented by images drawn from architecture.[18] In this case, Bede thinks through the meaning of *principium (creaturarum)* by constructing a mental picture of a building (the creation) whose construction is fully realized in an instant (the *principium*).[19] The fact that *principium* denotes "beginning (in time)," but also connotes "foundation (of a building)" facilitates this image, but its resonance depends on an established Biblical and patristic tradition of imagining creation as architecture. Comparisons of God's Creation to human acts of architectural construction also had a singular appeal for Old English writers. Indeed, as Jennifer Neville has observed, architecture is almost the only metaphor for the physical cosmos in Old English literature.[20]

18 Carruthers, *Craft of Thought*, esp. ch. 1.
19 Huppé, *Doctrine and Poetry*, pp. 104–6, also examines *In Genesim* in relation to Cædmon's hymn, but (a) does not connect *In principio* . . . to the *principium creaturarum*, and (b) does not mention this particular architectural image. Huppé's comparisons of the architecture imagery of Creation in the Fathers to the Hymn should be treated with some caution. For example, he translates Isaiah 40:22 (p. 113–14) as "God made heaven like a room [*sicut cameram*]"—but *camera* means "vault" or "arched roof," which is certainly how Basil and Ambrose understood it. Bede does not cite this passage from Isaiah in his commentary. Bede's equation of "in the beginning" with "all at once" and his literal approach to the meaning of "heaven and earth" derive ultimately from the exegeses of Basil of Caesarea and Gregory of Nyssa: see J. C. M. van Winden, "The Early Christian Exegesis of 'Heaven and Earth' in Genesis 1:1," in *Romanitas et Christianitas. Studia Iano Henrico Waszink . . . oblata*, ed. W. den Boer, P.G. van der Nat, C.M.J. Sicking and J.C.M. van Winden (Amsterdam, 1973), p. 374.
20 Jennifer Neville, *Representations of the Natural World in Old English*

It is also the only metaphorical image in Cædmon's hymn: the first of God's *miracula* (Latin) / *wundra* (OE), the object of his *potentia* / *meahte* and *consilium* / *modgeþanc* is not (as in the text of Genesis—or *Genesis A* for that matter) to create light, or to divide the primal waters, but to make the heavens as a roof (*caelum pro culmine tecti* / *heofon to hrofe*).[21]

However, critics have not been comfortable aligning the world-hall of Old English poetry, including the hymn, with the cosmic architecture of Latin exegesis such as Bede's. The Anglo-Saxon world-hall, it is often argued, carried a distinctive native charge incommensurate with architectural allegories based on Mediterranean sources.[22] The essence of this difference is that in the Anglo-Saxon milieu, the accent falls on the "hall" rather than the "world." To approach this transformation another

---

Poetry, Cambridge Studies in Anglo-Saxon England 27 (Cambridge, 1999), pp. 146–47.

21 The phrase *culmina tecti* (the summit or ridgepole of the roof) occurs in *Aeneid* 2.695 and 4.186, but is not used there as a metaphor for the heavens. This metaphorical transformation may have been an Anglo-Saxon innovation: *cf.* Aldhelm, *Carmen de virginitate*, ed. R. Ehwald, *Aldhelmi opera omnia*, Monumenta Germaniae Historica Auctores antiquissimi 15 (Berlin, 1919), p. 353: "Omnipotens genitor, mundum ditione gubernans / Lucida stelligeri qui condis culmina caeli." *Cf.* Schwab, "Miracle," p. 13. See also n. 56 below.

22 On the world-hall as a distinctive feature of Old English literature, see Wehlau, *"Riddle"* ch. 1, and Alvin A. Lee, *The Guest-Hall of Eden: Four Essays on the Design of Old English Poetry* (New Haven and London, 1972), esp. p. 24. Much of the literature devoted to the hall as an image does not, however, address the cosmic theme, but concentrates on the social imagery discussed below: e.g. H. Magennis, *Images of Community in Old English Poetry*, Cambridge Studies in Anglo-Saxon England 18 (Cambridge, 1993), esp. ch. 3; K. Hume, "The Concept of the Hall in Old English Poetry," *Anglo-Saxon England* 3 (1974), 63–74.

way, we should say that the social meanings attached to "hall" in Anglo-Saxon culture are projected onto the cosmos and its Creator, but that cosmological ideas are not expressed through the image of the hall. For example, Neville argues that for the hall to function as a cosmological metaphor, it would have to resemble visually the physical structure of the universe. We have no idea how the pre-Christian Germans visualized the shape of the universe, but most Mediterranean and patristic sources pictured the universe in the Hellenistic manner, that is, as a sphere, which disqualifies the hall as figure.

The only cosmos the world-hall could represent is the archaic Biblical-Mesopotamian one—a rectangular platform floating on the waters of the abyss, with a roof ("firmament") upheld on pillars at the four corners. This is the picture painted by a handful of Greek authors like Cosmas Indicopleustes; but while Neville speculates that Cosmas' text might have entered the Anglo-Saxon world with Theodore and Hadrian, she admits this in unlikely.[23] She concludes, then, that the world-hall is not a cosmological figure, because the Anglo-Saxons seem not to have had any articulate ideas about the form of the universe, or indeed any interest in this topic. Rather, the world-hall is a symbol of God's power to protect and provide. His act of Creation is comparable to Hrothgar's construction of Heorot as an enclosure for his people, where they can enjoy light, warmth, and fellowship, shielded from their enemies and from the chaotic and unbounded world of nature.[24]

---

23 Neville, *Representations of the Natural World*, pp. 146–47.
24 Neville, *Representations of the Natural World*, pp. 54–68, esp. 57; *cf.* Wehlau, *"Riddle"* pp. 20–1. The theme of protection and peace is the burden of Maginnis, *Images of Community*, and Hume, "The Concept of the Hall." On the other hand, Heorot's analogous relationship to God's Creation has also been interpreted as a macrocosm-microcosm metaphor with both Christian and pagan references; here the accent is on the threat from the builder/Creator's enemy, and the final destruction of the world-hall by fire:

Faith Wallis

The juxtaposition of the account of Hrothgar's construction of Heorot to the *scop*'s song of creation[25] speaks to a social meaning for the world-hall image—a meaning which J. B. Bessinger invokes by verbally braiding Cædmon's hymn and the description of the building of Heorot together into a medley. Like the *scop*'s song, Cædmon's hymn is a praise-song or panegyric, specifically "a half-definable sub-genre, the heroic encomium praising a structure along with its builder." Hence, the Old English text multiplies epithets of lordship for God, while Bede's Latin refers to him as *deus* rather than *dominus*.[26] The relationship of man to the Creator is one of loyalty to an ideally and incomparably strong and provident lord, not of admiration for a divine artist-craftsman's rational and expressive design.[27]

---

see Paul Beekman Taylor, "Heorot, Earth and Asgard: Christian Poetry and Pagan Myth," *Tennessee Studies in Literature* 11 (1966), 119–43.

25 *Beowulf*, lines 90b-98, ed. Elliott Van Kirk Dobbie, *Beowulf and Judith*, Anglo-Saxon Poetic records 4 (New York, 1953), p. 5.

26 "Homage to Cædmon and Others: a Beowulfian Praise Song," in *Old English Studies in Honour of John C. Pope*, ed. R. B. Burlin and E. B. Irving, Jr. (Toronto, 1974), pp. 92–93. Bessinger argues that the *Beowulf* poet modeled his "encomiastic association between cosmic and worldly rulers and their creations" (p. 94) on Cædmon. The idea that Cædmon's hymn is a transposed praise-song is developed by Jeff Opland, *Anglo-Saxon Oral Poetry: a Study of the Tradition* (New Haven, 1980), p. 117, and "From Horseback to Monastic Cell: The Impact on English Literature of the Introduction of Writing," in *Old English Literature in Context: Ten Essays*, ed. John Niles (Cambridge and Totowa, 1980), p. 42. See also John C. Pope, *Seven Old English Poems* (Indianapolis, 1966), 55, who suggests that Cædmon's imagination was stimulated not only by royal panegyric, but by the building of Hild's monastery itself.

27 Lee, *Guest-hall of Eden*, pp. 12 *sqq.*; Wehlau, *"Riddle"* pp. 20–1; Neville, *Representations of the Natural World*, p. 67; and P. J. Lucas, "Loyalty and Obedience in the Old English *Genesis* and the Interpolation of

For Neville, the world-hall motif is thus symptomatic of the poverty of Anglo-Saxon cosmological conceptions. Even *Genesis A*'s description of the sky as *hyrstedne hrof halgum tunglum* ("roof adorned with holy stars") contains nothing more than "a hint of a fuller vision of the cosmos than [the one] actually presented in the poem, a hint of a classical image divorced from its original context, but there is nothing else in the poem to make a connection more than tenuous." She doubts that the *Genesis A* poet borrowed the image from Bede, and, in any case, Bede himself shows little appreciation for cosmology, being preoccupied by *computus*.[28]

Bede's computistical works, on the other hand, invite us to take a fresh look at the world-hall image in Cædmon's hymn. To begin with, even though the hymn is the oldest evidence of vernacular use of the world-hall image, there is not enough internal evidence to prove that Cædmon thought of the image in either cosmological or social terms. Inferences must be based on assumptions about the nature of Cædmon's poetic practice (for example, whether he was an oral-formulaic poet), and this is a problem for philologists, not historians, to address. However, there is no need to assume that Cædmon's first audience did not think the image was about the structure of the cosmos. This is true even if the monks of Whitby thought about nature only in connection with the *computus*. Secondly, it is important to bear in mind that Cædmon articulates only one architectural metaphor, namely that the heavens are a roof. Bede's thinking about the cosmos suggests that he would not have read Cædmon's image as merely a statement of the obvious—that the heavens are overhead. For Bede, cosmology, *computus*, and the Creator's provision for the "sons of men" converged in specifically architectural images of the world that placed special emphasis on the

---

Genesis B into *Genesis A*," *Neophilologus* 76 (1992), 121–35.

28 Neville, *Representations of the Natural World*, p. 156; *Genesis A*, line 965, ed. George Philip Krapp, *The Junius Manuscript*, Anglo-Saxon Poetic Records 1 (New York, 1931), p. 31.

heaven-roof, including its construction, its motion, and above all its permanence and stability.

In the course of his commentary on Genesis, Bede re-activates the image of architecture precisely at the moment when he has to confront the text's most difficult structural issue: the waters above the firmament. The superior waters, he explains (drawing on Ambrose and Augustine), are the crystalline heavens in which the planets and stars are fixed. This crystalline material is water, but water concreted into solid *firmitas*, like quartz.[29] There is no need, however, to be anxious that the waters above the firmament might melt and run downward, for the form of the heavens is spherical; if vaporous clouds can remain aloft without shedding their waters, so much more can these waters be held up over the sphere of the heavens on the foundation (*crepidine*) of a much firmer substance (*In Genesim* I,i,6–8, pp. 10 line 252–11, line 268). Here the precise composition and shape of heaven's roof matters, because it poses a concrete structural problem. It is no accident that Bede closes this section with a quotation from the pseudo-Clementine *Recognitiones* that emphasizes the integrity of the cosmic house. *In principio* God made heaven and earth a single house (*tamquam domum unum*). The crystalline waters are the created heavens. They divide the entire *machina* of the world into two spaces (*regiones*), even though it remains a single *domus*. "Upstairs" is the *habitaculum* of the angels, the eternal heaven of God; "downstairs" lives humankind in the created cosmos (*In Genesim* I,i,6–8, p. 12, lines 309–24).[30]

This attention to structural stability and coherence underpins the way in which Bede uses the term *natura*. When he is writing about the physical world, Bede uses this word almost exclusively to mean the "property" or "attribute" of a specific entity. He never uses *natura* to mean the ensemble of the universe,

---

29 That crystal stones were formed by ice which had been "petrified" by cold was held by Pliny, *Historia naturalis* 37.23, 26; see also Isidore of Seville, *Etymologiae* 16.13.1.
30 See Huppé, *Doctrine and Poetry*, pp. 113–4.

or an abstract principle or power. Rather than define *natura*, he consistently associates it with the terms *ratio* and *ordo*, which almost serve as synonyms. However, when he is writing about time in *De temporum ratione*, he uses *natura* in a very precise and original manner to denote the way a particular kind of time is measured. *Natura* refers to God's "real time," established at Creation, embodied in the motions of the sun and moon, and measured by the physical movements of the heavens. The distinction between the two "natures" is particularly striking in *De temporum ratione*, where cosmology and *computus* are fused. It is in *De temporum ratione* as well that the terms *ordo* and *ratio* make their most distinctive appearance as quasi-synonyms for *natura*.[31] All these terms point upwards, to the heaven-roof.

Correct computistical *ratio* of Easter hinges on the "natural time" of the sun and moon at the moment of their creation: the sun must be at the equinox, where it stood on the fourth day, and the moon must be full. This *ratio* is embodied in the Dionysian Paschal table, the diagram that spatializes the true laws which order Christian time-reckoning. In *De temporum ratione* chapters 47–62, Bede describes the eight columns of this Paschal table using terms which evoke architecture, particularly spatial boundaries (*versus, meta*), extent (*regio, locus*), and arrangement (*linea, trames, ordo*). From the perspective of our interest in the heaven-roof, however, it is the discussion of the moon as a marker of time (*De temporum ratione* ch. 26) that presents the greatest interest. Bede presents an experiment to prove that when the moon appears higher in the sky (*i.e.* further above the horizon) than the sun, it does not necessarily mean it is physically above the sun in the heavens. Go into a church at night, he says, and sight along two hanging lamps, the nearer one being lower down than the further one. As you walk forward (Bede says), you will see that the flame in the nearer lamp, although actually lower, appears to be above the more distant, higher one.[32] Now the

---

31 Wallis, "*Si naturam quaeras,*" *passim.*
32 Bede, *De temporum ratione*, ed. C. W. Jones, Corpus christianorum

interesting feature of this demonstration is that a church building is actually unnecessary: the optical effect can be replicated by holding two candles at arm's length. Bede specifies a church, I believe, because he and his readers are deeply attuned to the cosmological meaning of the world-hall. The sun and moon tell God's natural time by being in specific, predictable places in a three-dimensional and mobile heaven, and this constitutes the divinely ordained basis of the Christian calendar. However, it is worth remarking that Bede, who definitely believed in the Hellenistic spherical universe, could use a rectangular church building with vertical walls and a (probably) flat roof as an improvised planetarium.[33] So also could his monastic readers. The early ninth century Northumbrian poet Æthelwulf, in his *De abbatibus*, likewise imagines the lamps hanging from the ceiling of Abbot Sigbald's monastery church as stars: "As the whole sky shines with gleaming stars, so beneath the roof of the church hanging torches dangle their tremulous flames in a number of rows. . . . Many men wished to hang up numerous bowls, which would give soft light in the rectangular church . . ."[34] The way these writers

series latina 123B (Turnhout, 1977), p. 361 line 34–362 line 55; trans. Faith Wallis, *Bede: The Reckoning of Time*, Translated Texts for Historians 29 (Liverpool, 1999, rev. ed. 2004), p. 78, and commentary on pp. 304–6.

33 It is worth noting that one branch of the Byzantine iconographic tradition of the zodiacal sphere transmitted to the west during the Carolingian period depicted the sphere within a classical temple, with colonnaded facade and pitched roof: see Barbara Obrist, "La représentation carolingienne du zodiaque. À propos du manuscrit de Bâle, Universitätsbibliothek, F III 15a," *Cahiers de civilisation médiévalé* 44 (2001), 3–33.

34 " . . . ut celum rutilat stellis fulgentibus omne, / sic tremulas uibrant subter testudine templi / ordinibus uariis funalia pendula flammas . . . nam plures multi cupiebant pendere caucos, / limpida qui tribuant quadrato lumina templo . . .": *De abbatibus* 20, ed. and trans. A. Campbell (Oxford, 1967), lines 625–27, 631–

deploy architecture as a model for the physical cosmos without literally equating the shape of the building with the shape of the universe brings to the fore another important element of medieval memory and meditation. To be functional, even in a "scientific" context, visual representation did not necessarily have to be mimetic,[35] though it could be mimetic if it so chose.

Architecture and the Monastic Encyclopedia: Time, Stability, and Edification

Bede's computistical writings reveal an interest in the real structure of the universe in relation to natural (that is, divinely created) time; his exegetical writings manifest that same interest in relation to stability, unity, and integrity of the fabric of the world. The two meanings of cosmic architecture, time and stability, cross-pollinate. This is made possible by the fact that exegesis and *computus* are facets of a single Christian program of knowledge, which we might call the "monastic encyclopedia." The process of *meditatio* links the two together in the moral and symbolic act of "edification."

What I understand by the "monastic encyclopedia" is the framework of Christian erudition set out in Augustine's *De doctrina christiana*, as "operationalized" by monastic practices of instruction, reading, and prayer. The encyclopedia is not a dis-

---

32. Compare the stars as *heofoncondelle* ("heaven-candles") in *The Order of the World* 54: ed. George Philip Krapp and Elliott Van Kirk Dobbie, *The Exeter Book*, Anglo-Saxon Poetic Records 3 (New York, 1936, 165. On Æthelwulf's imagery, see George Henderson, *Vision and Image in Early Christian England* (Cambridge, 1999), p. 181, and H. M. Taylor, "The Architectural Interest of Æthelwulf's *De Abbatibus*," *Anglo-Saxon England* 3 (1974), pp. 164–73, esp. p. 172.

35 This principle of *adaequatio* in fully elaborated in the memory theory of the High Middle Ages: see Mary Carruthers, *The Book of Memory: A Study of Memory in Medieval Culture*, Cambridge Studies in Medieval Literature, 10 (Cambridge, 1990), pp. 22–23.

crete body of knowledge, but a web of reference points in Scripture, liturgy, doctrine, and discipline, onto which elements of ancient profane learning, including scientific learning, could be hung. These elements do not necessarily have to be coherent with one another, but they do have to cohere to the node on the spiritual web which they address. The encyclopedia supported a paradoxically credulous agnosticism about nature: almost anything one could say about the natural world might be true, but almost nothing had to be true. Augustine, for example, thought that the validity of the spherical Hellenistic model of the cosmos was extremely probable, but ultimately the truth of Genesis did not depend on that probability.[36] I shall examine

---

36 These reflections on the "monastic encyclopedia" are indebted to a magisterial analysis of the transformation of ancient secular learning into this new religious encyclopedia, Hervé Inglebert's *Interpretatio christiana. Les mutations des savoirs (cosmographie, géographie, ethnographie, histoire) dans l'Antiquité chrétienne 30–630 après J.-C.* (Paris, 2001). They have also been formed by the work of the following scholars: Jacques Fontaine on Isidore of Seville, notably his commentary on Isidore's *De natura rerum* in *Traité de la nature* (Bordeaux, 1960) and his *Isidore de Seville et la culture classique en Espagne wisigothique* 2 v. (Paris, 1959); Giselle de Nie on Gregory of Tours, particularly *Views from a Many-Windowed Tower: Studies of Imagination in the Works of Gregory of Tours* (Amsterdam, 1987) and the essays collected in de Nie, *Word, Image, Experience: Dynamics of Miracle and Self-Perception in Sixth-Century Gaul* (Aldershot, 2003); Marina Smyth's *Understanding the Universe in Seventh-Century Ireland,* Studies in Celtic History 15 (Woodbridge, 1996); and the studies of *computus* and the re-configuration of ancient mathematics and astronomy by Brigitte Englisch, Stephen McCluskey, C. W. Jones, and Wesley Stevens. Though largely focused on terrestrial rather than cosmic "nature," Bühler's *Présence, sentiment et rhétorique de la nature* is particularly illuminating for its attention to exegesis. The monastic dimension has been profoundly influenced by the scholarship of Mary Carruthers, but also by studies of pre-

briefly how Bede works within the encyclopedia to elaborate the notion of the heaven-roof as both "time" and "stability," because I believe that his emphasis on the power of Cædmon's poetry to "edify" (which is, in the end, his principle message about Cædmon) rests on the meaning he attached to the architectural metaphor in the hymn.

Bede was deeply interested in Biblical architecture. He is famous for being the first exegete to comment on the construction of the Tabernacle and Temple,[37] but the allegory of building also penetrates his account of Noah's Ark in *In Genesim*, and of the new Jerusalem in the *Expositio Apocalypseos*.[38] In monastic culture, architecture was also a widely-used trope for monastic *meditatio*; in particular, it stood for the process of building thoughts about God, and thereby building up—edifying—the individual and the community.[39] Patristic authors proposed architecture as a subject of meditation, and extended the concept to include the architecture of the world. "If you have a taste for building," wrote Quodvultdeus, commending the variety of topics in the Bible open to the contemplative reader, "you have the construction of the world, the measurements of the

---

Carolingian monastic culture by Pierre Riché and Detlef Illmer, particular the latter's *Formen der Erziehung und Wissenvermittlung im frühen Mittelalter*, Münchner Beiträge zur Mediävistik und Renaissanceforschung 7 (Munich, 1971).

37 See *De tabernaculo*, ed. D. Hurst, CCSL 119B (Turnhout, 1969), pp. 1–139, trans. Arthur G. Holder, *Bede: On the Tabernacle*, TTH 18 (Liverpool, 1994); *De templo*, ed. D. Hurst, CCSL 119A (Turnhout, 1969), 143–234, trans. Seán Connolly, *Bede: On the Temple*, TTH 21 (Liverpool, 1995). For additional commentary, see Holder, "New Treasures and Old in Bede's *De tabernaculo* and *De templo*," *Revue Bénédictine* 99 (1989), 237–49.

38 *Expositio Apocalypseos*, ed. Roger Gryson, Corpus christianorum series latina 121A (Turnhout, 2001); I am presently preparing an English translation and commentary on this work.

39 Carruthers, *Craft of Thought*, *passim* and esp. ch. 1.

Ark, the enclosure of the Tabernacle, the soaring structure of the temple of Solomon, all of which symbolize the members of the Church throughout the world." ("Aedificandi si est affectio, habes fabricam mundi, mensuras arcae, ambitum tabernaculi, fastigium templi Salomonis, ipsiusque per mundum membra ecclesiae quam illa omnia figurabant.")[40] Not only could any building be a figure of the Church, but any of God's created works could be imagined as a building. In his commentary on Genesis 2:20–22, Bede expresses satisfaction that the Scriptural text says that God *built* (*aedificavit*) the body of Eve, symbol of the church, "not just as a human body, but also as a house; and we are that house, if we hold fast to our trust and the glory of our hope until the end." " . . . non tamquam corpus humanum, sed tamquam domum, quae domus nos sumus, si fiduciam et gloriam spei usque ad finem firmam retineamus" (*In Genesim* I.ii.20–22, pp. 56, line 1795–57, line 1805).[41]

Within the monastic encyclopedia, *computus* was not just a technique in the service of ecclesiastical discipline, but a manifestation of the divine and rational design of the physical universe according to "measure, number and weight." This coupling of counting and creation is a patristic commonplace that resonated with Anglo-Saxon poets, as the opening lines of *Christ and Satan* attest, where the Creator's *orðonc* numbers (*ariman*) the raindrops, and fixes the limit of the days (*Daga enderim / seolua he gesette*).[42] But architecture also invites Bede to represent

---

40   Quodvultdeus, *Liber promissionum* 13.17, ed. R. Braun, Corpus christianorum series latina 60 (Turnhout, 1976), p. 221, lines 59–62 (my translation). *Cf.* H. de Lubac, *Exégèse médiévale: Les quatre sens de l'Écriture* (Paris, 1964), pt. 2, v. 2, pp. 41–60 "Symboles architecturaux," esp. p. 41; Carruthers, *Craft of Thought*, p. 18.
41   *Cf.* de Lubac, p. 47.
42   *Christ and Satan* 11–13b, 18, ed. Krapp, *The Junius Manuscript*, p. 135. The image probably derives from Cassian, Conferences 15.1: we can see God indirectly through his creation "when we think that he knows the sands of the sea and that he has measured the number

computus as the framework of a distinctive quality of the creation, namely its stability. An Irish computistical text known to Bede

of the waves; when we contemplate with amazement the raindrops, the days and hours of the ages, how all things past and future are present to his knowledge" ("cum harenam maris undarumque numerum dimensum ei et cognitum cogitamus, cum pluuiarum guttas, cum saeculorum dies et horas, cum praeterita futuraue uniuersa obstupescentes scientiae eius adsistere contemplamur"): Iohannis Cassiani Conlationes XXIIII, ed. Michael Petchenig, Corpus scriptorum ecclesiasticorum latinorum 13, pt. 2 (Vienna, 1886), p. 25, lines 12–15, trans. Boniface Ramsey, John Cassian: The Conferences, Ancient Christian Writers, 57 (New York, 1997), p. 55. It should be pointed out that the word *meotod* which appears in vernacular versions of the hymn, as well as in *Christ and Satan*, to designate the Creator, can connote, *inter alia*, someone who measures or metes out; see Wehlau, *"Riddle,"* p. 30. This too may have Patristic origins. For example, Gregory calls Christ the "measurer" (*mensor*): *Moralia in Iob* 28.6, ed. M. Adriaen, Corpus christianorum series latina 143B, p. 1408, line 55. The image of God with compass and scales makes its first medieval appearance in Anglo-Saxon manuscript illumination, *e.g.* the Tiberius Psalter: see Dorothy Glass, *"In Principio*: The Creation in the Middle Ages," in *Approaches to Nature in the Middle Ages*, ed. Lawrence D. Roberts (Binghamton, 1982), pp. 88–92. I must decline, however, Glass's attractive suggestion that the compass signals God's role as architect of the universe: it represents measurement in general, the way the scales represent weight in general. The compass does not appear as an attribute of the builder until the twelfth century (personal communication, Prof. Hans J. Böker, Karlsruhe University). It is only in the thirteenth-century *Bible moralisé* that the compass appears by itself as an attribute of God, in a scene evoking the Creation: see John Block Friedman, "The Architect's Compass in Creation Miniatures of the Later Middle Ages," *Traditio* 30 (1974), 419–29.

establishes the place of "number" in the encyclopedia, and proclaims its special vocation to stabilize:

> Concerning the four divisions of Scripture, Augustine says: Four things are necessary in the Church of God: the divine law in which the future life is described and foretold/preached; history, in which deeds are recounted; number, in which future events and divine celebrations are reckoned up; grammar, in which the science of words is understood. Therefore there are four parts of Scripture: divine law, history, number, and grammar. In praise of *computus*, Isidore says: "The calculation of numbers is not to be scorned, for it reveals the mystery contained in many passages of Holy Scripture. Not in vain is it said of God [Wisdom 11.21]: 'Thou hast made all things in measure, number and weight.' . . . Using the science of numbers, we have an ability to stand firm to some degree, when through this science we discuss the course of the months or learn the span of the revolving year. Indeed through number we are taught so that we do not fall into confusion. Take number away, and everything lapses into ruin. Remove *computus* from the world, and blind ignorance will envelop everything, nor can men who are ignorant of how to calculate be distinguished from other animals.[43]

---

43 "Augustinus dixit de quatuor divisionibus scripturae: Quatuor necessaria sunt in Ecclesia Dei: Canon divinus, in quo narratur et praedicatur vita futura; Historia, in qua rerum gesta narrantur; Numerus, in quo facta futurorum et solemnitates divinae dinumerantur; Grammatica, in qua verborum scientia intelligitur. Igitur quatuor sunt partes Scripturae: Canon divinus, Historia, Numerus, Grammatica. Istae autem divisiones sunt quasi Scripturae quatuor fundamenta. Isidorus in Computi laude dicit: Ratio numerorum contemnenda non est. In multis locis sanctarum Scripturarum, quantum mysterium habet, elucet. Non enim frustra in laudibus Dei dictum est: Omnia in mensura et numero et pondere fecisti. . . . Datum enim nobis est, ex aliqua

Cædmon's Created World and the Monastic Encyclopedia

When Bede wants to imagine the counterintuitive concept of "standing fast" in time, he summons architecture to his aid. The time in question can be the whole span of history, of which the Ark of Noah, the Tabernacle and the Temple are spatialized, materialized schemata. Their design and measurements bind the Old Covenant to the New, the Church Militant to the Church Expectant, and the six ages of the world to the Eighth Age of the world-to-come. Reflecting on the mortised boards that are assembled into the walls of the Tabernacle, for example, Bede remarks that

> when the tabernacle is built and the boards are joined together in accordance with the pattern prescribed above, the form of the mortises is not perceived at all; nevertheless, the firm stability of the unwavering wall (*parietis inconcussi firma stabilitas*) itself shows with what great strength it is joined together through the boards.[44]

---

parte sub numerorum consistere disciplina, quando mensium curricula disputamus, quando anni spatium redeuntis per numerum agnoscimus. Per numerum siquidem ne confundamur, instruimur. Tolle numerum a rebus omnibus, et omnia pereunt. Adime saeculo computum, et omnia caeca ignorantia complectitur. Nec differri possunt a caeteris animalibus, qui calculi nesciunt rationem." *De computo dialogus, Patrologia Latina* (Paris, 1844–82) v. 90, cols. 647–48. The quotation from Isidore is from *Etymologiae* 3.4. For commentary on this text, see Wallis, *Bede: The Reckoning of Time*, pp. xxiii–xxv, and Faith Wallis, "'Number Mystique' in Early Medieval Computus Texts," in *Mathematics and the Divine: a Historical Study*, ed. Tuen Koetsier and L. Bergmans (Amsterdam, 2005), pp. 181–99.

44 "Et quidem erecto tabernaculo regulariter ante ordinata compage tabularum figura incastraturarum non cernitur, quanta tamen uirtute per tabulas sibimet coadunauerit ipsa parietis inconcussi firma stabilitas ostendit." Bede, *De tabernaculo* 2, p. 62, lines 794–97, trans. Holder, p. 69.

Faith Wallis

The way in which the boards are mortised together at their corners also demonstrates

> how our present manner of life remains stable and unshaken . . . because it believes in, hopes for, and loves the gifts of recompense to come, and because with the continual help of the citizens of heaven it is held together lest it should fall down amidst the stormy blasts of unclean spirits.[45]

The architecture of the Tabernacle is *stabilis*. It stands for the "eternal stability and stable eternity (*aeterna stabilitate ac stabili aeternitate*)" that promises safety, order, and purpose in the "fleeting and wave-tossed course of time (*uolubili ac fluctiuagu temporis lapsu*)." These last phrases, however, come from *De temporum ratione* (ch. 71, p. 544, lines 91–93); and indeed, *stabilitas* is a word which figures prominently in Bede's computistical lexicon.[46] For example, in chapter 43, he says "We are bolstered by the aid of the authority of the Fathers when we follow the decrees of the Council of Nicaea, which fixed the fourteenth Moons of the Paschal feast with such firm stability [*firma stabilitas*] that the 19-year cycle can never waver [*vacillare*] and never fail." (p. 415, lines 62–6)[47] The common denominator of *stabilitas* equates the

---

45 "Angulares tabulae sunt tabulis parietum per omnia coniunctae quia futurae requiei et immortalitatis gloria praesenti nostrae conuersationi per fidem spem et caritatem firmissime conexa est immo ideo stabilis et inconcussa praesens nostra conuersatio perdurat quia futurae dona retributionis credit sperat diligit quia crebro supernorum ciuium adiutorio ne flatibus turbulentis immundorum spirituum decidere possit continetur." Bede, *De tabernaculo* 2, p. 67, lines 1003–9; trans. Holder, p. 75.
46 Faith Wallis, "Images of Order in the Medieval Computus," in *ACTA XIV: Ideas of Order in the Middle Ages*, ed. Warren Ginsberg (Binghamton, 1990), pp. 45–67.
47 Trans. Wallis, *Bede: The Reckoning of Time*, p. 117.

calendar to the wall-boards of the Tabernacle through *ratio*, our perception of a structure.

Bede uses the world-hall image, both in his commentaries and in his computus, to proclaim and embody stability. So also does the author of *Genesis A* in the image of the star-strewn roof of heaven mentioned above, for the image is part of a catalogue of the goodness of a creation that persists unchanged, even after Adam and Eve have forfeited paradise through their disobedience.[48] Heorot will be destroyed, like the work of the giants in *The Ruin*,[49] or the shattered walls in *The Wanderer*;[50] but God's work partakes of a unique stability. Bede even argues in *De temporum ratione* (ch. 70) that the fires of the Last Judgement will not touch the starry heaven, or the sun and moon; nor will the new heaven and earth replace the old, but rather purify it.[51] His logic is based on a very clear picture of the physical structure of the world—the "heavens" which will be affected by the fires are only the atmosphere, not the region of the planets and stars, which will simply be temporarily occluded by the smoke from the conflagration.

This concept of cosmic stability is also articulated through the world-hall image in other Old English poetry, notably in tropes of "fastening" and "fastness" connected with the structure of the physical cosmos in poems like *The Order of the World*.[52]

---

48   *Genesis A* 952–960, ed. Krapp, *The Junius Manuscript*, p. 31.
49   Ed. Krapp and Dobbie, *The Exeter Book*, pp. 227–9.
50   *The Wanderer* 64–87, ed. Krapp and Dobbie, *The Exeter Book*, pp. 135–36.
51   *De temporum ratione* 70, p. 540. 5–35; Wallis, *Bede: The Reckoning of Time* p. 244, and commentary pp. 370–73.
52   Wehlau, "*Riddle*," pp. 39–40. The architect in *The Gifts of Men* 44–48 is "One [who] can marvelously devise the work of each sort of high building; his hand is learned, wise and controlled, as it is right for a builder to build a hall, he knows how to join fast a broad hall against sudden collapses." See Krapp and Dobbie, *The Exeter Book*, p. 138, trans. Wehlau, "*Riddle*," p. 16. A comparable

Faith Wallis

The heaven-roof plays a critical role because it embodies the capacity of the world-hall to literally stay standing up: God's cosmos is a unique edifice whose vertiginous dimensions pose no risk to its stability.[53] Indeed, on those occasions when he allegorized Biblical buildings as symbols of divine protection, Bede expressed this idea through the theme of height, and the process whereby height is stabilized. Commenting on the New Jerusalem of Apocalypse 21.12, "And it had a wall great and high, . . . ," Bede says:

> That is, an unassailable stability of faith, hope and love. This can also be understood as the Lord, who is the great wall protecting the Church everywhere of which Isaiah spoke: *a wall and a bulwark shall be set therein*[54]—that is, the protection of the Lord and the intercession of the saints, who make a path for Him by teaching the hearts of the faithful.

Explaining Apocalypse 21.16–17, he adds:

---

case is presented by the first of the Advent Lyrics in *Christ I* which invites "the head [-stone] of the great hall" to "draw together the vast walls," "leave standing wall against wall" and repair the "house under its roof"—the cosmos and the human body; ed. Krapp and Dobbie, *The Exeter Book*, p. 3, trans. Brown, "Old English Verse," pp. 19–21.

53 "Architecture represents the opposite of the inevitable downward movement of things natural. The declining world of *The Wanderer* is one in which things fall down and fall apart. Successful buildings, on the other hand, not only stay together, but they stay up. God's creative ability is, therefore, the ability specifically to raise up the creation." Wehlau, "*Riddle*," p. 52.

54 "This can also be . . . *therein*": *cf.* Primasius of Hadrumentum, *Commentarius in Apocalypsim*, ed. A. W. Adams, Corpus christianorum series latina 92 (Turnhout, 1985), pp. 288, lines 102–3 and 105–289, line 108, who also quotes Isaiah 26:1.

"and the length and the height and the breadth thereof are equal." This is that solidity of unconquered truth by which the Church, supported from below by the length of faith, the breadth of charity and the height of hope, is not suffered to be "carried about with every wind of doctrine."[55] 'And [the angel] measured the wall thereof, a hundred forty-four cubits, . . .' This sum contains the square of the number 12, for 12 times 12 makes 144, signifying that stable perfection of the holy city itself. (*Expositio Apocalypseos* 37, pp. 525, lines 24–29; 529, line 72–531, line 81)[56]

Bede knew Cædmon was a monk because Cædmon (in his view) had made a monastic song about the cosmos. It is a song about *principium creaturarum* that operated within the monastic encyclopedia by likening the universe to a building. The unique architectural manifestation of God's *potentia* and *consilium* is the heaven-roof, a metaphor which conveyed a many-layered monastic experience. Under the lamp-lit roof of their church,

---

55 "This is that solidity . . . doctrine": Bede is quoting Primasius (p. 293 lines 213–15), who in turn is quoting Ephesians 4:14.
56 "ET HABEBAT MVRVM MAGNVM ET ALTVM, id est inexpugnabilem fidei spei caritatisque firmitatem. Potest et ipse dominus ecclesiam undique protegens murus magnus intellegi, de quo Esaias ait: *Ponetur in ea murus et antemurale*, id est domini protectio et intercessio sanctorum, qui iter faciunt ei docendo ad corda credentium. . . . LONGITVDO ET LATITVDO ET ALTITVDO EIVS AEQVALIA SVNT. Haec est illa soliditas ueritatis inuictae, qua ecclesia longitudine fidei, latitudine caritatis, altitudine spei subnixa circumferri non sinitur omni uento doctrinae; quarum si una minus habuerit, perfecta ecclesiae stabilitas non erit. ET MENSVS EST MVRVS EIVS CENTVM QVADRAGINTA QVATTVOR CVBITORVM. Haec summa quadraturam duodenarii numeri continet,—duodecies enim duodeni centrum quadraginta quattuor,—significans et ipsa stabilem ciuitatis sanctae perfectionem" (my translation).

monks vowed to *stabilitas* lived a life of *ordo* and *ratio*—including a *ratio* of time indexed to God's "natural" time—which consciously sought to anticipate heaven. Beneath that same roof, the monk mined his *lectio* for ideas and images which he could fasten together to "edify" himself and others. In chapters 38 and 42 of his *Rule*, St. Benedict uses the term *aedificare* to describe the work of *lectio divina*. Gregory the Great, in the letter to Leander of Seville that prefaces the *Moralia in Iob*, likens the modes of scriptural exegesis to the stages of architectural construction. *Historia* lays the foundation of understanding, allegory raises the walls, and the moral meaning of the text crowns the heights.[57] Aldhelm transforms the motif by boldly extending Gregory's trope to literary production in general: its foundations are rhetoric, its walls are prose, and its celestial roof (*culmen*) is poetry.[58] This last phrase is suggestive, for it connects Cædmon's gift of poetry with the same constructive act that the hymn ascribes to God: *qui primo filiis hominum caelum pro culmine tecti*. The hymn's world-hall image, to Bede, was proof that Cædmon would think within the monastic encyclopedia of Biblical allusions, ideas about cosmos and time, and meditative practice. This was one of the keys, perhaps *the* key, that opened the cloister to Cædmon, and Old English poetry to the cloister.

---

57 Gregory the Great, *Moralia in Iob*, "Ad Leandrum" 3, p. 4, lines 106–14.

58 "Velut jactis jam rhetoricis fundamentis, ac constructis prosae parietibus, cum regulis trochaicis et dactilicis metrororum imbricibus firmissimum culmen caelesti confixus suffragio imponam." Prose *De virginitate*, 60 (ed. Ehwald, p. 80). For discussion see Carruthers *Craft of Thought*, pp. 18–19; Wehlau, *"Riddle"* pp. 23–24; de Lubac, v. 4, pp. 49–54. See Augustine, *Enarrationes in Psalmos* 95:2, who describes the new song which the renewed earth will one day sing: "ipsum cantare, aedificare est." Ed. E. Dekkers and J. Fraipont, Corpus christianorum series latina 39 (Turnhout, 1966), p. 1343, line 3.

All Created Things:
Material Contexts for Bede's Story of Cædmon

Allen J. Frantzen

IN THE FOURTH BOOK of the *Ecclesiastical History*, Bede recounts miracles associated with the double monastery at Barking. During a time of plague, monks were being buried in the cemetery every day; the abbess wondered where the nuns would lie when the catastrophe spread to them. Her question was answered when the sisters went to the cemetery to sing "their accustomed praises to the Lord." Suddenly a light "appeared from heaven like a great sheet and came upon them all, striking such terror into them that they broke off the chant they were singing in alarm."[1] The light then moved to a spot west of the oratory and remained there before being withdrawn to heaven, showing the nuns where their cemetery should be located and also guiding them along the path to salvation. Bede ends the chapter with an interior perspective. A brother in the oratory "declared in the morning that the rays of light which penetrated the cracks of the doors and windows seemed brighter than the brightest daylight."[2]

---

1 "Solitas Domino laudes decantarent, ecce subito lux emissa caelitus, ueluti linteum magnum uenit super omnes, tantoque eas stupore perculit, ut etiam canticum quod canebant tremefactae intermitterent." *Bede's Ecclesiastical History of the English People*, 4.7, ed. and trans. Bertram Colgrave and R. A. B. Mynors (Oxford, 1969), pp. 356–57. All subsequent references are to this edition and translation and are given, as here, by book, chapter, and page number.

2 "Cujus radius lucis tantus extitit, ut quidam de fratribus senior,

Allen J. Frantzen

In the next chapter, Bede describes another miracle of light at Barking. A plague-stricken nun twice asked the sisters around her to put out their lamp because it seemed to her to be "utterly dark" when compared to the light filling the room ("uestra illa lucerna mihi omnimodis esse uideatur obscura"). No one responded to the request, presumably because the sisters thought the dying nun was hallucinating and they needed the lamp in order to see (4.8, pp. 358–59). Bede offers no commentary, and no doubt the meaning of the event was obvious: if miraculous light in the cemetery could outshine the sun, certainly it could obscure the glimmer of an ordinary lamp.

Lamps, cracks around doors and windows, and the location of cemeteries are not the sorts of things that draw readers to Bede's *Ecclesiastical History*. Some texts seem to tell us about the things of Anglo-Saxon England and some do not. Ælfric's *Colloquy* and the riddles belong in the former category; Bede's *Ecclesiastical History*, which demonstrates more interest in the miraculous than in the mundane, does not. Modern historians have done their best, as Benedicta Ward once noted, not to be embarrassed by Bede's many miracles and their reminder of the work's spiritual goals. Ward herself observed that Bede embraced wondrous events less as *miracula* or amazing tales than as *signa*, signs pointing to "moral truth and inner meaning." Miracles in the *Ecclesiastical History* always serve a purpose other than inciting readers to wonder or asserting the marvelous for its own sake, Ward argued. Instead, Bede adapted miracles to develop his major themes—the need for unity in the English Church, for example, a theme emphasized by the miraculous appearance of St. Peter to Laurence (2.6).[3] Bede's miracle of

> qui ipsa hora in oratio eorum cum alio iuniore positus fuerat, referret mane quod ingressi per rimas ostiorum uel fenestrarum radii lucis omnem diurni luminis uiderentur superare fulgorem." *Ecclesiastical History*, 4.7, pp. 358–59.

3 Benedicta Ward, "Miracles and History: A Reconsideration of the Miracle Stories used by Bede," *Famulus Christi: Essays in*

All Created Things

Cædmon had, for Ward, little sense of wonder about it. Instead, the event motivates "a piece of literary criticism" in which Bede establishes the *principium creaturarum*, the beginning of all created things, as "the basic subject of all poetry." This subject matter, in Ward's view, liberated the hitherto "frustrated poet" and made him "a better poet than all the rest" (73). In this essay, I attribute another effect to Bede's miracles, including the story of Cædmon, which is that they inadvertently call our attention to the everyday world and the ordinary objects in it.

Miracles and the Everyday

In Book 4 of the *Ecclesiastical History*, according to Bertram Colgrave and R. A. B. Mynors, Bede "describes the great revival of Church life which followed the coming of Theodore."[4] Miracles demonstrate the vigor of the faith and its leaders. Eighteen of the book's thirty chapters contain visions or miracles, a higher proportion than in the other four books of the *Ecclesiastical History*.[5] A miracle is an event outside natural causation, attributable to divine agency, and used to demonstrate control over nature so that the agent of the miracle will be seen as divinely favored (*OED*). Hence, as we see in the case of the nun who finds lamplight dim and dispensable, a miracle can be used to put an object in its place, exposing the limits of the merely material by demonstrating the power of the supernatural over it.

Commemoration of the 13th Centenary of the Birth of Bede (London, 1976), pp. 70–76.

4 Colgrave and Mynors, *Bede's Ecclesiastical History*, pp. xxiii-xxiv.

5 Colgrave and Mynors use two numbering systems, yielding either thirty or thirty-two chapters in Book 4, since chapter 14 has no heading (it is added in one manuscript only) and chapter 15 is continuous with it. See *Bede's Ecclesiastical History*, p. 326. By my count, only five of thirty-four chapters in Book 1 contain miracles or visions; only three of twenty chapters in Book 2; nine of thirty chapters in Book 3; and nine of twenty-four chapters in Book 5.

Allen J. Frantzen

The chains binding the prisoner Imma are unlocked when his distant brother says Mass on his behalf (4.22). When the Abbess Hild dies at Whitby, a nun at Hackness awakes to see the roof of the dormitory rolled back. As the dormitory is flooded with light, Hild's soul is guided to heaven by angels. This vision is shared by a nun at Whitby "in the remotest part of the monastery," as Bede notes, so that "a beautify harmony of events" joined two foundations some thirteen miles apart (4.23, pp. 414–15).

Rather than focus on their theological or typological meaning, I propose that we see the miracles in the context of the everyday observances and things that form continuities beneath Bede's notice and, in some cases, contradict his purposes.[6] I will focus on ordinary objects and their functions rather than on high-status objects—swords, helmets, crosses, brooches, grave goods, and similar materials—and their functions. As John Hines has written, the latter objects use "straightforward symbolism" to denote "group-association or identity," and have rarely been overlooked by art historians, archaeologists, or literary historians.[7] We cannot say the same for ordinary objects. Bede writes about them only because he writes about miracles, and his indifference to them is hardly unusual.

In asking "why things were forgotten," the Norwegian archaeologist Bjørnar Olsen juxtaposes materialist studies that focus on objects to cultural studies that focus on discourse. Olsen asserts that "material culture" has become "a contradictory term for reaching a culture that is not material."[8] In cultural studies, life seems to be nothing more than discursive practice in a world "held together almost solely by human cognition," he

---

6 The standard discussion is William D. McCready, *Miracles and the Venerable Bede* (Toronto, 1994).

7 John Hines, *Voices in the Past: English Literature and Archaeology* (Cambridge, 2004), p. 11.

8 Bjørnar Olsen, "Material Culture after Text: Re-Membering Things," *Norwegian Archaeological Review* 36 (2003), 87–104; quote from p. 90.

writes (88–89). Things in such a world are important chiefly because, as signs, metaphors, and symbols, they reveal social and cultural meanings shaped by human consciousness. Olsen's corrective is to bring archaeology, which he calls "the discipline of things *par excellence*," to focus on things in their functional rather than their symbolic roles.

Hines, who has made similar arguments, proposes that archaeology can be seen either as a discipline that studies the past by looking through its material remains to their broader significance or as a discipline that approaches material remains as ends in themselves. To see objects as ends rather than as means or as lenses requires us to ask why "physical products such as buildings, tombs, tools and utensils should have taken a particular form in particular contexts," Hines writes, rather than how they acquire or manipulate their symbolic content.[9] This perspective also concentrates our attention on the social relations that explain the function of ordinary objects in daily life; these relations, obviously, also exploit symbolic levels of meaning, but they are, in the first instance, functional, or what Hines describes as "distinct configurations of practice traceable in the material record" (15).

Olsen proposes that we conceive of "a symmetrical archaeology founded on the premise that things, all those physical entities we refer to as material culture, are beings in the world alongside other beings, such a humans, plants and animals." Olsen sees the object as a "silent thing" and as "a new and unknown actor" in partnership with human agency.[10] At first this sounds suspiciously New Age, I admit, and Olsen's examples are not reassuring. "One thousand years ago the Vikings ascribed personality, intention, and social identity to their swords," he writes; by naming their weapons, the Vikings bridged what we

---

9   John Hines, *Voices in the Past*, p. 9 and pp. 32–33; he cites Anders Andrén, *Between Artifacts and Texts: Historical Archaeology in Global Perspective* (London, 2001).

10 Olsen, "Material Culture," pp. 88–89.

see as separate human and non-human worlds. Reindeer herders of northern Scandinavia who "hugged and greeted pine trees" and "had long conversations with drums and stones" offer another example (95). These relations are not good indices to the social life of everyday things, however, for they mystify ordinary objects and elevate them above their everyday functions. The pine tree signifies something other trees do not; the drums and stones likewise support specific cultural symbolism.

To modern ways of thinking, Olsen writes, Viking warriors and reindeer herders did not understand "where reality ends and its metaphorical representation begins." They did not regard things as symbols or metaphors but rather as their partners, leading to what Olsen calls an "appalling mixture of people and things" (95).[11] Unlike the medieval folk Olsen describes, modern readers intuitively acknowledge the "Great Divide," described by Bruno Latour in *We Have Never Been Modern* as thinking subjects on the one side and as unthinking objects on the other.[12] Bede and his contemporaries also seem to have objected to that "appalling mixture of people and things" and set out not only to discredit the pagans' amulets and auguries—the aim of many miracles in the *Ecclesiastical History*—but to replace the mixture with a pattern of subject-object relations that supported the Christian perspective of the material world. Another writer who describes the subject-object dichotomy is Aron Gurevich. In the pagan world, he writes, "the relationship of men and natural phenomena was conceived as one of interaction or even as mutual aid. The natural forces can help or harm man, who in turn is able to influence them in ways that are advantageous for him." In a system characterized by "archaic beliefs" such as these, Gurevich claims, "men think of themselves in the same

---

11 Olsen notes that modern people do, however, "fall in love" with things like jackets, cars, and gadgets and "mourn them when they fall to pieces—when they die." See "Material Culture," p. 95.

12 Bruno Latour, *We Have Never Been Modern* (Cambridge, Mass., 1993), p. 13, cited by Olsen, p. 95.

All Created Things

categories as the rest of the world, not isolating themselves from it and construing an 'object-subject' dichotomy." Gurevich, and Olsen after him, describe "an ultimate unity" predicated on a "reciprocal penetration of nature and humankind, organically connected with each other and magically interactive."[13]

The Church, in Gurevich's words, disapproved of pagan "identification of man and nature" and attempted "to tear people away from it, for the only clerically approved contact with a higher power was in and through the church of God" (97). Humans can then be seen as alienated from nature so that "the link between them ceases to be organic and becomes symbolic" (96).[14] If one must embrace a tree, let the tree symbolize the cross; as for talking to stones, think, as does Bede, of the "living stones" of 1 Peter 2:5, Ephesians 2:21, or 2 Corinthians 5:1.[15] Objects in the pre-Christian world needed to be brought into a proper relationship with their Christian masters. The "natural forces" that, in Gurevich's words, "can help or harm man," had to be seen as expressions of God's favor or disfavor. Adam named the animals in the Garden, "and whatever the man called every living creature, that was its name" (Genesis 2:19); Adam's dominion rested on an apparently innate relationship

---

13 Aron Gurevich, *Medieval Popular Culture: Problems of Belief and Perception*, trans. János M. Bak and Paul A. Hollingsworth (Cambridge, 1988), p. 81.

14 Compare Raymond Williams' discussion of the alienation of "a whole body of activities" (i.e., ordinary cultural practices) as art, aesthetics, or ideology, with the result that "none of these things can then be grasped for what they are: as real practice, elements of a whole material social process." See *Marxism and Literature* (Oxford, 1977), p. 5. Quoted by Perry, *Material Culture and Cultural Materialisms*, pp. x-xi.

15 See Colgrave and Mynors, *Bede's Ecclesiastical History*, 4.3, p. 338, note 2, where these citations are found in comments on Bede's reference to "uiuos ecclesiae lapides," the living stones of the Church.

that connected him and Eve to the natural world. After the Fall, however, this easy mastery was transformed into struggle. "By the sweat of your face you shall eat bread until you return to the ground," God said to Adam; and to Eve, "I will greatly multiply your pain in childbearing; in pain you will bring forth children" (Genesis 3:19).[16]

Once the unity of "man and nature" had been broken by sin, human relations with objects had to be reconceived. Miracles were instrumental to this process, which relied on the saints and God's intervention through them to wrench ordinary things out of their functional or organic relation to humanity and to emphasize their place in God's plan. Bede's *Ecclesiastical History* recounts the English Church's ages-long struggle to instill this alien view and to manage what Gurevich calls the "divergence between clerical civilization and popular consciousness" (99). Magic and superstition framed things in "popular consciousness," and miracles sought to contest their longstanding control over the symbolic. Christianity's struggle against "popular consciousness," the main subject of Gurevich's discussion, had to be pursued both on this level and also on a second, which concerned ordinary rather than symbolic (i.e., magical) objects. Miracles attributed to Wilfrid, Cuthbert, and others in Book 4 of the *Ecclesiastical History* operate on both levels. While some miracle-workers divest amulets of their power, others expose the inadequacy of popular control over ordinary things so that the superior force of Christianity can be displayed.

The contest on the first level, between competing symbolic systems, is familiar to all readers of Bede's account of Pope Gregory's reply to the inquiries of Abbot Mellitus (*Ecclesiastical History*, 1.30). The abbot's followers were to preserve pagan shrines, but to substitute the relics of the saints for statues of idols. The missionaries were directed to keep the pagans' feast days but to celebrate them on the festivals of the martyrs, since, as Gregory

---

16 Herbert G. May and Bruce M. Metzger, ed. and trans., *The Oxford Annotated Bible* (New York, 1962), pp. 4–6.

observed of the pagans, it is "impossible to cut out everything at once from their stubborn minds" ("Nam duris mentibus simul omnia abscidere inpossible esse non dubium est").[17] This strategy assumes that pagans would associate relics with idols, hardly an appropriate connection, and feast days with holy days, as if Christians and pagans were merely carrying out different forms of the same activity. Indeed, on the material level there is no obvious difference in the attitudes that these two systems of belief manifest: special powers are attributed to certain objects, places, and rituals, which thereby become sacred. Observers may look at these objects, but do so only to look through them to find their symbolic meanings. Gregory's strategy rested on this habit of looking through an object rather than at it.

Some archaeological evidence from the early Anglo-Saxon period suggests that Christian leaders might have taken Gregory's advice literally. In the Bernician royal residence at Yeavering (Bede's "Adgefrin," 2.14) was a temple now designated as Building D_2. Within its precincts Brian Hope-Taylor found extensive evidence of burned animal bones—that is, of sacrificial offerings.[18] Around the remains of this structure he found traces of a structure that Hope-Taylor described as a "rebuild" of an earlier ceremonial building. He designated the temple as Building D_2a, and the "rebuild," which enclosed the foundation trenches and postholes of Building D_2a, as Building D_2b. Hope-Taylor

---

17 Colgrave and Mynors, *Bede's Ecclesiastical History*, 1.30, pp. 105–8, quotation p. 108.

18 Brian Hope-Taylor, *Yeavering: An Anglo-British Centre of Early Northumbria* (London, 1977), pp. 97–100 and 277–78. For recent discussions of Yeavering (which leave most of Hope-Taylor's conclusions standing), see Sarah Zaluckyj (with Marge Feryok and John Zaluckyj), *Mercia: The Anglo-Saxon Kingdom of Central England* (Woonton, Herefordshire, 2001), pp. 43–49; and D. A. Hinton, *Archaeology, Economy and Society: England from the Fifth to the Fifteenth Century* (London, 1990), pp. 7–10.

suggested that the second structure was a wooden church that closely followed the temple's structural outline and would have been built after A.D. 632, when Bishop Paulinus catechized the royal household at Yeavering.[19] How the original temple was destroyed we do not know, but we must recall that Coifi, counselor to the Northumbrian king Edwin, declared that the king's court should "commit to the flames the temples and the altars which we have held sacred without reaping any benefit." The counselor volunteered to be the first "to profane the altars and the shrines of the idols, together with their precincts."[20]

Hope-Taylor describes the culture at Yeavering as conservatively pagan, a phrase that suits the settlement's ancient and monumental pre-Christian structures and also suggests how implausible Coifi's bluster must have seemed.[21] It is easy to see why a conversion at such a site might be, as Sir Frank Stenton called the spread of Christianity in this area, "rapid, if superficial."[22] The presence of massive pagan buildings would have discouraged a change of faith and would have made such a transformation as that suggested by Gregory into a momentous undertaking. References in *The Wanderer* to the "ancient work of giants"

---

19 Hope-Taylor, *Yeavering*, pp. 97–100 and pp. 277–78. See also Richard Morris, *The Church In British Archaeology*, BAR 47 (London, 1983), pp. 39–40.

20 Colgrave and Mynors, ed., *Bede's Ecclesiastical History*, Book 2.9–14, pp. 162–89; Coifi's speech is quoted ch. 13, pp. 182–87. This too had been Gregory's policy at one point, communicated in a letter to Æthelberht; see 1.32, pp. 112–13.

21 Recent investigations have questioned some of Hope-Taylor's conclusions about Yeavering; see, most recently, Tim Gates, "Yeavering and Air Photography: Discovery and Interpretation," in Paul Frodsham and Colm O'Brien, eds., *Yeavering: People, Power, Place* (Stroud, Gloucestershire, 2005), pp. 65-83.

22 Sir Frank Stenton, *Anglo-Saxon England*, 3rd ed. (Oxford, 1971), p. 115.

are often taken as a bow to Roman ruins.[23] At Yeavering and elsewhere, it is entirely possible that pagan structures in wood qualified for that description. Signs of animal sacrifice such as those found in Building D_2a would have taken a long time to disappear from popular memory; those signs have, after all, survived into the present. As if conceding that Gregory's strategy, however shrewdly conceived it might have been, was not practical in the face of entrenched and remembered ancient traditions, Bede refers to persistent pagan worship alongside Christianity in East Anglia. There Rædwald kept two altars in his temple, one for "the Christian sacrifice and another small altar on which to offer victims to devils" ("atque in eodem fano et altare haberet ad sacrificium Christi et arulam ad uictimas daemoniorum," 2.15, pp. 190–91).[24] With leaders hedging their bets so conspicuously, lower social groups might well have approached the new religion with even greater ambivalence.

We expect Bede's miracles to demonstrate the superiority of Christian belief and its symbolic system, and many do. But the Church also had to struggle to reorient pagans toward the material on a second level, that of ordinary things and their participation in a social world in which the human and the material were closely connected. Some of the most important miracles

---

23 See P. J. Frankis, "The Thematic Significance of *enta geweorc* and Related Imagery in 'The Wanderer,'" *Anglo-Saxon England* 2 (1973), 253–69, and, for a recent discussion, R. M. Liuzza, "The Tower of Babel: The Wanderer and The Ruins of History," *Studies in the Literary Imagination* 36 (2003), 1–35 (Liuzza comments on "The Ruin" and the Cotton Maxims).

24 Rædwald has sometimes been thought to be the figure in the first burial mound at Sutton Hoo. See Jane Roberts, "Anglo-Saxon Vocabulary as a Reflection of Material Culture," in *The Age of Sutton Hoo: The Seventh Century in North-Western Europe*, ed. M. O. H. Carver (Woodbridge, Suffolk, 1992), pp. 185–202. The authoritative report is Rupert Bruce-Mitford, *The Sutton Hoo Ship Burial*, 3 vols. (London, 1975, 1978, 1982).

in the fourth book of Bede's *Ecclesiastical History* assert Christian control over this level of pagan materialism and its assumptions about the natural world. These miracles do not contest the relative powers of symbolic systems, as do those on the first level, but rather impose a model of subject-object relations on the material world in order to demonstrate that ordinary things serve the will of God and the Church. Bede uses miracles to show how humans should be properly connected to the things around them; the new faith helps to achieve mastery over the material world and to overcome obstacles that have frustrated the pagans. But the objects in these accounts are functional rather than symbolic, and by focusing on them we see that many miracles in Book 4 are concerned with the transformation of social rather than of symbolic systems. Objects involved in social relations rather than cultural symbolism assert themselves in five episodes: Wilfrid's work among the South Saxons (4.13), Cuthbert's retirement in the Farne islands (4.28), Adamnan's vision at Coldingham (4.25), the wood-working monk Owine (4.3), and the story of Cædmon (4.24). Bede does not use these episodes to develop stages of an argument, I should note; that is my concern, not his. I have grouped together two miracles that show how Christianity confronts the material world in pagan or in unconverted territories and three that show how miracles make use of ordinary things within Christian communities.

Pagan Materialism: Wilfrid and Cuthbert

Wilfrid went to the South Saxons in A.D. 681, after he was imprisoned in Northumbria by a council that refused to restore the see of York to him. He preached among the South Saxons for five years, attaching his mission first to Æthelwealh, the South Saxons' Christian king, and then to Cædwalla, the king of Wessex who killed Æthelwealh. Bede underscores the failure of the South Saxons and their paganism to master the material world. When Wilfrid arrived, he found that a famine had ravaged the population and that forty or fifty men "wasted with hunger"

All Created Things

("inedia macerati") had joined hands and thrown themselves into the sea (4.13, pp. 372–75). On the very day when the South Saxons accepted baptism, however, the three-year drought ended: rain fell, the earth revived, "and a happy and fruitful season followed." The people cast off "ancient superstitions" and renounced "idolatry" ("abiecta prisca superstitione, exsufflata idolatria") because they understood that God, "by his heavenly grace, endowed them with both outward and inward blessings" ("qui uerus est Deus, et interioribus se bonis et exterioribus caelesti gratia ditasse," pp. 374–75). Bede exposes the failure of the supposedly harmonious relationship between pagans and the natural world. The starving South Saxons were destroying themselves because their "ancient superstitions" and "idolatry" had failed to subject the natural world to their needs. The first reward of their baptism, accordingly, was a demonstration of the power of Christian belief over the environment.

The indictment of a failed religion of superstition and idolatry is only the first of the chapter's objectives, as we see when Bede turns to Wilfrid's concern with fishing and its evidence of the South Saxons' faulty subject-object relations. Although in this region "both the sea and the rivers abounded in fish," Bede writes, "the people had no knowledge of fishing except for eels alone" ("piscandi peritia genti nulla nisi ad anguillas tantum inerat," pp. 374–75). When the bishop's men showed them that eel nets could be cast into the sea to catch fish, 300 fish were quickly captured and divided equally among the poor, those who supplied the nets, and the bishop's men. The episode recalls various miracles involving Christ and the sea, and the division of the catch is no doubt symbolic.[25] Fresh-water and

---

25 The purpose of the claim, no doubt, is to evoke biblical parallels: John 21: 1–14, when Peter, Thomas, and the sons of Zebedee fish without success and Jesus tells them to cast their net to the right of the boat, causing the net to be filled to overflowing with fish; and John 6: 9–14, the miracle of the loaves and fishes (rather than Matthew 4:19, when Christ calls the disciples "fishers of men" and

ocean fishing practices are imagined to be so different in this account, and the means of catching eels so unrelated to other kinds of fishing, that the South Saxons were unable to transfer techniques successful in one endeavor to the other, even during a time of starvation so severe as to prompt mass suicide. We might suppose that a people living near the sea who knew how to use nets to catch eel might also have caught fish by accident and realized that fish could be caught in the sea the same way.

Bede's aim is to show that the pagans lack a proper model of subject-object relations and hence do not have the good sense to exploit natural resources. Wilfrid's knowledge of fishing was enough to persuade the Saxons of his holiness; the people had "greater hope of heavenly blessings from the preaching of one by whose aid they had gained temporal blessings" ("libentius eo praedicante caelestia sperare coeperunt, cuius ministerio temporalia bona sumserunt," pp. 374–75). When the things of the world are properly aligned with Christian will, they are revealed as blessings that had been invisible to those who did not believe.

The episode exploits a symbolic contrast between death in the sea and the Christian view of the sea as a source of life, but Bede's narrative—this one, like many, acquired second-hand—does not connect ignorance of fishing practices to either superstition or idolatry. His aim is to demonstrate that interior and exterior welfare, the spiritual and the material, are interdependent, and that adherence to true belief and successful exploitation of natural resources cannot be separated. The materiality of fishing challenges his claim, however, and forces us to question his knowledge of the practice. Other sources give us reason to doubt that Wilfrid introduced the practice.[26] Large

---

prompts them to leave their nets behind).

26 Skepticism about the story has sometimes been in short supply. John Thrupp, for example, regarded fishing as a gentlemanly occupation in *The Anglo-Saxon Home: A History of the Domestic Institutions and Customs of England from the Fifth to the Eleventh*

fishing weirs in Essex, in the Blackwater estuary, have produced radiocarbon dates corresponding to the Middle Anglo-Saxon period (ca. A.D. 650–850), "with a particular emphasis on the eighth century."[27] Fifth- and sixth-century evidence from Bishopstone shows that "shellfish were gathered from the coast, and conger eel and whiting were caught at sea." Although whalebone has been found at nearby Botolphs, it is thought to have come from a stranded, rather than a hunted, cetacean.[28] One can understand Bede's enthusiasm for the *exemplum*, but it is not likely that Wilfrid taught the South Saxons to fish from the sea. Recent analysis suggests that deep-sea fishing—as opposed to estuarine fishing—was fully developed only in the late Anglo-Saxon period (that is, tenth-century and after).[29]

In his account of Cuthbert's settlement on the Farne islands off Lindisfarne, Bede again looks at, rather than through, the production of food, and again his narrative illuminates continuities of practice where his rhetoric calls for radical change. As prior of Melrose, Cuthbert preached among lay folk who reverted to "foolish customs" involving amulets and incantations and forsook the true faith in time of plague ("per incantations

---

Century (London, 1862), pp. 375–78, including it under "Sports and Pastimes." A reviewer in *The Gentlemen's Magazine* (July 1862) archly observed that Augustine and Paulinus had already taught "the gentle pastime to the men of Kent and Northumberland" (p. 555).

27 Anon., "No Small Fry in Saxon Fishing Industry," *British Archaeology* 41 (February 1999), http://www.britarch.ac.uk/BA/ba41/ba41 news.html#fry (July 2006).

28 See Mark Gardiner, "Economy and Landscape Change in Post-Roman and Early Medieval Sussex, 450–1175," in David Rudling, ed., *The Archaeology of Sussex to AD 2000* (Norfolk, 2003), pp. 153–54.

29 See James H. Barrett, A. M. Locker, and C. M. Roberts, "'Dark Age Economics' Revisited: the English Fish Bone Evidence, A.D. 600–1600," *Antiquity* 78 [301] (2004), 618-36.

uel fylacteria uel alia quaelibet daemonicae artis arcane," 4.27, pp. 432–33). The confrontation between symbolic systems and the persistence of pagan views of magic are clear. After becoming prior at Lindisfarne, Cuthbert withdrew for a time to an island that, Bede notes, offered nothing—no water, corn, or trees—and was populated by evil spirits. Arriving there, as he said, "to support myself in this place with the work of my hands" so long as he lived, Cuthbert banished the evil spirits ("de opere manuum mearum uiuere queam," 4.28, pp. 434–35). Hence the contest between symbolic systems—a monk armed with faith, battling a hostile landscape—does not materialize. Instead, Bede concentrates on the ordinary things that Cuthbert used for his work.

Devoted to the Benedictine Rule, Cuthbert built a settlement that included a "small dwelling-place" ("domus"), an oratory, and a room for common use ("oratorium et habitaculum commune"), surrounded by a rampart ("circumuallante"). His brothers sank a well into the floor of the "habitaculum commune" at Cuthbert's request, and although the ground was rocky, the well quickly filled with water. Cuthbert also asked for farming implements ("ferramenta ruralia") and wheat ("frument[um]"), which he planted at the proper time. When none grew, Cuthbert asked for barley ("hordeum") instead. His reasoning is important. "So when the brothers were making their accustomed visit, he ordered them to bring barley to see if perhaps *the nature of the soil or the will of the heavenly Giver* demanded rather that a crop of this kind should grow there" (my emphasis). The barley was brought "long after the proper time of sowing," but "an abundant crop quickly appeared, providing the man of God with the means of supporting himself by his own labor" ("Vnde uisitantibus se ex more fratribus hordeum iussit adferri, *si forte uel natura soli illius uel uoluntas esset superni Largitoris*, ut illius frugis ibi potius seges oriretur. . . . mox copiosa seges exorta desideratam proprii laboris uiro Dei refectionem praebebat," pp. 436–37).

All Created Things

Bede assigns the holy man's success to his piety and does not explain why even the saintly and industrious Cuthbert failed in his first effort to grow grain, although the saint's reference to the "nature of the soil" ("natura soli") points to an obvious explanation. Wheat, like barley, could be planted either in the fall or the spring, and, if planted in the fall, could be lost to a severe winter; that might have been the fate of the wheat crop. The barley may have needed a boost from the divine, but if it were planted in the spring instead of the fall—a planting that might have seemed late to Bede—its flourishing might, to one unfamiliar with crop cycles, have seemed a special blessing. Barley and wheat flourish in different soil types, another consideration that Bede, as we would expect, fails to consider.[30] Yet this chapter demonstrates Christian mastery of the material world even more impressive than Wilfrid's, since Farne was both uninhabited and uninhabitable before Cuthbert arrived. More fundamentally than Wilfrid's or Cuthbert's own prior triumphs over pagan customs, the success of the monastic settlement of Farne seems to represent a triumph over the force of evil itself. Miracles might have cleared away the evil spirits, and prayers alone, Bede no doubt wished to believe, might have made the crops flourish. But Cuthbert himself did not think so, and consequently Bede had to acknowledge the place of the things and material processes in the saint's success. Without his tools and his fellow workers, the saint could not have grown the abundant crops that would later signify his spiritual victory.

---

30   But Francis J. Green warns that it is "perhaps unwise to simply equate different soil types with different crops." See "Cereals and Plant Food: A Reassessment of the Saxon Economic Evidence from Wessex," in *Environment and Economy in Anglo-Saxon England: A Review of Recent Work on the Environmental Archaeology of Rural and Urban Anglo-Saxon Settlements in England,* ed. James Rackham. BAR Report 89 (London, 1994), pp. 83–88.

Allen J. Frantzen

Miracles and Monastic Materialism: Adamnan, Owine, and Cædmon

The next three miracles I discuss take place within monastic settlements. Bede's account of Coldingham reverses the perspective on tools and labor that the account of Cuthbert demonstrates. The conflict between symbolic systems had long since been resolved in monastic cultures, but, as Bede shows, ordinary things failed to remain in the subordinate position to which Christian symbolism consigns them. At Coldingham, such things exert power without the aid of magic and indeed seem to use the people who ought to have mastered the objects. As Scott DeGregorio argues in his essay in this volume, Coldingham illustrates Bede's interest in monastic reform. Bede sets the sinfulness of monks and nuns against the piety of the Irishman Adamnan, a penitent ("uir de genere Scottorum, Adamnanus uocabulo," pp. 422–23). "Guilty of a certain sin" in his youth, Adamnan "came to his senses, repented, and sought to confess to a priest" ("siquidem in adulescentia sua sceleris aliquid commiserat"). The phrase "sceleris aliquid" and the conjunction of vagueness, severity, and the sinner's youthfulness probably indicate a sexual sin. Irish and Anglo-Saxon penitentials contain many provisions covering such offenses as committed by young men and boys.[31] Using the medical analogy common in penitential literature, Adamnan's priest described the Irishman's sin as "a severe wound" and prescribed

---

31 Penances for them range from "six special fasts" ("vi. superpositionibus") for innocent kissing to two years for boys "practicing homosexuality," Ludwig Bieler's translation of "in terga uero fornicantes," or anal intercourse. Quoted from the *Penitential of Cummean* (chapter ten, canon 15) in *The Irish Penitentials*, ed. and trans. Ludwig Bieler, Scriptores Latini Hiberniae 5 (Dublin, 1963), pp. 128–29. For penances for same-sex acts, see Allen J. Frantzen, *Before the Closet: Same-sex Love from "Beowulf" to "Angels in America"* (Chicago, 1998), pp. 149–62.

"an even more severe remedy."[32] Adamnan volunteered to fast for a week or to stand in prayer all night; he was, plainly, a good student of Irish hagiography.[33] The priest rejected a week-long fast as too extreme, however, and instead assigned a fast of two or three days. He then left for Ireland, promising that on his return he would specify how long the sinner should fast (this shows that the priest was not following the penitential, which would have required him to specify the period of penance on the spot). But the priest died in Ireland, abandoning the sinner—whose signs of scrupulousness might be considered worrying—to his own devices. Adamnan did not fast two days each week but rather ate on only two days and fasted on the other five; he continued this fast for his whole life. Bede seems to approve of this unwearying repentance.[34]

One day, Adamnan and a companion left the monastery for a journey. When, on their return, they approached Coldingham and "its lofty buildings," Adamnan burst into tears. Asked why, he replied that he had learned that "All these buildings which you now see, both communal and private, will shortly be burnt to ashes" (4.25, pp. 424–25). He had seen a vision in which he was told that those around him were obsessed with "worldly occupations." An unknown figure in the vision reported his findings on a tour of the monastery:

---

32 On the "medical metaphor" in early medieval penitential literature, see Frantzen, *The Literature of Penance*, pp. 30–31, 84–89.

33 Colgrave and Minors note that Bede respected but possibly did not approve of the acts of asceticism for which Irish monks were famous; see *Bede's Ecclesiastical History*, p. xxiii.

34 Alan Thacker assumes that this indicates Bede's approval of lifelong penance; see "Monks, Preaching and Pastoral Care in Early Anglo-Saxon England," in *Pastoral Care Before the Parish*, ed. John Blair and Richard Sharpe (Leicester, 1992), p. 159. Lifelong penance was not required even for sodomy, however, and seems to have been prescribed only for fratricide. See Frantzen, *Before the Closet*, pp. 151–52.

> I have visited every part of this monastery in turn: I have examined their cells and their beds, and I have found no one except you concerned with his soul's welfare; but all of them, men and women alike, are sunk in slothful slumbers or else they remain awake for the purposes of sin. And the cells that were built for praying and for reading have become haunts of feasting, drinking, gossip, and other delights; even the virgins who are dedicated to God put aside all respect for their profession, and, whenever they have leisure, spend their time weaving elaborate garments with which to adorn themselves as if they were brides, so imperilling their virginity, or else to make friends with strange men.[35]

When Adamnan spoke to the abbess about the vision, she prompted a reform that preserved the community during her lifetime, but subsequent lapses lead to the monastery's destruction.

This vision contrasts Adamnan's asceticism—and possibly his identity as a reformed sexual sinner—with the self-indulgence of the inhabitants of Coldingham. Adamnan rejected the most basic dependence on materiality—the need for food. His example underscores the failure of the monks and nuns

---

35 "Siquidem modo totum hoc monasterium ex ordine perlustrans, singulorum casas ac lectos inspexi, et neminem ex omnibus praeter te erga sanitatem animae suae occupatum repperi; sed omnes prorsus, et uiri et feminae, aud somno torpent inerit aut ad peccata uigilant. Nam et domunculae, quae ad orandum uel legendum factae erant, nunc in comesationum, potationum, fabulationum et ceterarum sunt inlecebrarum cubilia conuersae; uirgines quoque Deo dicatae, contemta reuerentiae suae professionis, quotiescumque uacant, texendis subtilioribus indumentis operam dant, quibus aut se ipsas ad uicem sponsarum in periculum sui status adornent, aut externorum sibi uirorum amicitiam conparent." Colgrave and Mynors, *Bede's Ecclesiastical History*, pp. 424–27.

All Created Things

to use things properly. Instead, they are obsessed with luxury (fine clothes, eating, drinking, sleep) and triviality (sexual banter, gossip, amusement); their clothes are a form of competition; and they pursue sexual relationships, misusing even their bodies. Bede shows a strong interest in objects for what they are—things, not symbols, that tempt the monks and nuns to sin. He also imagines the continuity of daily life at Coldingham, which is seen as a social network of luxurious living and sinfulness rather than of prayer and repentance. The vision asserts the continuity of such behavior and its material roots only to repudiate them, of course. The figure who appeared to Adamnan had seen these abuses when he "visited every part" of the monastery. His inspection, which took place without the awareness of those being observed, encompassed private as well as communal spaces, a warning to Bede's audience that walls and rooms provide temptation in the form of secrecy, but that they also offer only superficial—one wants to say *merely* material—privacy.

The mysterious figure's account to Adamnan is a judgment on those who assume that their sins, since unknown, can go unconfessed and unrepented. At the start of the chapter, Bede notes that the monastery is said to have burned down "through carelessness" ("per culpam incuriae," 4.25, pp. 420–21). Later he dismisses the material cause. "All who knew the truth," he claims, are aware that the disaster punished "the wickedness of those who dwelt there and especially those who were supposed to be its leaders" ("Quod tamen a malitia inhabitantium in eo, et praecipue illorum qui maiores esse uidebantur, contigisse omnes qui nouere facillime potuerunt aduertere," pp. 420–21). Proper and godly use, in Bede's view, would have turned the things of Coldingham into blessings for the inhabitants. But the drama of judgment depends on Bede's *fiat* alone, for the pursuit of things as ends in themselves could not have transformed those things into curses. Made into ashes by accident, they become symbols for God's curse only through Bede's rhetoric.

Allen J. Frantzen

The scandal of Coldingham's materiality, a synecdoche for the corruption of the monastic world Bede wanted to reform, and in particular for the corrupting power of the material world, is implicitly repudiated by all the honest laborers of Book 4. The last two miracles I will discuss, those of Owine (4.3) and Cædmon (4.24), emphasize the continuity of such labor most clearly. Owine was a monk attached to Lastingham, a small monastery built by Chad near his episcopal seat in Litchfield. Owine had been the chief thegn of Queen Æthelthryth. When she went to Coldingham, at Wilfrid's urging, Owine renounced his office and "stripped himself so completely of his worldly possessions that he left all that he had and, dressed only in a plain garment and carrying an axe and an adze in his hands," came to Lastingham ("sed adeo se mundi rebus exuit, ut relictis omnibus quae habebat, simiplici tantum habitu indutus et securim atque ascian in manu ferens," 4.3, pp. 338–39). By keeping his tools with him, Owine "show[ed] that he was not entering the monastery for the sake of ease, as some did, but to work hard" ("Non enim ad otium, ut quidam, sed ad laborem se monasterium intrare signabat," pp. 338–39)—an anticipation of the depravity of Coldingham and similar foundations.

Unlearned and "less capable of the study of the Scriptures" than others, Owine "used to work outside at whatever seemed necessary," while the bishop and the brothers read ("nam quo minus sufficiebat meditationi scripturarum, eo amplius operi manuum studium inpendebat," pp. 338–39). One day, "occupied with some task outside" ("quadam tale aliquid foris ageret," pp. 338–39), Owine heard "sweet and joyful singing" descend from the sky, coming first from the southeast (Bede describes it precisely: "from the highest point of the rising of the winter sun," "ab alto brumalis exortus") and reaching the oratory where Chad prayed, filling it with music for half an hour (pp. 340–41). Thereafter, Chad, who had been praying alone, came to the window and summoned Owine, telling him to bring the other monks, who had gone to the church. When they returned, they were told that the bishop had learned through a visitation

All Created Things

by his deceased brother, Cedd, that his death was at hand. Only after the others had left did Owine ask Chad to explain "the song of joyful voices" that he heard ("quod erat canticum illud laetantium quod audiui"). The bishop did not answer the question but instead ordered Owine to tell no one that "angel spirits" ("angelorum spiritus") visited him (pp. 342–43).

Bede's chapter focuses on the power of Chad's faith over the material world. According to Trumberht, one of the monks at Lastingham (and one of Bede's teachers, "quidam de his qui me in scripturis erudiebant," pp. 342–43), Chad would interrupt his reading when the wind rose and ask for God's mercy on the human race. If the wind increased, he would pray more earnestly, falling on his face; and if there were a violent storm, the bishop would enter the church and pray until the storm had passed. "For the Lord moves the air, raises the winds, hurls the lightnings, and thunders forth from heaven to arouse the inhabitants of the world to fear Him," Chad would tell his people, warning them that they must purge "the dregs of our sins" lest a God so powerful strike them down ("Mouet enim aera Dominus, uentos excitat, iaculatur fulgora, de caelo intonat, ut terrigenas ad timendum se suscitet," pp. 342–45).[36] Chad recognized the power of nature as a sign of the power of God; his prayers during a storm were acts of instruction as well as of piety, intended not to alter the course of events but to point to the true power behind things, lest the onlookers be confused. The chapter ends with a brief description of miraculous cures that signify the bishop's virtue, including the curing of sick cattle by water mixed with dust from the saint's shrine. The chapter moves from the glorious—Cedd's appearance to Chad, and the sweeping example of God's control of the skies—to the hum-

---

36 This episode is discussed by McCready, *Miracles and the Venerable Bede*; McCready suggests that Bede shared Chad's view that storms were to be understood not "as products of an inherently natural process but as indications of divine displeasure and intimations of the judgment to come," p. 25.

ble matter of sick cattle. Surely God's power over the latter can be taken for granted if his power over the former has been made clear. Bede implicitly underscores the persistence of pagan traditions associated with animal husbandry, including the amulets that Chad inveighed against earlier in his career. But the chapter emphasizes the competition between symbolic sign systems less than it emphasizes ordinary things and the continuities they create beneath the invocations and demonstrations of the saints.

Although he illustrates Bede's belief that monks, contemplative or not, should engage in manual labor (an ideal better exemplified by Cuthbert), Owine is noted less for piety than for hard work.[37] Unlike others who witness visions and miracles, Owine does not have credibility. When he asks what the song was, Chad replies, "*If* you heard the sound of singing . . ." ("*Si* uocem carminis audisti . . . ," pp. 340–43; my emphasis); "carmina," "song" or "verse," is also the word used later for Cædmon's music (4.24, pp. 416–17). Although Owine appears to have understood the vision as Chad explained it, Owine was not permitted to talk about it. He himself saw no messenger, and any power or influence he would have acquired from witnessing the miracle is suppressed, both by the bishop and by Bede—although Bede does note that Owine later told the story to someone ("ut postea referebat," pp. 340–41).

We see a pointed contrast in the miracle of Cædmon, who both comprehends his vision and is commanded to speak about it. Owine never becomes a subject who reflects on his experience. One soon forgets his single act of signification, his arrival at the monastery with his tools in hand—"ad laborem se monasterium intrare signabat" ("he did this to show that he was entering the monastery to work hard," pp. 338–39). Instead, Owine barely stands above the dumb matter that music envelops. He might be said to be more like his tools than he is like his breth-

---

37 Colgrave and Mynors, *Bede's Ecclesiastical History*, p. 124 (n. 1), p. 338, and p. 339 (n. 6).

ren—that is, he seems to be an object, not a subject; not an end, but a means to it.

Like Owine, Cædmon works in an environment in which Christian orthodoxy already superintends human attitudes toward the material world. Workers go about their routine functions while learned brothers pursue their occupations outside the workers' view. Owine and Cædmon are both seen as loners. Owine works while the learned brothers study and pray. Already isolated from the workers at the feast, Cædmon leaves them behind permanently when he joins the learned community. He does not connect these worlds but rather moves from one sphere to another, even though his departure from the "gebeorscip," as the Old English version translates Bede's "convivium," or feast, is occasioned by duty, not simply by Cædmon's desire to avoid his turn with the harp. Cædmon went "to the cattle byre, as it was his turn to take charge of them that night," Bede writes ("ad stabula iumentorum, quorum ei custodia nocte illa erat delegata," pp. 416–17).[38] Owine overhears but does not comprehend heavenly music. Cædmon is likewise alienated from the native songs of his fellow workers and has no understanding of the music he himself makes until its purpose is explained to him. Less the creator of music than the instrument through which it is played, Cædmon masters a form for content created by others. The song tradition he rejects, whatever its origins and character, is the practice of Christian workers, a thing if not an object, and in this chapter, a synecdoche for all the popular practices and beliefs that the Christian tradition challenges.

There is music everywhere in Book 4, but only at Whitby is there music that is not Christian in content and purpose. The "great revival of Church life" that follows Theodore's arrival is, in Book 4 of the *Ecclesiastical History*, manifested nearly as of-

---

38 Thomas Miller, ed., *The Old English Version of Bede's Ecclesiastical History of the English People*, Early English Text Society, Original Series 95, 96, 110, 111 (1890-1898; London, 1959-1963), pp. 342–43.

ten in references to sacred music as to the miraculous.[39] Near the beginning of the book, Bede describes Wilfrid's success in bringing Eddius Stephanus, the first singing master to come to Northumbria since James, the deacon of Paulinus (4.2).[40] In Rochester, Theodore consecrated Putta, who was "especially skilled in liturgical chanting after the Roman manner, which he had learned from the disciples of the blessed Gregory" (4.2, pp. 334–37). When his church was destroyed by Æthelred, the Mercian king, Putta retired from his bishopric but continued to teach music (4.12, pp. 368–69). John, the arch-cantor, brought music to Monkwearmouth at Benedict Biscop's behest and taught "the mode of chanting throughout the year as it was practised at St. Peter's in Rome" (4.18, pp. 388–89).

These teachers, it would seem, had many pupils; Book 4 is filled with those who sing. Music prefigures the announcement of Chad's death to his followers in Owine's vision (4.3). The nuns' singing precedes the first miracle of light at Barking (4.7). Singing also accompanies the translation of Æthelthryth's body (4.19), and Bede's hymn in her honor, taken up in the next chapter, is replete with its own references to musical skills, both his and hers (4.20): "Chaste is my song," Bede begins. Describing the nun in the afterlife, he writes, "Ever on the sweetest harp thou sing'st new songs, / Hymning thy Spouse ever on sweetest harp" (pp. 400–401). The nuns at Hackness sing when they learn of Hild's death (4.23, pp. 412–13). Singing is at the center of Bede's account of Cædmon, and singing accompanies his own death (4.24, pp. 420–21). Adamnan was singing psalms when he was warned in a vision of the destruction of Coldingham as well (4.25, pp. 424–25).

Music belongs both to the material world of those whose bodies are required to sing, play instruments, and make musi-

---

39 Colgrave and Mynors, *Bede's Ecclesiastical History*, pp. xxiii-xxiv.
40 On James's work with church music, which is mentioned here by Bede, see Colgrave and Mynors, *Bede's Ecclesiastical History*, 2.20, pp. 206–7. Eddius Stephanus was also Wilfrid's biographer.

cal sounds, and to the symbolic world of discourse. Bruce W. Holsinger has used "a materialist focus upon the musical body" to demonstrate the relevance of the musical body to "social formations"—such as the feast in the beer-hall—in which music played a central role.[41] Music is material not only in the sounds that constitute it but in the physical, social, and institutional unities required to produce it, especially according to the strict Roman standards Bede discusses in several chapters in Book 4. Music symbolizes that unity of worship, so important after the tension between Irish and Roman observances often mentioned in Bede's *History*; however, singing forms the many into one among pagans as well. Cædmon's self-imposed exile from the feast scene is remedied by his central importance to the learned community once his musical gift has been made known. His change in social standing is a material transformation, and so too is the transformation of poetry that his gift brings.

Bede emphasizes the wealth of themes that flow into native verse once the native tradition is connected to sacred teaching. After his gift is discovered, Cædmon puts the formal elements of the native tradition to the new and noble purpose of instruction. His innovation is an appropriation, not an exchange, for the flow works in only one direction. Bede says that after his vi-

---

41 Bruce W. Holsinger, *Music, Body, and Desire of Medieval Culture* (Stanford, 2001), pp. 10–15. Bede and Cædmon do not figure into this book, but see Holsinger's forthcoming essay in *JEGP* 2007. See also Robert Boenig, "Musical Instruments as Iconographical Artifacts in Medieval Poetry," in Perry, ed., *Material Culture and Cultural Materialisms*, pp. 1–16. As Gerry Bloustein writes, music is "central both to the materiality of social context and the symbolism of the self"—to the social practices around ordinary things, that is, as well as to symbolic systems. Gerry Bloustein, "On Not Dancing Like a 'Try Hard,'" Musical Visions : Selected Conference Proceedings from 6th National Australian/New Zealand IASPM and Inaugural Arnhem Land Performance Conference (Kent Town, Australia, 1999), pp. 8–20 at p. 11.

sion, Cædmon could not compose any "foolish or trivial poem," but only those poems "which were concerned with devotion and so were fitting for his devout tongue to utter" ("Unde nil umquam friuoli et superuacui poematis facere potuit, sed ea tantummodo, quae ad religionem pertinent, religiosam eius linguam decebant," 4.14, pp. 414–15). After his vision, Cædmon was unable—as well as unwilling—to compose "foolish" and "trivial" poems; that is, he would not compose vernacular verse on secular topics.

But the native tradition remained strong and, we must assume, unchanged, however little Bede thought of it. Bede downplayed the indisputably hybrid nature of the new musical tradition Cædmon helped to launch. Although we have come to think of Cædmon's music as exclusively sacred, it integrates two traditions that, within Olsen's framework, would be seen as interdependent partners. In Gurevich's work, such hybridity is seen as characteristic of "popular culture," which he sees as a synthesis of pagan and Christian traditions, and which he juxtaposes to the learned, written tradition.[42] Other scholars, including Richard Kieckhefer, for example, in his discussion of medieval magic, define "popular culture" as pagan culture outside the Christian tradition.[43] Gurevich makes the more persuasive case, arguing that pagan culture was, after a point, unavoidably infused with Christian elements and—the important point here—that Christian culture was likewise infused with folk elements, an admixture Bede would have been loathe to acknowledge. Bede looks with scorn on the native tradition and sets Cædmon's song over it, but the cowherd's co-workers would not have adopted that view of their own tradition any more than they would have discontinued feasting and singing once

---

42 Gurevich, *Medieval Popular Culture*, pp. 7–8, where he reminds us that Aldhelm's famous comment about the relationship of Ingeld to Christ was a protest against monks who would rather listen to the harpist than to a (monastic) reader. Gurevich finds much later evidence of the tenacious hold of folk tales on learned minds.

43 Richard Kieckhefer, *Magic in the Middle Ages* (Cambridge, 1988), p. 1.

Cædmon had left their number (his participation had been dispensable in any case).[44] Like other elements of the everyday, the native tradition persisted within a Christianized popular culture and even within sacred song; amid the other claims routinely advanced on its behalf, Cædmon's hymn also makes that point about the material culture of Bede's world.

The Limits to Things

The miracles I have described form a small part of those Bede catalogues in Book 4 of the *Ecclesiastical History*. I have suggested that each episode presents us with a double perspective. Even as Bede draws attention to God's miraculous power over ordinary things, his narrative is forced to allude to the everyday practices and social relations that wonders do not transform. William D. McCready has argued that Bede's belief in miracles did not preclude his understanding of a "coherent natural order" and its operations, and that his "dual perspective" appears in "Bede's account of human events as well."[45] It must be said that skepticism or search for causation outside the divine—and in particular the agency of things or people—is not obvious in Book 4 of the *Ecclesiastical History*. All the same, the things that appear in Bede's miraculous accounts retain their materiality and their functions once the miraculous has flowed around or through them. Bede's miracles point to the limitations of such things—the lamp that shines darkness, shutters that cannot keep out light, and shackles that cannot bind the slave. But such limitations are only temporary, the fleeting trace of a symbolic meaning that often eludes those before whom it is displayed—the dying nun's companions, for example, Imma's captors, Owine, and others, including Cædmon. Ordinary things and routines per-

44 See Frantzen, *Desire for Origins: New Language, Old English, and Teaching the Tradition* (New Brunswick, 1983), pp. 139–44.
45 See the discussion in McCready, *Miracles and the Venerable Bede*, pp. 27–29, and arguments about Bede's attitudes especially in *De natura rerum*.

sist; Cædmon does not sing about them because they represent human handiwork rather than God's. Once they have served their rhetorical purpose and have been mastered by human subjects, they cease to matter to Bede, if not to the women and men whose social relations those objects and routines mediated.

It is the nature of miraculous power—as it has been the function of the *Ecclesiastical History* itself, Book 4 especially—to transfigure pre-existing contexts in order to illustrate a new Anglo-Saxon world order. Bede usually focuses the reader's attention on what Ward considers the "moral truth and inner meaning of miracle stories," diminishing the power of the material world.[46] But if we refocus on the circumstances in which these miracles have taken place, we find that the material world has not been diminished after all. Imma's chains will bind a less fortunate captive; the nuns' lamp will continue to glow; the oratory shutters will keep out daylight; and more monks and nuns will die of the plague. Likewise, the workers of Whitby will go on singing their favorite songs with or without Cædmon's company. That continuity offers little competition for Bede's miracles, since their spectacular effects defeat and overwhelm the everyday. But the everyday did not, in the end, require texts to preserve it, while the miracles, it must be said, could have survived no other way.

The idea that the *Ecclesiastical History* should tell us anything about everyday life and ordinary things seems to be a novel one. Yet Bede's text and the monastic culture to which it belonged has long influenced the study of material culture. Prior to the 1980s, Chris Loveluck writes, "the vast majority of Middle Saxon sites [i.e., A.D. 650–850] which had been subject to excavation were documented major monastic centers," including Whitby and Monkwearmouth. Because these sites had royal patrons, finds recovered from them "were viewed as characteristic of high-status monastic settlements." Further analysis "seemed to corroborate textual evidence provided by Bede and other clerics" that these religious centers were also centers for certain

---

46 Ward, "Miracles and History," pp. 72–73.

kinds of craftwork. Loveluck has argued that archaeological criteria for identifying monastic settlements have to be reassessed, since features supposedly characteristic of monastic settlements have increasingly been found at wealthy rural settlements "for which there is no historical evidence to influence interpretations of their character and status."[47] Recent work by Tim Pestell supports this view.[48] Patrick Wormald's negative response to Loveluck's assertion of "independent archaeological criteria for defining settlement character and status" shows that this demarcation of disciplinary boundaries can be misunderstood. Wormald protested "the evaporation of historical insight from current archaeological studies," but he seems to have been objecting instead to the downgrading of text-based criteria as primary guides to the interpretation of archaeological evidence.[49] It is hardly a loss of "historical insight" to employ more diversified models for the analysis of settlement archaeology and the contexts it provides for our knowledge of ordinary things and the Anglo-Saxon everyday.

Loveluck has cast doubt on the wisdom of using texts to study archaeology more explicitly, stating that "it is seldom possible to marry textual and archaeological evidence" in relation to the study of settlements. Loveluck compares texts to "snapshots" that cannot capture the evidence of change (for example, the

47 C. P. Loveluck, "A High-status Anglo-Saxon Settlement at Flixborough, Lincolnshire," *Antiquity* 72 (1998), 146–81.
48 Tim Pestell, *Landscapes of Monastic Foundation: the Establishment of Religious Houses in East Anglia, c. 650–1200* (Woodbridge, Suffolk, 2004), pp. 22–64.
49 See Patrick Wormald's comments on Loveluck, "Wealth, Waste and Conspicuous Consumption: Flixborough and its Importance for Middle and Late Saxon Rural Settlement Studies," in *Image and Power in the Archaeology of Early Medieval Britain: Essays in Honour of Rosemary Cramp*, ed. Helena Hamerow and Arthur MacGregor (Oxford, 2001), pp. 78–130. Wormald reviews this collection in *English Historical Review* 119 (2004), p. 160.

phasing of settlements at a particular site) that makes the archaeological record difficult to interpret.[50] But texts have layers, too, and not only layers of meaning—they have layers of language, error, corruption, and scribal variation, any one of which might serve to connect some element of the text to a point or a process that the text's words itself do not directly address. Jane Roberts has made arguments similar to Loveluck's with different reasoning. While producing a long list of Old English words associated with the finds of Sutton Hoo, Roberts comments that it is "notoriously hard to match the words that remain to the artefacts removed from the earth."[51] She suggests that it is easier to get from things found in the ground to the Anglo-Saxon words for them than from the words to things that archaeologists are likely find.[52]

Roberts' comments remind us that Olsen describes archaeology as "the discipline of things *par excellence.*"[53] An attempt to do more with things in texts (or outside them) must begin with objects, not with words. As a first step (admittedly a large one), we must leave behind the idea that texts and objects should somehow mirror each other, so that they can be precisely matched. Social processes do not necessarily engage things in self-evident ways, and most texts point to processes as well as objects indirectly rather than directly. Nonetheless, important connections can be made, as we see in John Ruffing's powerful analysis of what he calls the "labor structure" of Ælfric's *Colloquy*.[54] Ruffing

50   Chris Loveluck, "Wealth, Waste, and Conspicuous Consumption," in Hamerow and MacGregor, *Image and Power*, p. 121.
51   Roberts, "Anglo-Saxon Vocabulary," p. 185.
52   Roberts, "Anglo-Saxon Vocabulary," pp. 185–86 and pp. 193–202 (the list).
53   Olsen, "Material Culture after the Text," p. 89; Hines, *Voices in the Past*, p. 18.
54   John Ruffing, "The Labor Structure of Ælfric's *Colloquy*," in *The Work of Work: Servitude, Slavery, and Labor in Medieval England*, ed. Allen J. Frantzen and Douglas Moffat (Glasgow, 1994), pp. 55–70.

All Created Things

shows how the competition among workers (baker, salter, etc.) intensifies in the course of the discussion until the master settles the question of the supremacy of professions. He makes it clear, as Ruffing writes, that agriculture is "the most important secular art" because "the plowman is merely the most essential of all those who must supply the monastery." In the end, as Ruffing sees it, the dialogue leads to a standoff between the monastic master, who controls language, and the ironworker, who argues for "a sociological reality in which the entire condition of food production, especially the crucial surplus that feeds non-producers like kings and monks, does depend on tool technology."[55] But in the end the master asserts the primacy of texts and those who create and parse them, making the learned the center and disguising their dependence on the skills of the unlearned.

The *Colloquy* is unusual in representing labor as a social process and in pointing to the objects on which labor itself depends. Since texts, objects, and processes are more often tied together by complementarity than by such direct association, we must ask how—with Bede's *Ecclesiastical History* and other texts in which labor and its attendant objects seem to matter only because they are proximate to monastic well-being, or to the advancement of the Church's mission—we can begin to uncover such ordinary social relations as the text might illuminate. One could compile a list of words associated with finds from any of the major Anglo-Saxon archaeological sites, especially those recently excavated, and index them so that all scholars could see what objects associated with a particular process—food preparation, for example—survive, and in what condition, and where. Next, one would try to situate those words in the lexical contexts established by the superb tools of the *Dictionary of Old English*. The results might seem to be meager, as we find, for example, when searching for certain words in the Old English kitchen vocabulary. The *Dictionary of Old English* lists only nine occurrences of *cruce*, designating a pot, jar, or pitcher, and only four for *crohha*,

---

55 Ruffing, "The Labor Structure of Ælfric's *Colloquy*," pp. 66–67.

a pot or crock used especially for cooking. There are thirty-five occurrences of *crocca*, however, a word for an earthenware pot or crock that also has a figurative meaning.[56] Glosses frequently include these words, as the *DOE* entries show, allowing us to extend the search to Latin equivalents and to the Latin corpus.

Some objects might be more rewarding. For example, there are twenty-five Old English references to the quernstone (a hand mill used to grind corn), which is one of the most common surviving food-related objects.[57] Many texts that mention it use the object to make didactic and figurative statements concerning the great millstone of Mark 9:42, which is to be hung around the neck of the one who causes children to sin. Alfred's translation of the *Cura Pastoralis* offers an example: "Đurh ða cweorne is getacnod se ymbhwyrft ðisse worolde & eac monna lifes & hira gesuinces" ("Through the millstone is signified the circuit of this world and also of man's life and their toil").[58] But other references to the quernstone are specific to the material, medieval world. A prognostication from a Worcester manuscript specifies that, in a certain phase of the moon, a plowman is to get out his plow, a miller to get out his mill, and a merchant to begin selling his merchandise:

> Se IIII nihta mona se byð god þæm ergendan hys sul ut to done, & þem grindere his cweorn, & þem cipemen hys cipinge to anginnane.

---

56 See Angus Cameron, Ashley Crandell Amos, and Antonette diPaolo Healey, eds., *Dictionary of Old English: A to F* (Toronto, 2003), s.v. *crocca, crohha, cruce*. Some words are found only in glosses (*crohha*, for example).

57 See Cameron, Amos, and Healey, eds., *Dictionary of Old English*, s.v. *cweorn, cwyrn*.

58 Henry Sweet, ed., *King Alfred's West-Saxon Version of Gregory's Pastoral Care*, Early English Text Society, O. S. 45, 50 (London, 1871; repr. New York, 1973), Book 1, ch. 2, pp. 30–31.

All Created Things

> On the fourth night of the moon, it is good for the plowman to take out his plow, and the miller his millstone, and the merchant to begin his selling.[59]

Here the quernstone appears in a strategic context linking two objects to what might be the first two of three stages of food-related labor: production (plowing), preparation (milling), and exchange (trading or selling).

It is possible that our attempts to match objects to texts might become easier, for just as new archaeological evidence is weakening the textual preconceptions that once dominated the field, that same evidence increases opportunities for textual scholars to make connections to material culture. Archaeology has, as Hines points out, a seemingly unique status among the disciplines of medieval studies. "Its basic source of information" is "constantly changing and growing: new finds are made at a faster rate than most archaeologists can cope with."[60] The ordinary objects routinely found in settlement archaeology—usually in middens and similar locations—can help to determine the relation of small sunken-floor buildings or craft huts to the longhouses that were the principle domestic space of Anglo-Saxon settlements. By locating centers of craftwork within the defined boundaries of settlements—within, for example, the rampart constructed at Cuthbert's behest on Lindisfarne—archaeologists can clarify a settlement's plan and begin to frame its social spaces. That evidence helps to define the working world within which social relations played out.

David Herlihy observed that "even archaeology, the one true frontier of early medieval history, does little to illuminate the softer aspects of culture, such as human relations or domestic

---

59 Cambridge, Corpus Christi College MS 391, pp. 720–21. For the text, see Max Förster "Beiträge zur mittelalterlichen Volkskunde VIII," *Archiv* 129 (1912), 16–49, c. 43–45.

60 Hines, *Voices in the Past*, p. 19; see also Hamerow, *Early Medieval Settlements*, who refers to "an abundance of new information regarding early medieval settlements" (p. 4).

ties."[61] Herlihy might have added that texts, literary or otherwise, are seldom better than archaeology at illuminating the Anglo-Saxon everyday. Ordinary objects and daily behavior, fundamental to the "softer aspects of culture," might be mentioned in passing in literary texts—as they are in Bede's *Ecclesiastical History*—without giving us much of an idea of their specific functions, shape, or, in the case of objects, their manufacture. More mundane sources, including prognostics, penitentials, and administrative texts such as laws, offer more overlap with objects and everyday life. If not likely to turn up a lexicon that resembles items commonly mentioned in site reports, such texts do sometimes refer directly to processes of production or consumption that imply the existence of those objects.[62] Even Bede's *Ecclesiastical History*, with its many sidelong glances at ordinary objects, including lamps, windows, and doorways, can contribute to our knowledge of objects. To begin that endeavor, we have to analyze the texts with objects in mind and notice what objects the texts mention and what (however little) the texts say about them. Any text, whether Bede's *Ecclesiastical History, Beowulf,* or less canonical works, is rich in references to things, and if not necessarily the ordinary things likely to turn up in excavations of Anglo-Saxon sites (pottery, ironwork, quernstones, spindle-whorls), then the processes of production and consumption to which such objects were indispensable.[63]

---

61 David Herlihy, *Medieval Households* (Cambridge, 1985), p. 29 (quoted, to quite different effect, by Hamerow, *Early Medieval Settlements*, p. 4).

62 See Frantzen, *The Anglo-Saxon Penitentials: A Cultural Database,* for a provisional material index to the vernacular handbooks of penance: http://www.Anglo-Saxon.net.

63 See Ann Hagen, *A Handbook of Anglo-Saxon Food and Drink: Processing and Consumption.* (Norfolk, 1992) and *A Second Handbook of Anglo-Saxon Food and Drink: Production and Distribution* (Norfolk, 1995).

Such things furnished the working world of Cædmon and Owine. Cædmon's hymn overlooks them even as it predicates on them the creative power the poem celebrates. The work of the wonder-father encompasses heaven as a roof for earth and all that exists in between. The cowherd was commanded to sing of *principium creaturarum* (4.24, pp. 416–17), of *frumsceaft*, "of the beginning of all things."[64] This has long been understood as a command to sing about the sacred moment of Creation and no more. But creation was not confined to the Creator, and the Creator himself, as Faith Wallis's essay shows, was understood by Cædmon, Bede, and Bede's contemporaries to be a craftsman who shaped "wundra gehwæs," "each of wonders." Wallis quotes an Irish computistical text known to Bede that quotes Wisdom 11.21: "Not in vain is it said of God: 'Thou hast made all things in measure, number and weight'" ("Sed omnia in mensura, et numero, et pondere disposuisti"). The command to sing of "the beginning of all created things" ("principium creaturarum") cannot be limited to a celebration of God's power over the material world. Inevitably, the praise must extend to "omnia," to all, in its measure, number, and weight, whether axe, adze, dormitory, fish nets, doors, or windows. Such things were shaped by humans, not by God, and given a place in the everyday social order. For textual and particularly for literary scholars such things have been subsumed into symbolic categories of identity and representation that alienate them from their use. Owine's axe does not need to be seen striking wood (and indeed never is so seen) to represent his status as a worker. The song Cædmon sings seems to refer only to the new tradition of sacred vernacular verse, not to the old tradition that forms its second voice.

Before ordinary things, whether axe or drinking song, were given representational meaning, they were used for shaping timber, cooking, weaving, butchering, grinding grain, forming and reinforcing social bonds. Sometimes those processes lent

---

64 Miller, *The Old English Version of Bede's Ecclesiastical History*, pp. 344–45.

Allen J. Frantzen

themselves to figuration. The twelfth-century capital reliefs in the cathedral at Vézelay (France) show agricultural labor in remarkable detail (honey-gatherers can be seen following procedures clear to modern apiculturists, for example).[65] That detail did not mean that some scenes—grain-grinding, for example—could not also be understood metaphorically. Abbot Suger of St. Denis compared the grinding of grain to the "mystic mill" that "urg[es] us onward from the material to the immaterial" by "converting the words of the prophets into the message of the New Testament."[66] No less familiar to Anglo-Saxonists is the preface to the *Soliloquies* attributed to King Alfred. The king describes himself as a woodsman traveling to the forest to secure posts, lumber, and other building materials for a house. Seeing on every tree "something that I needed at home" ("on ælcum treowo ic geseah hwæthwugu þæs þe ic æt ham beþorfte"), he exhorts each of his followers to "load his [wagons] with fair twigs" so that he too can build a house, a "fair dwelling" to inhabit both in winter and in summer "as I have not yet done" ("gefeðrige hys wænas mid fegrum gerdum ... swa swa ic nu ne gyt ne dyde").[67] These images of the timber-gatherer and cottage-builder describe the assimilation and reformulation of literary translation and transformation.[68] But Alfred did not leave

65 Henry Kraus, *The Living Theatre of Medieval Art* (Bloomington, 1967), p. 104, reproduces the capital showing the honey-gatherers.
66 Christopher Brooke, *The Monastic World 1000–1300* (New York, 1974), pp. 70–71, plate 112. The quotation from Suger is found in Erwin Panovsky and Gerda Panofsky-Soergel, eds., *Abbot Suger: On the Abbey Church of St. Denis and Its Art Treasures*, 2nd ed. (Princeton, 1979), pp. 74–75, and is quoted by Brooke in the caption to plate 112.
67 My translation from Thomas A. Carnicelli, ed., *King Alfred's Version of St. Augustine's "Soliloquies"* (Cambridge, Mass., 1969), p. 47.
68 See Milton McC. Gatch, "King Alfred's Version of Augustine's *Soliloquia*: Some Suggestions on its Rationale and Unity," in *Studies*

behind the worldly uses of the house, metaphorical or literal, that a loyal follower might build. One could rest in such a cottage, built "on his lord's lease and by his help," Alfred wrote, but could also use time there to gain ownership of the land and to enjoy the surroundings, and to hunt and fish at will ("he hine mote hwilum þar-on gerestan, and huntigan, and fuglian, and fiscian," p. 48). In the first instance, the things integral to such processes need to be understood in the context of what they were made to do, not in the context of what they could be made to mean. Bede and other subjects of Anglo-Saxon texts have passed away, but as Hines reminds us, the objects of the Anglo-Saxon world remain, even if sometimes only as traces in the soil, and are emerging at a greater rate today than ever before. Surely it is time for Anglo-Saxonists reading texts to look for these things and then to look at, rather than through, them to see what they can tell us about the matter of Bede's world.[69]

---

in Earlier Old English Prose, ed. Paul Szarmach (Albany, 1986), pp. 17–45.

69 My thanks to Fannon Alison, Bradley Fruhauff, and Scott DeGregorio for comments on drafts of this essay.

Cædmon's World: Secular and Monastic Lifestyles and Estate Organization in Northern England, A.D. 650–900

CHRISTOPHER LOVELUCK

Early-Medieval Settlement Archaeology and its Development

THE NARRATIVE PROVIDED by Bede concerning the cowherd Cædmon, the composition of his hymn, and his transformation in role to become a monk at the royal monastery of Streanaeshalch provides a most fortunate piece of "theater" within which to explore most of the recent developments in our understanding of the material world inhabited by both Cædmon and Bede. That physical world comprised northern England from the mid seventh to early eighth centuries A.D., within the political context of the Anglo-Saxon kingdom of Northumbria. The characters and circumstances of the Cædmon story, and its context within the *Ecclesiastical History*, reflect the material foundations of secular and ecclesiastical lives, and the extents of their social networks during the late seventh century.[1] We see the cowherd Cædmon at a feast within a building at a secular settlement; his tending of the animals in an attempt to avoid reciting his verse; his presentation by an estate or royal official (a reeve) before Hild, the royal abbess of Streanaeshalch; and his adoption of a monastic life on the advice of the abbess. Here in a microcosm, we see a suite of hierarchical relations associated

---

1   Bertram Colgrave and R.A.B. Mynors, ed. *Bede's Ecclesiastical History of the English People*, 4.24 (Oxford, 1969), pp. 414–21.

with different elements of the settlement and social hierarchy, ranging from the cowherd and his animals, his horizons focused on local affairs; to the reeve, who may have had both local and regional responsibilities at one or more estate centers; and to the abbess, a person at the heart of both secular aristocratic and ecclesiastical networks, and to a monastery that had recently hosted the synod which had resulted in the adoption of Roman Church practices across Anglo-Saxon England.

In combination, the context, the circumstances, the actors, and the transformations of the Cædmon story can provide touchstones or windows through which it is possible to examine specific aspects of the material world of Anglo-Saxon England, in what has been described as the Middle Anglo-Saxon period—between approximately 650 and 850. More specifically, the themes from the narrative allow an exploration of the current debates associated with the archaeological remains of different elements of the settlement hierarchy, and their provisioning structures and exchange networks. Furthermore, the narrative gives an entry-point into the exploration of the character of lifestyles on different types of settlement, especially those of the social elite. The distinguishing of social practices that may be associated with different group identities has been one of the key advances in recent years, in relation to the settlement archaeology of the seventh to eleventh centuries. This is increasingly achieved through the integrated analysis of structural, artifactual, and biological remains, when the preservation of deposits and stratigraphic relationships allows such an approach.[2]

---

2   Christopher Loveluck, "Wealth, Waste and Conspicuous Consumption. Flixborough and its Importance for Middle and Late Saxon Rural Settlement Studies," in *Image and Power in the Archaeology of Early Medieval Britain—Essays in honour of Rosemary Cramp*, ed. Helena Hamerow and Arthur MacGregor (Oxford, 2002), pp. 78–130; Christopher Loveluck, *Rural Settlement, Lifestyles and Social Change in the later First Millennium A.D. Excavations at Flixborough*, vol. 4 (Oxford, in press).

Christopher Loveluck

Even more importantly, an increasing number of settlements from parts of continental western Europe, formerly situated within the provinces of the Roman empire, are now providing strong archaeological evidence for transformation of settlement character—change from secular estate centers to monasteries and vice versa.[3] While the donation of estates and their settlement infrastructures for the foundation of monasteries has long been known from textual sources, it is only now that we can start to see particular archaeological signatures associated with different lifestyles and characters within the occupational histories of individual settlements. Just as transformation in social role is a key element of Cædmon's life, so too is transformation in character now becoming a key feature of settlement biographies as they are viewed through the filter of archaeological remains.

This contribution to the interdisciplinary discussion of Cædmon's world will, therefore, focus on the following themes in order to explore the different material vistas of seventh- to ninth-century northern England, and its world-view. The discussion begins with a brief summary of the origin of Middle Anglo-Saxon settlement archaeology and its legacy for the interpretation of settlement remains. It developed primarily from excavations at identifiable and documented centers, usually sites labeled as monasteries. One of the first sites investigated was located on the headland at Whitby, precisely because it was thought to be the location of Hild's monastery of Streanaeshalch, thus providing yet another link with the Cædmon story.[4] The con-

3   Discussed below, and see Christopher Loveluck, "L'habitat anglo-saxon de Flixborough: dynamiques sociales et styles de vie (VIIe-XIe siècle)," *Les Nouvelles de l'Archéologie* 92 (2e trimestre 2003), 16–20; Christopher Loveluck, "Rural Settlement Hierarchy in the Age of Charlemagne," in *Charlemagne: Empire and Society*, ed. Joanna Story (Manchester, 2005), pp. 230–58; Loveluck, *Rural Settlement, Lifestyles and Social Change*, Chapter 9.
4   Charles R. Peers and C. A. Ralegh Radford, "The Saxon Monastery of Whitby," *Archaeologia* 89 (1943), 27–88.

sideration of developmental influences and biases within past archaeological interpretation is followed by a discussion of the integrated material culture profiles, which can be associated with the settlements of the seventh- to ninth-century social elite, both secular and ecclesiastical. This review includes traits from settlements best characterized as estate centers and monasteries, and some of the lifestyles described by Bede are reflected at both. A geographical focus on settlements facing the North Sea coast, from East Anglia to Northumberland, also provides a corrective on impressions of the exclusivity of particular activities and artifacts at specific types of settlement (Figure 1). Finally, attention is given to the phenomenon of settlement transformation between the seventh to tenth centuries; this discussion also incorporates some emerging evidence from northern France and Germany (Figure 2).

The academic training of the pioneers of the settlement archaeology of seventh- to ninth-century England was grounded in medieval history, Old English/Norse, and classics. In this sense, and perhaps somewhat ironically in the perceptions of many younger archaeologists, scholars such as C. A. Ralegh Radford, Brian Hope-Taylor, Rosemary Cramp, and Philip Rahtz all approached the study of the Anglo-Saxon past from an interdisciplinary perspective. With archaeological survey techniques in their infancy, they followed the best available sources of information available to them. Namely, they followed seventh- to eleventh-century textual sources, often Bede's *Ecclesiastical History*, and located excavations at the sites of documented settlements, with a view to gaining the first insights into the nature of Anglo-Saxon society as reflected in the physical remains below the modern ground surface. All of the settlements targeted for excavation were associated with textual labels, and in many cases with Anglo-Saxon descriptions of buildings, events, and activities at specific sites.

In the vast majority of cases, the settlements described were monasteries, and as a corollary, most sites targeted for excavation were those of documented, major monasteries. The exca-

Christopher Loveluck

vations of Peers and Radford in the 1920s at Whitby (probably Streanaeshalch), North Yorkshire; those of Radford and Rahtz at Glastonbury, Somerset; and those of Rosemary Cramp at Monkwearmouth and Jarrow, County Durham—in the late 1950s and '60s—provide examples of the targeting of monastic sites.[5] In contrast, the excavations at Yeavering, Northumberland, by Brian Hope-Taylor from 1957–62, and at Cheddar, Somerset, by Philip Rahtz, from 1960–62, represented more limited targeting of secular centers. However, they too were textually attested: namely, a *caput* settlement of a Northumbrian royal *vill*, thought to be "Adgefrin" described by Bede (2.14), and a royal estate center or so-called palace of the ninth- and tenth-century West Saxon kings, respectively.[6]

The excavators of the above sites were all guided by sources of evidence other than the textual references: architectural fragments and earlier finds of artifacts at Whitby; standing Anglo-Saxon stone churches at Monkwearmouth and Jarrow; and a pioneering use of aerial photographs at Yeavering. The key point to note, is that in the absence of wider comparative data-sets, the excavators almost inevitably used the textual descriptions and impressions of these settlements to condition archaeological interpretation. Through no fault of these pioneers, the interpretations put forward on the basis of these early excavations, with the apparent support of textual sources, have

---

5 Peers and Radford, "Saxon Monastery of Whitby." See also Philip Rahtz, *Glastonbury* (London, 1993), pp. 67–73; Rosemary J. Cramp, "Excavations at the Saxon Monastic Sites of Wearmouth and Jarrow, Co. Durham: an Interim Report," *Medieval Archaeology* 13 (1969), 21–66; Rosemary J. Cramp, "Monkwearmouth and Jarrow in their Continental Context," in *Churches Built in Ancient Times: Recent Studies in Early Christian Archaeology*, ed. K. Painter, Society of Antiquaries Occasional Paper 16 (London, 1994), pp. 279–94.

6 Brian Hope-Taylor, *Yeavering—An Anglo-British Center of Early Northumbria* (London 1977); Philip Rahtz, *The Saxon and Medieval Palaces at Cheddar*, BAR British Series 65 (Oxford, 1979).

Cædmon's World

Figure 1: Locations of settlements in Britain discussed in the text (Drawn by David Taylor).

Christopher Loveluck

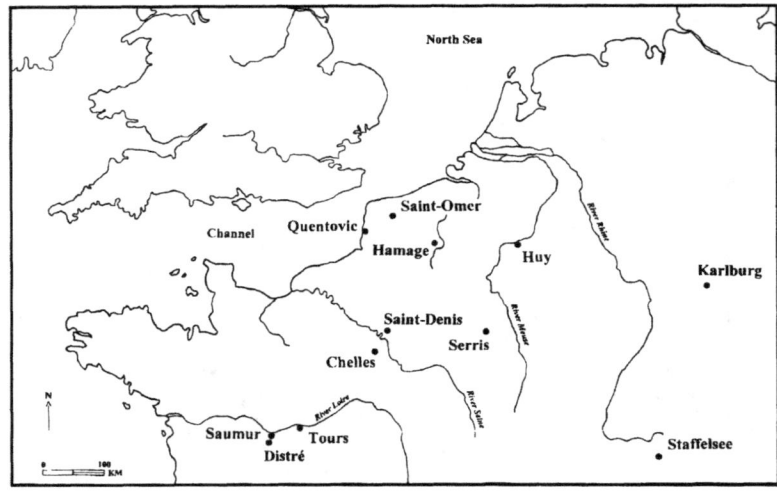

Figure 2: Location of settlements in Continental northwest Europe discussed in the text (Drawn by David Taylor).

produced something of an orthodoxy in archaeological interpretation over the past thirty years, in respect to the distinction between secular estate centers and monasteries. Recently, this has been stressed less by archaeologists and more by historians, who have interpreted archaeological evidence within the strict parameters perceived in textual sources.[7]

7 Especially by John Blair. See his essay, "Anglo-Saxon Minsters: A Topographical Review," in *Pastoral Care before the Parish*, ed. Blair and Richard Sharpe (Leicester, 1992), pp. 226–66; Blair, "Churches in the Early English Landscape: Social and Cultural Contexts," in *Church Archaeology: Research Directions for the Future*, ed. John Blair and Carol Pyrah, CBA Research Report 104 (York, 1996), pp. 6–18; Blair, "Palaces or Minsters?—Northampton and Cheddar Reconsidered," *Anglo-Saxon England* 25 (1996), 97–121; and to a certain extent in Blair, *The Church in Anglo-Saxon Society* (Oxford, 2005).

The documented center of Yeavering and the monasteries of Whitby, Jarrow, and Monkwearmouth seemed to provide a distinct contrast. Yeavering yielded evidence of a sixth- to early eighth-century occupation sequence comprising large rectangular timber buildings, display structures (the assembly structure and great enclosure), two cemeteries, and religious buildings—one identified as a temple (D_2), and the other a timber church (Building B).[8] Artifact remains were limited, but the settlement appeared to have acted as a focus for the consumption of local surpluses. The only indication of integration within the wider world came from an imported imitation of a Merovingian Frankish gold coin.[9] In contrast, the monastic centers were provided with stone churches and display buildings, and had relatively abundant evidence of integration within long-distance exchange links along the North Sea coast and to the continent of Europe, between the later seventh and ninth centuries. They also yielded evidence of specialist artisan activity, in the form of fine metalworking and other crafts; and, in addition, evidence of a literate element amongst their populations, in the form of inscribed and sculpted stone monuments and styli. All of these traits seemed to be supported by textual sources.

Up until the late 1970s, this distinction seemed clear for the Middle Anglo-Saxon period. However, it rested largely upon the extent to which a so-called type-site like Yeavering was indeed representative of a royal estate center of the seventh to eighth century at a national level within England. Insufficiently detailed attention was paid to the geographical situation of Yeavering. This site lies in the Glen valley, in Northumberland—a region of England located to the north of the former Roman province of Britannia, which comprised much of the northern Northumbrian kingdom of Bernicia. This Anglo-Saxon kingdom (also

8   Hope-Taylor, *Yeavering*, pp. 158–69.
9   The coin was a very debased copy of a *triens* of the moneyer Bertoaldus of Huy, in the Meuse valley, probably minted in the 650s. See comments of Lafaurie and Kent in Hope Taylor, *Yeavering*, p. 183.

incorporating modern south-east Scotland), its settlement hierarchy, and its society appear as an acculturated native society of the post-Roman Iron Age,[10] with coastal, fortified royal centers, such as Bamburgh, Northumberland, and Dunbar, Lothian;[11] lowland royal estate centers further inland, such as Yeavering and Milfield in Northumberland, and Sprouston, Borders;[12]

10   Christopher Loveluck, "The Romano-British to Anglo-Saxon Transition: Social Transformations from the Late Roman to Early Medieval Period in Northern England, A.D. 400–700," *Past, Present and Future: The Archaeology of Northern England*, ed. Catherine Brooks, Robin Daniels, and Anthony Harding, Architectural and Archaeological Society of Durham and Northumberland Research Report 5 (Durham, 2002), pp. 127–48.

11   Excavations were undertaken in the west ward of Bamburgh castle by Brian Hope-Taylor, revealing Anglo-Saxon remains, but those who inherited his site archive have yet to publish the evidence. Some of the Anglo-Saxon artefacts discovered have been published, for example a seventh-century gold plaque with zoomorphic ornament. See Richard Bailey, "Gold Plaque, Bamburgh, Northumberland," in *The Making of England: Anglo-Saxon Art and Culture A.D. 600–900*, ed. Leslie Webster and Janet Backhouse (London, 1991), pp. 58–59. Larger scale excavations have been undertaken at Dunbar, revealing an exceptional occupation sequence from the sixth/seventh to ninth centuries A.D. See David R. Perry, *Castle Park, Dunbar: Two Thousand Years on a Fortified Headland*, Society of Antiquaries of Scotland Monograph 16 (Edinburgh, 2000).

12   The remains at Milfield and Sprouston are best known from aerial photographic evidence. For Milfield, see Tim Gates and Colm O'Brien, "Cropmarks at Milfield and New Bewick and the Recognition of *Grubenhäuser* in Northumberland," *Archaeologia Aeliana*, 5th series, No 16 (1988), 1–12. For Sprouston, see Ian Smith, "Patterns of Settlement and Land Use of the Late Anglian Period in the Tweed Basin," in *Studies in Late Anglo-Saxon Settlement*, ed. Margaret Faull (Oxford, 1984), pp. 177–96.

lowland hamlets; and both lowland and upland farmsteads.[13] Outside the coastal royal centers, wealth seems to have been expressed in native media, such as cattle, rather than exotic imports; a lack of integration within international networks or rather, a lack of archaeological expression of such links, was a regional phenomenon and may have been a particular cultural choice for the supposedly Anglo-Saxon society of Bernicia. Furthermore, the apparent contrast in activities relating to craft specialization between Yeavering and the northern monasteries became less distinct through the 1970s. Fine metalworking crucibles and textile-working evidence were recovered during excavations at Yeavering henge on the opposite side of the road from Hope Taylor's excavations, although this fact is rarely noted.[14] Hence, apparent differences increasingly appear to be a consequence of extent of excavation and regional trends.[15]

With the Yeavering evidence less than convincing as a type-site for Middle Anglo-Saxon England as a whole, traits from other

13 For a lowland hamlet, see Thirlings; Colm O'Brien and Roger Miket, "The Early Medieval Settlement of Thirlings, Northumberland," *Durham Archaeological Journal* 7 (1991), 57–91. For a lowland farmstead, see New Bewick, in Gates and O'Brien, "Cropmarks at Milfield and New Bewick." For upland farmsteads, see Huckhoe and Ingram Hill—although their occupation into the seventh century is uncertain; George Jobey, "Excavations at the Native Settlement at Huckhoe, Northumberland, 1955–57," *Archaeologia Aeliana*, 4th Series, No 37 (1959), 217–78; George Jobey, "A Radiocarbon Date for the Palisaded Settlement at Huckhoe," *Archaeologia Aeliana*, 4th Series, No 46 (1968), 293–5; George Jobey, "Excavations at Brough Law and Ingram Hill," *Archaeologia Aeliana*, 4th Series, No 49 (1970), 71–93.

14 Alison Tinniswood and Anthony Harding, "Anglo-Saxon Occupation and Industrial Features in the Henge Monument at Yeavering, Northumberland," *Durham Archaeological Journal* 7 (1991), 93–108.

15 Loveluck, *Rural Settlement, Lifestyles and Social Change*, Chapter 9.

settlements were brought into the debate over the identification of settlement character from archaeological remains. Two key settlements in this debate were from Portchester Castle, Hampshire, and Wicken Bonhunt, Essex—both in southern England, and both near coastal waterways (the Channel and the Thames estuary respectively). These settlements were excavated between the late 1960s and mid 1970s; both had rectangular timber buildings—some of them large—and both were in receipt of imported goods from northern France and the Rhineland, and supported artisan activities to cater for the needs of the settlements.[16] Both were interpreted as estate centers, and indicated that secular estate centers, housing members of the aristocracy or royalty, were integrated within long-distance exchange or provisioning networks. Nevertheless, stone buildings dating from the seventh to ninth centuries were absent, and literacy was not evident in any element of their populations. Thus, a distinction between the material worlds of the secular and ecclesiastical elites still seemed to exist, albeit based on very limited evidence from so-called secular sites. Numbers of excavations

16 At Portchester Castle, Barry Cunliffe uncovered a complex settlement sequence dating predominantly from the seventh to eleventh centuries, although with an Early Anglo-Saxon phase as well. Imports from the Continent between the seventh and ninth centuries included small quantities of pottery and a fragment of a reticella-decorated glass drinking vessel. See Barry Cunliffe, *Excavations at Portchester Castle, Volume II: Saxon*, Report of the Research Committee of the Society of Antiquaries, No 33 (London, 1976). At Wicken Bonhunt, Keith Wade and Andrew Rogerson discovered a series of large Middle Anglo-Saxon buildings, a mill leat, and a provisioned settlement which included a pottery assemblage that was predominantly composed of imported Continental wares and Ipswich ware. See Keith Wade, "A Settlement at Bonhunt Farm, Wicken Bonhunt, Essex," in *Archaeology in Essex to AD 1500*, ed. David Buckley, CBA Research Report 34 (London, 1980), pp. 96–102.

at documented monasteries dwarfed the number of identified secular centers (as they still do today).

Since the late 1980s and 1990s, many of our past assumptions have increasingly been shown to be consequences of small comparative data-sets and over-reliance on textual sources. New discoveries of settlements such as Staunch Meadow, Brandon, in Suffolk; Bawsey in Norfolk; and above all, Flixborough in North Lincolnshire, have emphasized the need for a re-evaluation of the criteria which have been used to define settlement character from the seventh to ninth centuries.[17] All of these more recent discoveries are materially very wealthy settlements and none are associated with documentary labels to influence interpretation. All have yielded styli, all have evidence for craft-working, and all are located in east coast locations ideal for long-distance exchange. Initial reactions, primarily resulting from the presence of the small numbers of styli, were that these settlements were undocumented monasteries.[18] Yet, by the late 1990s, most

17 The settlement at Staunch Meadow, Brandon, is currently the subject of a detailed post-excavation analysis and publication program, funded by English Heritage, although the only published interim to date is Robert Carr, Andrew Tester, and Peter Murphy, "The Middle Saxon settlement at Staunch Meadow, Brandon," *Antiquity* 62, No. 235 (1988), 371–77. For Bawsey, see Andrew Rogerson, "Six Middle Anglo-Saxon Sites in West Norfolk," in *Markets in Early Medieval Europe. Trading and "Productive" Sites, 650–850*, eds. Tim Pestell and Katharina Ulmschneider (Macclesfield, 2003), pp. 110–21. For the history of interpretation of Flixborough, see Christopher Loveluck, "A High-status Anglo-Saxon Settlement at Flixborough, Lincolnshire," *Antiquity* 72, No 275 (1998), 146–61; Loveluck, "Wealth, Waste and Conspicuous Consumption"; and Loveluck, *Rural Settlement, Lifestyles and Social Change*.
18 For example those of Ben Whitwell and Barbara Yorke. Ben Whitwell, "Flixborough," *Current Archaeology* 126, 11.6 (1991), 244–47. Barbara Yorke, "Lindsey: The Lost Kingdom Found?," in *Pre-Viking Lindsey*, ed., Alan Vince (Lincoln, 1993), pp. 141–50.

materially wealthy settlements of Middle Anglo-Saxon date in eastern England possessed a material signature previously associated with documented, monastic labels; the number of such signatures grows all the time with new metal-detected finds.[19] Many have also yielded small numbers of styli.[20] For some, most, if not all, of these wealthy settlements represent *minsters*—that is, monasteries. But if that is the case, we have to accept that it is all but impossible to identify secular centers, and this does not seem credible.

Since the late 1990s, there has also been a significant increase in the array of known Middle Anglo-Saxon rural settlement types from an archaeological standpoint, including small

---

19 See the work of Katharina Ulmschneider based on metal-detected evidence from Hampshire and the Isle of Wight and Lincolnshire: Katharina Ulmschneider, "History, Archaeology, and the Isle of Wight in the Middle Saxon Period," *Medieval Archaeology* 43 (1999), 19–44; Ulmschneider, "Settlement, Economy and the 'Productive Site' in Anglo-Saxon Lincolnshire, A.D. 650–780," *Medieval Archaeology* 44 (2000), 53–79; Ulmschneider, *Markets, Minsters and Metal-Detectors: The Archaeology of Middle Saxon Lincolnshire and Hampshire Compared*, BAR British Series 307 (Oxford, 2000). Also, Kevin Leahy, "Middle Anglo-Saxon Lincolnshire: An Emerging Picture," in Pestell and Ulmschneider, ed., *Markets in Early Medieval Europe*, pp. 138–54. For East Anglia, see Andrew Rogerson, "Six Middle Anglo-Saxon Sites"; Tim Pestell, "The Afterlife of "Productive" Sites in East Anglia," in Pestell and Ulmschneider, ed., *Markets in Early Medieval Europe*, pp. 122–37; and Tim Pestell, *Landscapes of Monastic Foundation. The Establishment of Religious Houses in East Anglia, c. 650–1200* (Woodbridge, 2004), pp. 31–36. For Yorkshire, see John Naylor, *An Archaeology of Trade in Middle Saxon England*, BAR British Series 376 (Oxford, 2004), especially appendix 1, pp. 137–44; and also the current project "Viking and Anglo-Saxon Landscape and Economy," University of York, largely based on metal-detected data.

20 See Tim Pestell, *Landscapes of Monastic Foundation*, pp. 36–48.

coastal trading and fishing settlements, such as Sandtun at West Hythe, Kent, and periodically occupied artisan and trading sites, as at Eton on the River Thames.[21] Archaeologists have been forced to reassess the use of textual evidence in archaeological interpretation. We are undoubtedly faced with a much more complex range of elements within seventh- to ninth-century settlement and social hierarchies than previously envisaged. The body of evidence now available can no longer be framed totally within the textually-led interpretations of the past. This is not to suggest abandonment of awareness of the vital textual evidence of writers like Bede. Instead, the use of textual sources by archaeologists (and archaeological sources by historians) has to be amended in light of the complex reality now represented in the physical remains of what is often called the Age of Bede. The exclusive association of certain traits with monastic centers, in particular, has to be amended, especially evidence of literacy, often represented by several styli over occupation sequences lasting over two hundred years—which are as likely to represent a cleric or an occasional literate individual on a secular aristocratic center as they are a monastery.[22]

The Cædmon story provides an avenue to illustrate the positive use of textual and artistic evidence in archaeological inter-

21 Mark Gardiner *et al.,* "Continental Trade and Non-Urban Ports in Middle Anglo-Saxon England. Excavations at Sandtun, West Hythe, Kent," *Archaeological Journal* 158 (2001), 161–290; Jonathan Hiller, David Petts, and Tim Allen, "Discussion of the Anglo-Saxon Archaeology," in *Gathering the People, Settling the Land. The Archaeology of a Middle Thames Landscape, Anglo-Saxon to Post-medieval,* ed. Stuart Foreman, Jonathan Hiller, and David Petts (Oxford, 2002), pp. 57–72.

22 See Rosamond McKitterick, *The Carolingians and the Written Word* (Cambridge, 1989), pp. 222–23; Richard Morris, *Churches in the Landscape* (London, 1989), p. 75; Loveluck, "Wealth, Waste and Conspicuous Consumption," pp. 112–13; Pestell, *Landscapes of Monastic Foundation,* pp. 38–40.

pretation, as well as to illustrate the strengths and limitations of all the forms of information. Firstly, all of us as medievalists have often sought to draw too strong a distinction between the secular and ecclesiastical elements of seventh- to ninth-century Anglo-Saxon society, with an expectation that the material reflections of both would look different. Yet the presence of Hild, the Northumbrian royal princess-*cum*-abbess, and the ease of access of a local reeve to her community, demonstrates the long-known fact that the ecclesiastical and secular elites were different sides of the same coin. Perhaps we should not expect clear distinction in the material worlds and social relations of secular and ecclesiastical settlements at the elite level. The social spectrum of the populations of royal estate centers, fortresses (Bamburgh and Dunbar), and monasteries was also complex. The extent of the lay and artisan populations at major monasteries, and the extent of the presence of clerics at secular centers, are still tantalizing unknowns.

The three cemeteries located in different zones of the monastery at Hartlepool, County Durham (Hild's base before the foundation of Streaneshalch) provide the best indications of lay and ecclesiastical population elements at a single monastic center, dating from the seventh to ninth centuries. The cemetery at Cross Close, associated with the famous name stones in runic and majuscule scripts, may have been the cemetery of the religious women of the community, while the cemetery at Church Walk seems to have been the burial zone of the monks of the community, together with discrete secular family groups, probably of high social status. A cemetery at Gladstone Road seems to have contained the majority of the lay population of the settlement. It has to be kept in mind, however, that burial at a monastery after death does not necessarily equate with residence at a monastery in life, and it is not possible to know what proportion of the probable lay/secular burial groups at Hartlepool actually lived and worked at the monastery and on its estate. Procurement of a burial space at a monastery in prox-

Cædmon's World

imity to sacred relics was much sought after.[23] Equally, there are increasing signs of differentiated burial locations within, and in association with, settlements interpreted as secular estate centers or secular phases of settlements down the east coast of England: from Yeavering in Northumberland to Thwing, East Yorkshire, and Flixborough, North Lincolnshire, to Bramford and Staunch Meadow, Brandon, in Suffolk. Again, the multiple choices for the higher ranking members of Middle Anglo-Saxon society, in terms of burial location, may also be providing archaeologists with an unrepresentative reflection of aristocratic elements among settlement populations.[24] Some members of

23 For a discussion of the Hartlepool name stones, see Rosemary Cramp, *Corpus of Anglo-Saxon Stone Sculpture, Vol 1, Pt. 1, County Durham and Northumberland* (Oxford, 1984), pp. 97–101. For a detailed discussion of the Cross Close, Church Walk, and Gladstone Street cemeteries, see chapters by Robin Daniels, Sue Anderson, and Christopher Loveluck on the nature of the cemeteries, their demographic structure and their interpretation, in Robin Daniels and Christopher Loveluck, ed., *Anglo-Saxon Hartlepool and the Foundations of English Christianity. An Archaeology of the Anglo-Saxon Monastery* (Durham, in press). The Cross Close (name stone) cemetery seems to have contained almost exclusively female graves—although at least one of the name stones also lists a male name alongside a female name. The Church Walk cemetery has several spatially distinct groups: the largest group being exclusively males, and two discrete "family groups" of adult males, females and children, distinguished by exclusive burial practices. There is also a separate cluster of children's graves around a possible shrine associated with a founder grave (again of a child). The Gladstone Street cemetery is composed of the full demographic range expected of a "normal" settlement population, in terms of males, females, children, and the full spectrum of age ranges.

24 For Yeavering, see Hope-Taylor, *Yeavering*; for Thwing, see Terry Manby, *Excavations at Thwing, East Yorkshire* (English Heritage, forthcoming). For a recent account of the Bramford evidence,

leading families living at secular centers could have been buried in monastic graveyards along with the clerics or priests who may have served the religious needs and assisted in the administration of their centers.

In addition to these gaps in our knowledge, the social transformation embodied in Cædmon's story, from secular to monastic life, also illustrates a huge previous shortcoming in the textually led interpretation of archaeological settlement remains. Once a site with a documented label of "monastery" or "royal vill" had been targeted for excavation, the tendency was to ascribe one character to the settlement for its entire occupational history. Yet, this runs against the textual evidence for settlement transformation, in both England and continental Europe, where secular estate centers were given over to become monasteries or monastic estate centers. This is abundantly clear in relation

---

see Pestell, *Landscapes of Monastic Foundation*, pp. 52–3. For Flixborough and Brandon see below. For the Anglo-Saxon aristocracy there is no doubt that major monasteries constituted desired burial locations, following continental Frankish models, such as Saint-Denis and Saint Martin de Tours in France; see Michael Wyss, "Saint-Denis (France): Du mausolée hypothetique du Bas-Empire à l'ensemble basilical carolingien," in *Death and Burial in Medieval Europe*, Papers of the Medieval Europe Brugge 1997 Conference, vol. 2, ed. Guy De Boe and Frans Verhaeghe (Zellik, 1997), pp. 111–14; and Henri Galinié, "Tours from an archaeological standpoint," in *Spaces of the Living and the Dead: An Archaeological Dialogue*, American Early Medieval Studies 3, ed. Catherine Karkov, Kelly Wickham-Crowley, and Bailey Young (Oxford, 1999), pp. 87–105. Streaneshalch/Whitby was one of these desired burial locations, like Hartlepool. Such procurement of burial places was a key component of the interaction between the secular and ecclesiastical elites, which may have been facilitated through gifts from leading families during life, and also entry of members of these families into the religious communities of leading monasteries.

to the early Northumbrian monastic foundations. Some of the earliest foundations, such as Lindisfarne and Hartlepool, between A.D. 635–640, were initially given only small land grants, probably carved out from parts of royal estates. From 655, however, we see King Oswiu granting larger estates of ten hides to major monasteries such as Lindisfarne. Some of the estate centers associated with these became monasteries, while others remained estate centers.[25] The monastery of Streaneshalch was also founded within a ten-hide estate, presumably given to Hild by Oswiu in 657, along with its *caput* central settlement.[26] Within the Merovingian and the later Carolingian Frankish realms, major monasteries such as that of St. Bertin at Saint-Omer, Nord, and Staffelsee, Bavaria, were religious settlements founded on the take-over of existing secular estate centers; monasteries were also supported by the gifting of parts of royal estates, as at Karlburg, Bavaria.[27] Given the textual evidence for dynamic

---

25 The limited endowment of the earliest Northumbrian monasteries prior to 655 has been commented upon in detail by Nick Higham, *The Kingdom of Northumbria AD 350–1100* (Stroud, 1993), p. 133. The donation of parts rather than the entirety of the "Hartness" estate to the Hartlepool monastery is discussed by Daniels and Loveluck in *Anglo-Saxon Hartlepool and the Foundations of English Christianity*, Chapters 9 and 10. Oswiu granted a series of ten-hide estates to the community of St. Cuthbert, Lindisfarne. These were located along the River Tweed and its hinterland, including grants adjacent to the Yeavering settlement and estate. Only two of the settlements within these landholdings are known to have become monasteries, namely Norham and Melrose; see Ian Smith, "Patterns of Settlement and Land Use," pp. 179–80.

26 Colgrave and Mynors, *Bede's Ecclesiastical History of the English People*, 3.24, pp. 288–95.

27 The monastery of St. Bertin was founded on the basis of the gift of the estate (*villa*) of Sithiu in 651. See Hervé Barbé, Michel Barret, Jean-Claude Routier and Eddy Roy, "Aménagement du réseau hydrographique et urbanisation aux bords de l'abbaye Saint-

transformation of estates and estate centers, it is surprising that the potential indications of such change have not been sought more readily in the archaeological record. The approach has been more conservative when dealing with Anglo-Saxon archaeological evidence than with that from the Frankish kingdoms.

Considering the biases passed down from the interpretative heritage of the development of Middle Anglo-Saxon rural settlement studies, and the complexities which might be expected on the basis of textual sources, archaeologists face the following key problems and research questions in relation to interpretation of the material remains of rural settlements, from the seventh to ninth centuries. First, how do we analyze the material signatures of lifestyles from different phases of occupation on individual settlements, to identify the potential for dynamic change of character in settlement histories? In this venture, single, textually-derived, character-based labels may be completely inappropriate. Second, have excavation biases, and the targeting of certain zones in monasteries and other settlements, rendered it particularly difficult to compare data from settlements on a like-with-like basis? Third, what would be the expected differences in the archaeological signature among a secular aristocratic estate center with one or two clerics; an aristocratic estate

---

Bertin. Donnés récentes de l'archéologie à Saint-Omer," *Revue du Nord—Archéologie de la Picardie et du Nord de la France* 53 (1998), 7–50, especially pp. 40–41. At Staffelsee, Bavaria, archaeological evidence demonstrates the existence of a seventh-century mortuary church and settlement associated with an aristocratic family, prior to becoming a major monastery during the eighth century; see Brigitte Haas-Gebhard, *Die Insel Wörth im Staffelsee* (Stuttgart, 2000), pp. 59–61 and 68–72. For Karlburg, see Peter Ettel, "Karlburg—Entwicklung eines Königlich-Bischöflichen Zentralortes am Main mit Burg und Talsiedlung vom 7. Bis 13. Jahrhundert," *Château Gaillard* 18 (1998), 75–85. For discussion of these sites in English, see Loveluck, "Rural Settlement Hierarchy in the Age of Charlemagne."

center tied to a monastery with occasional visits by clerics for administration; and a small family monastery sited in a particular zone of a larger, secular aristocratic estate center complex (a poly-focal settlement)?

Flixborough, North Lincolnshire: The Paradigm of Variation and Change

Since the late 1990s, it has become possible to address aspects of the questions and problems that can be generated from an appreciation of the social setting and the themes of the Cædmon narrative. The post-excavation analysis program of the seventh- to eleventh-century settlement sequence at Flixborough, North Lincolnshire, in particular, has enabled the development of a methodological approach to analyzing the integrated material signatures relating to settlement character, and a wider evaluation of the question of settlement transformation.[28]

The settlement remains from Flixborough were uncovered during sand quarrying in 1988 and 1989, and are located eight kilometers south of the Humber estuary, on two sand spurs overlooking the River Trent (Figure 3). With the support of English Heritage and local sponsors, a two-year excavation program was undertaken between 1989 and 1991, and a post-excavation and publication program has been directed by the author since 1995 (again funded by English Heritage). The length of the period of analysis and publication of the remains reflects their exceptional nature and scale. Approximately forty rectangular buildings were excavated, associated with huge refuse dumps incorporating 15,000 individually recorded artifacts—including 1,000 items of copper alloy, silver and gold jewelry, 6,000 iron artifacts, fragments of 65 glass drinking vessels, numerous worked bone and stone artifacts, 5,000 pottery fragments, thousands

---

28 See Loveluck, "Wealth, Waste and Conspicuous Consumption"; Loveluck, "L'habitat anglo-saxon de Flixborough"; and Loveluck, *Rural Settlement, Lifestyles and Social Change.*

Christopher Loveluck

Figure 3: View looking eastward across the River Trent and its floodplain toward Flixborough (center of picture) and the Lincoln Edge escarpment (Photograph: C. Loveluck).

of other fragmentary finds and craft-working debris, and more than 200,000 hand-collected animal, bird and fish bones, plus hundreds of thousands more retrieved from sieving (Figure 4). Even more exceptionally for a rural settlement, the buildings and refuse dumps containing the artifact and biological remains were superimposed in an unprecedented vertical stratigraphic sequence, akin to a Middle Eastern Tel.[29]

---

29 The research on Flixborough and its wider importance is published in four monographs, in press at time of writing of this chapter: Christopher Loveluck and David Atkinson, *The Early Medieval Settlement Remains from Flixborough, Lincolnshire: The Occupation Sequence, c. A.D. 600–1000*, Excavations at Flixborough, vol. 1 (Oxford, in press); Christopher Loveluck and David Evans, *Life and Economy at Early Medieval Flixborough: The Artefact Evidence*, Excavations at Flixborough, vol. 2 (Oxford, in press); Keith Dobney,

Cædmon's World

Figure 4: View of the excavations, showing building foundations and refuse dumps, looking westward from the sand spurs, down to the River Trent (Photograph: Humber Field Archaeology).

Having analyzed the stratigraphic sequence and all the datable indicators from the excavated site, it is possible to identify six major structural periods of occupation from the seventh century until the early eleventh century, and a seventh phase of peripheral settlement activity between the twelfth and fourteenth centuries, following Anglo-Norman re-planning. Our understanding and interpretation of life on the Anglo-Saxon settlement is, of necessity, viewed through the filter of archaeological site formation processes and patterns in the discard of artifacts and osteological remains. Our ability to examine the

---

Deborah Jaques, James Barrett, and Cluny Johnstone, *Farmers, Monks and Aristocrats. The Environmental Archaeology of an Anglo-Saxon Estate Center at Flixborough, North Lincolnshire,* Excavations at Flixborough, vol. 3. (Oxford, in press); Loveluck, *Rural Settlement, Lifestyles and Social Change in the later First Millennium AD.*

Figure 5: Open refuse dumps (dark deposits against the lighter sand spur in the background) in the central shallow valley, traversed by gravel paths between building plots and a zone of ovens, dating from the mid- to late ninth century (Photograph: Humber Field Archaeology).

character of the settlement through time was reliant upon understanding the refuse disposal strategies followed during the occupation sequence, survival factors relating to different forms of evidence, and the survival of intact occupation surfaces, within or in association with buildings. Understanding these waste streams behind deposit accumulation was critical in assessing the limits of inference possible from the huge structural, artifactual, and biological assemblages.[30] It had to be established whether the finds were likely to be representative of the entire Anglo-Saxon settlement or just part of it, at different times in the site's history.

With the analysis of all the material constituents of each of the deposits from the site, it became evident that the material discarded from the end of the seventh through to the early eleventh centuries was likely to be representative of the full range of activities undertaken on the settlement as a whole (periods 2 to 6 of the occupation sequence). This was mainly due to the presence of external middens around buildings and the regular use of a shallow valley in the center of the excavated area for large-scale refuse disposal, sometimes as leveling prior to new phases of buildings, and sometimes as open refuse heaps (Figure 5). The huge refuse deposits in the shallow valley and in ditch fills contained large quantities of finds and industrial residues from activities that were not undertaken in the excavated area, such as iron smithing and non-ferrous metalworking. Hence, it could be demonstrated that the huge refuse deposits probably acted as a communal refuse zone for the settlement from the end of the seventh to the early eleventh century.[31] By studying the inte-

---

30 Michael B. Schiffer, *Formation Processes of the Archaeological Record* (Albuquerque, 1987), pp. 66–68.
31 Loveluck, "Wealth, Waste and Conspicuous Consumption," pp. 91–92; Loveluck, "*Terres Noires* and Early Medieval Rural Settlement Sequences: Conceptual Problems, Descriptive Limitations and Deposit Diversity," in *Terres Noires-Dark Earth. Collection D'Archéologie Jospeh Mertens* 14, eds. Laurent Verslype and Raymond Brulet

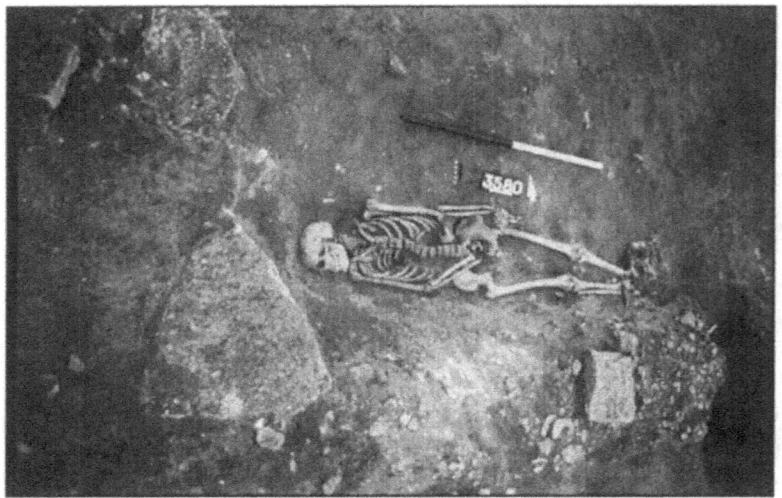

Figure 6: Body of an adult woman, between 25 and 30 years of age, with a perinatal fetus at her feet, buried inside Building 1a (Photograph: Humber Field Archaeology).

grated material culture profiles from the different phases of occupation (using structural, artifactual, and biological remains on a huge scale), it has been possible to identify social practices relating to lifestyles of consumption and production suggesting a dynamically changing settlement character between the seventh and late tenth centuries, which can in turn be compared to the archaeological reflections of other settlements. A basic summary of the changing character of the settlement and associated lifestyles through time is presented below.

Between the seventh and late eighth centuries, we see a series of three superimposed structural phases of substantial rectangular, timber buildings (normally between 14m x 7.5m in dimensions), with one building constructed on a dry-stone sill used as a burial focus for 6 individuals, both male and female (Figure 6).

(Louvain-la-Neuve, 2004), pp. 86–96; Loveluck, *Rural Settlement, Lifestyles and Social Change*, Chapter 2.

Other inhabitants were buried in a second cemetery, again housing both males and females, to the south of the habitation zone. The burial of the individuals in the building marks them out as special; the stone-footings reflect adoption of the northern French, Flemish, and Rhineland style of stone sills for significant buildings. These can also be seen in monastic contexts at Whitby, Hartlepool and Whithorn, Dumfries and Galloway, but equally, they are found at high-status secular centers, such as the Northumbrian royal stronghold of Dunbar.[32] The buildings from these end of seventh- to late eighth-century phases at Flixborough are also significantly larger than those found on most contemporary monastic sites, such as Hartlepool. So the use of the stone sills at Flixborough, in an early eighth-century context, reflects high social standing rather than a particular secular or religious elite identity; the building is best interpreted as a mortuary chapel for a leading family on the settlement—although the use as a burial focus was not maintained beyond the late eighth century.

The demographics of the buried individuals in Building 1a may also reflect the mobility in death of elements of the Anglo-Saxon aristocracy at this time, as well as the inter-relationship

---

32 For Whitby, see Peers and Radford, "The Saxon Monastery of Whitby"; Philip Rahtz, "The Building Plan of the Anglo-Saxon Monastery Whitby Abbey," in *The Archaeology of Anglo-Saxon England,* ed. David Wilson (Cambridge, 1976), pp. 459–62; and Rosemary Cramp, "A Reconsideration of the Monastic Site of Whitby," in *The Age of Migrating Ideas. Early Medieval Art in Early Medieval Britain and Ireland,* eds. R. Michael Spearman and J. Higgitt (Edinburgh, 1993), pp. 64–73. For Hartlepool, see Robin Daniels, "The Anglo-Saxon Monastery at Church Close, Hartlepool, Cleveland," *Archaeological Journal* 145 (1988), 158–210, and Daniels and Loveluck, *Anglo-Saxon Hartlepool and the Foundations of English Christianity,* Chapter 3. For Whithorn, see Peter Hill, *Whithorn and St. Ninian. The Excavation of a Monastic Town 1984–91* (Stroud, 1997). For Dunbar, see David Perry, *Castle Park, Dunbar,* pp. 64–76.

of secular and religious centers, as we see in the Cædmon story. The building (Building 1a) with graves cut through its floors and one external burial contained an adult woman, with a newborn baby at her feet, together with four adolescents. No adult men were present. It is possible that other elements of this potential elite group were buried at a nearby monastery, such as West Halton. Differentiation by social rank, or gender and age, is also seen at other settlements deemed as secular centers of the seventh to ninth centuries in England and northern France. Sue Anderson has observed that the populations of the two cemeteries at Staunch Meadow, Brandon, taken together represent a normal population of men, women, and children, although the children are buried in a separate cemetery around a possible shrine.[33] At Serris, Seine-et-Marne, in northern France, there are two cemeteries, one around the elite settlement focus of the estate center and another, much larger cemetery for an attendant agricultural community, focused on a cemetery chapel with a dry-stone sill.[34] It would increasingly appear that as

33 See Carr, Tester and Murphy, "The Middle Saxon Settlement at Staunch Meadow, Brandon," p. 374. For Sue Anderson's observations on the demographics of the Brandon cemeteries, and the fact that the Brandon research team currently believes that the site represents a secular "proto-urban" settlement, see Sue Anderson, "The Human Population," in Daniels and Loveluck, eds., *Anglo-Saxon Hartlepool and the Foundations of English Christianity*, Chapter 5.

34 See Bruno Foucray and François Gentili, "Le village du Haut Moyen Age de Serris (Seine-et-Marne), lieudit 'Les Ruelles' (VIIe-Xe siècle)," in *L'Habitat Rural du Haut Moyen Age (France, Pays-Bas, Danemark et Grande-Bretagne)*, ed. Claude Lorren and Patrick Périn (Condé-sur-Noireau, 1995), Mémoires publiés par l'Association française d'archéologie mérovingienne, 6: 139–43; Bruno Foucray and François Gentili, "Serris—Chapelle cimétériale des Ruelles," in *Les premiers monuments chrétiens de la France*, vol. 3, ed. Noel Duval (Paris, 1998).

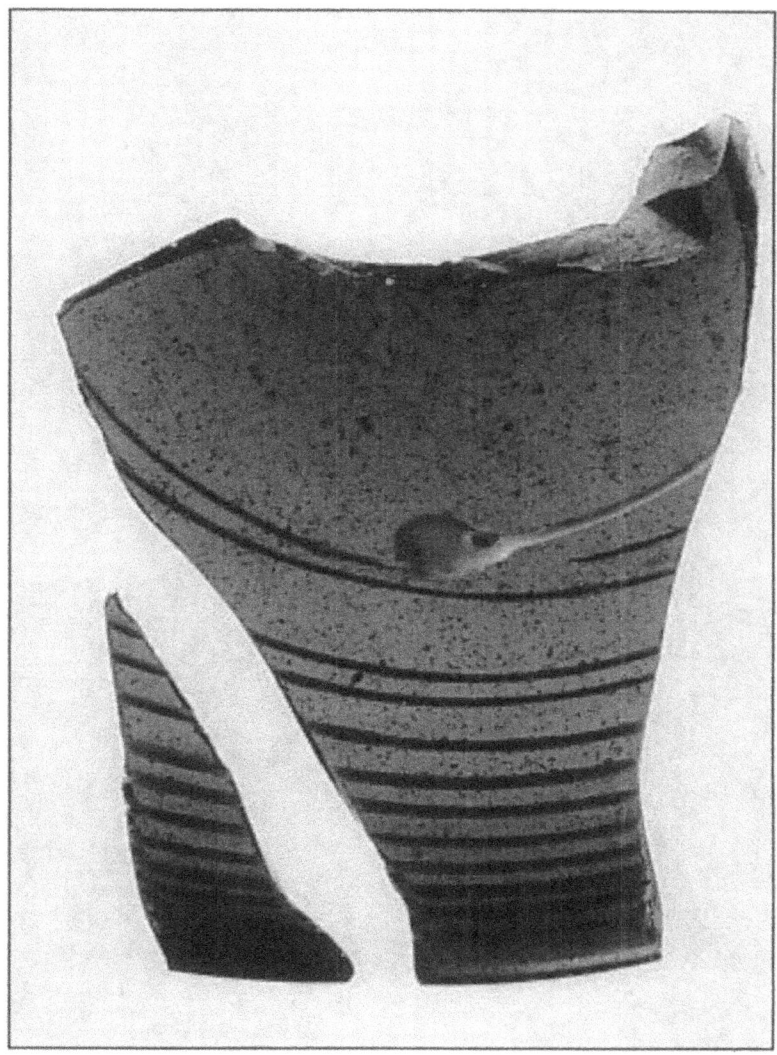

Figure 7: Fragment of a cobalt-blue glass drinking vessel (Photograph: Bill Marsden).

Cædmon's World

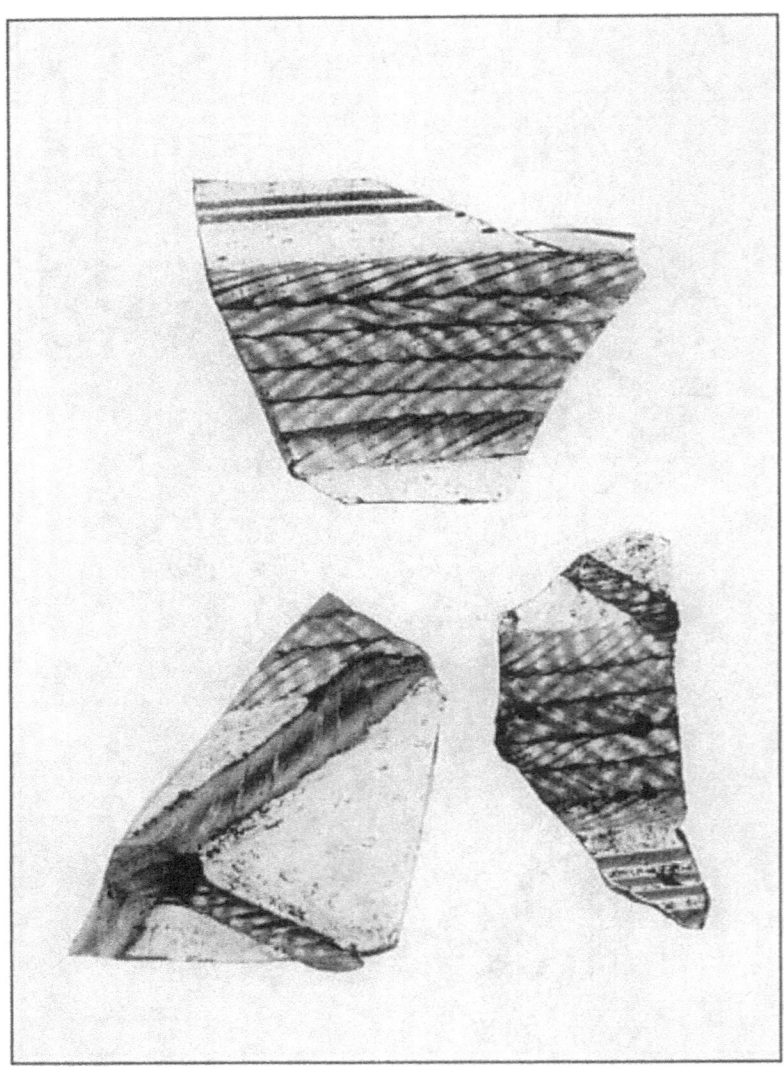

Figure 8: Fragments of a reticella-decorated glass drinking vessel (Photograph: Bill Marsden).

are much rarer farther north. Indeed, Hild's change of focus from her initial monastery at Hartlepool to her newer foundation at Whitby may well reflect a desire for greater proximity to this key communication zone with the continent and the larger resource base provided by Whitby's ten-hide estate.

In addition to the presence of feasting kits provided by long-distance exchange, the consumption pattern of the animal resources reflects conspicuous consumption and the secular elite pastimes of hunting and falconry. From the late seventh century, the Flixborough settlement was in receipt of the largest cattle (in terms of stature) known in Anglo-Saxon England, with the closest parallels known to be in Flanders. Almost all cattle consumed were adults or sub-adults, which suggests their submission as renders arriving on the hoof; approximately forty percent of all animals consumed were these cattle—a huge proportion.[37] This predominance of cattle and the age range at Flixborough are mirrored on the settlements of Portchester Castle and Wicken Bonhunt, identified as estate centers, and also at the *wic* trading and artisan settlements.[38] At Flixborough,

37 See Dobney, Jaques, Barrett, and Johnstone, *Farmers, Monks and Aristocrats*.

38 See Annie Grant, "The Animal Bones," in Barry Cunliffe, *Excavations at Portchester Castle, Volume II: Saxon,* Report of the Research Committee of the Society of Antiquaries No 33 (London, 1976), pp. 262–87; Jennifer Bourdillon, "The Animal Provisioning of Saxon Southampton," in *Environment and Economy in Anglo-Saxon England,* ed. James Rackham, CBA Research Report 89 (York, 1994), pp. 120–25; Pam Crabtree, "Animal Exploitation in East Anglian Villages," in *Environment and Economy in Anglo-Saxon England,* ed. Rackham, pp. 40–54; Crabtree, "Production and Consumption in an Early Complex Society: Animal Use in Middle Saxon East Anglia," *World Archaeology* 28.1 (1996), 58–75; Terry O'Connor, *Bones from 46–54 Fishergate,* The Archaeology of York, Volume 15: The Animal Bones, Fascicule 4 (London, 1991); O'Connor, "8th-11th Century Economy and Environment in York," in *Environment and Economy in Anglo-Saxon England,* ed. Rackham,

however, the consumption of wild species is much greater than at *wic* settlements and monastic sites, based on published data. This proportionately large assemblage of wild fauna, especially the large number of cranes and other wildfowl, reflects hunting, netting, and probably falconry. Again, the closest parallels in terms of the wildfowl exploitation pattern at Flixborough are from Wicken Bonhunt and Portchester Castle.[39] Cranes were a much-documented elite prey species for falconry and also a feast species in eighth-century sources and later.[40] Cranes are also presented as a favored species in the Cotton Tiberius Calendar's portrayal of falconry, from the eleventh century. Other exceptional species consumed were dolphins, again documented as an Anglo-Saxon feast food.[41] All the reflections of feasting, hunting, and conspicuous consumption very much mirror the picture of life at a secular estate center, as suggested by the first stage of Cædmon's life; we can probably envisage the Flixborough settlement under the control of an aristocratic family or reeve during the seventh and eighth centuries.

From the end of the eighth century or the early decades of the ninth century, however, we see a huge change in the lifestyles reflected at Flixborough. The settlement is cleared and rebuilt with a range of slightly smaller buildings, and the abandonment and demolition of the earlier mortuary chapel. Whereas the artisan activity of the seventh and eighth centuries had comprised fine metalworking, ironworking and textile-working for the settlement's needs, the range, scale, and degree of specializa-

pp. 136–47.
39   See Keith Dobney and Deborah Jaques, "Avian Signatures for Identity and Status in Anglo-Saxon England," *Acta zoologica cracoviensia* 45 (2002), special issue, 7–21, especially p. 10.
40   See E. Emerton, *The Letters of Saint Boniface* (New York, 1940), p. 179. King Æthelberht of Kent asked St. Boniface if he could send him falcons that would take cranes.
41   See Mark Gardiner, "The Exploitation of Sea Mammals in Medieval England: Bones and their Social Context," *Archaeological Journal* 154 (1997), 173–95.

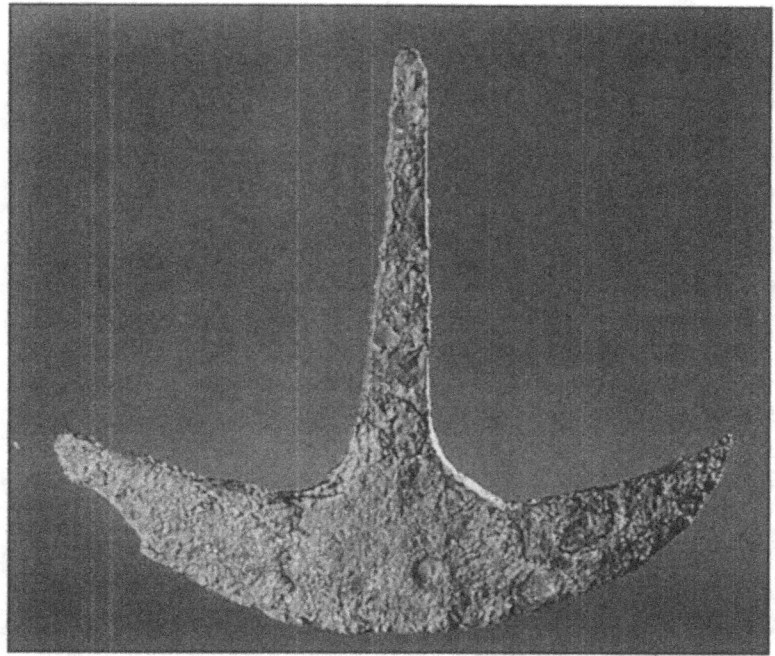

Figure 9: *Lunette* Knife, or *Lunellum*, for leather-working, found in a mid- to late ninth-century refuse dump (Photograph: Bill Marsden).

tion in the artisanal activity of the ninth century expanded to create products for export—including the production of fine quality textiles, leather goods, and metalwork (Figures 9 and 10). At the same time, small numbers of styli made their appearance, mostly iron, but several in copper alloy and one in silver (Figure 11). Window glass and an inscribed lead plaque with seven names, both male and female, and a paleographic script most closely associated with charters of Offa of Mercia,[42] also

---

42   Michelle Brown and Elisabeth Okasha, "Inscribed Objects," in Loveluck and Evans, ed., *Life and Economy at Early Medieval Flixborough, c. AD 600–1000: The Artefact Evidence,* Chapter 3.

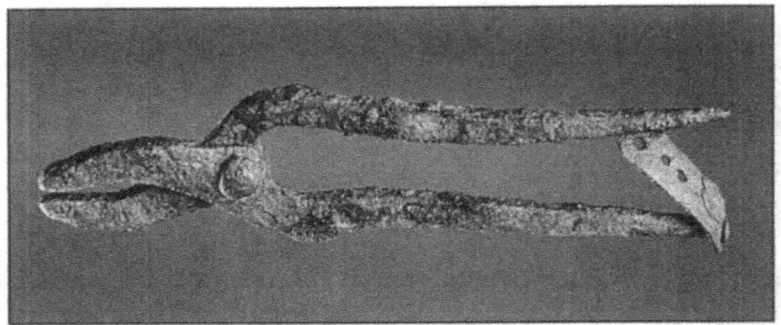

Figure 10: Small metal-working tongs/hand vise, found in a mid-ninth-century refuse dump (Photograph: Bill Marsden).

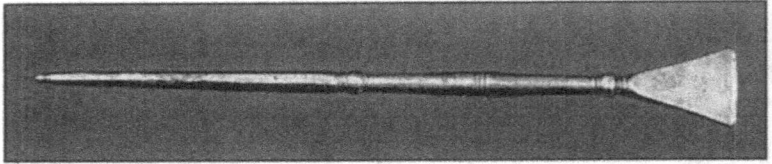

Figure 11: Silver stylus found in a mid-ninth-century refuse dump (Photograph: Bill Marsden).

occurred from the end of the eighth to the mid-ninth century. The quantity of imported commodities, in the form of silver coinage and pottery, diminished in this period, but West Saxon and Mercian pennies and Ipswich Ware pottery still attest to the operation of east coast communications into the 860s and 870s. However, there is no evidence for the new arrival of glass drinking vessels.

Furthermore, there was a complete transformation of the consumption practices relating to the biological profile of the settlement. Cattle dropped from approximately forty percent of the domesticated species consumed to below ten percent. Infant cattle also began to be slaughtered. Sheep rose to almost fifty percent of animals consumed, and all were old when killed, probably reflecting sheep husbandry to support the specialized and increased textile production on the settlement at this period. During the ninth century, the quantity of wild species consumed declined greatly, despite the fact that the species were available in the local environment.[43] This suggests that hunting was no longer a significant pastime enjoyed or practiced by the settlement's inhabitants. Overall, if we compare the biological signature from ninth-century Flixborough with other settlements from the Middle Anglo-Saxon period, its similarities with settlements like Hartlepool, Whithorn, Jarrow, and Monkwearmouth are now apparent. Where it is possible to tell, exploitation of wild species was also very limited at those centers, as was overt evidence of feasting. Some evidence of consumption of small quantities of red deer, and the occasional seabird and seal have been encountered at the monasteries of Hartlepool, Whithorn, and the Dal Riadan monastery of Iona, but this level of consumption is minute compared to the consumption of wild resources at eighth-century Flixborough, Wicken Bonhunt, and Portchester Castle. Such occasional consumption at Iona and Hartlepool can be accounted for by the gifting of food resources by secular aristocrats to the monasteries, which seem to have had limited provisioning of domestic animals from beyond their immediate monastic lands.[44]

---

43 See Dobney, Jaques, Barrett, and Johnstone, *Farmers, Monks and Aristocrats*. Percentages are based on thousands of bones, percentages relate to what are called "Minimum Number of Individuals" calculations.

44 For Hartlepool see chapters by James Rackham and Chris Loveluck in Daniels and Loveluck, ed., *Anglo-Saxon Hartlepool and the Foundations of English Christianity*, Chapters 6 and 10. For Whithorn, see Finbar McCormick and E. Murphy, "The Animal Bones," in Peter Hill, *Whithorn and St Ninian. The Excavation of a Monastic Town 1984–91*, pp. 605–13. For Iona, see Finbar McCormick, "The Animal Bones from Ditch 1," in John Barber, "Excavations on Iona, 1979," *Proceedings of the Society of Antiquaries*

Cædmon's World

The managed slaughter of young animals also seems to be part of monastic husbandry regimes for vellum production, as is possibly indicated on Lindisfarne.[45] The small number of younger calves killed at Flixborough in the ninth century is very unlikely to reflect support of a scriptorium on the site. Instead, such a kill pattern is more likely to show the normal killing of a small number of young animals within a cattle husbandry regime. In the absence of any biological indications for a scriptorium at Flixborough, despite thousands of domesticated animal bones, it is also unlikely that the "lunette-knife," or *lunellum* (Figure 9), found in a mid to late ninth-century refuse deposit was used exclusively for vellum preparation, rather than the preparation of ordinary leather.[46]

However, despite similarities between ninth-century Flixborough and documented monastic sites, there are still differences from major monasteries like Whitby, Jarrow, Monkwearmouth, Lindisfarne, and Hartlepool. There is primarily the absence of stone sculpted and inscribed monuments. Perhaps, then, we should view the Flixborough settlement as a small monastery or monastic estate center in its ninth-century incarnation. There

---

of Scotland 111 (1981), 313–18. For exploitation of wild birds at Jarrow and other monasteries, see Dobney and Jaques, "Avian Signatures for Identity and Status in Anglo-Saxon England."

45 Deirdre O'Sullivan, "Space, Silence and Shortage on Lindisfarne: The Archaeology of Asceticism," in Hamerow and MacGregor, ed., *Image and Power in the Archaeology of Early Medieval Britain*, pp. 33–53, especially p. 42.

46 The absence of biological evidence from Flixborough for the support of a scriptorium and the occurrence of the lunette-knife indicate that such knives were not used exclusively in vellum preparation, as has recently been suggested in Martin Carver and Cecily Spall's, "Excavating a *Parchmenerie*: Archaeological Correlates of Making Parchment at the Pictish Monastery at Portmahomack, Easter Ross," *Proceedings of the Society of Antiquaries of Scotland* 134 (2004), 183–200, especially pp. 192–95.

is no evidence of a consuming elite on the settlement at this period, and in this respect it agrees with the communal lifestyle described by Bede for Cædmon's home monastery at Streanaeshalch/Whitby. It is difficult to assess, however, the extent of communal living in the smaller monasteries and the larger double-houses like Whitby. The nature of the excavations by Peers and Radford do not enable us to identify communal buildings from this site's pre-stone, seventh-century phases. Only Jarrow has yielded a likely communal refectory. Communal dormitory buildings are currently unknown in England, although a single example from the seventh century has recently been discovered at Hamage, Nord, in northern France[47]—the region that provided Hild, who had a sister at the monastery of Chelles, with her Christian inspiration. Perhaps future excavation may redress this current absence in England.

By the end of the ninth century, all had changed again at Flixborough. Indeed, it is probably from this time that the name "Conesby"—that is, *Konungsbyr*, "King's farmstead" in Old Danish/Norse—now associated with a deserted medieval settlement immediately adjacent to the excavations, came to be associated with the Anglo-Saxon settlement. The excavated site has become known by the name Flixborough, only by association with the existing village of Flixborough some three hundred meters away. The settlement of the ninth century was totally cleared and replaced in the early tenth century with the largest residential buildings in the occupation sequence (not respecting any earlier element of the settlement plan), as a form of status display. The largest of these buildings measured 20 meters by 7.5 meters. All the wild feast species reflecting hunting, falconry, and feasting were also present, reflecting the return of the settlement's character to a residence exploited by a king

---

47 See Etienne Louis, "Archéologie des bâtiments monastiques, VIIème—IXème siècles: Le cas de Hamage (France, Département du Nord)," in *Religion and Belief in Medieval Europe*, ed. De Boe and Verhaeghe, pp. 55–63.

or secular aristocrat, for whom the feast and the hunt were key elements associated with rural high-status identity in the tenth century. At the same time, the indications of specialist craft and industrial activities fell to their minimum, with only iron-working and textile manufacture practiced for the needs of the settlement alone (and no evidence of a literate element here either). Furthermore, consumption of exotic goods derived via long-distance exchange with the Continent, for purposes of social display, had also disappeared. The pattern of the conspicuous consumption of local resources at Conesby reflects the definition of "the countryside" and rural media of display, as opposed to the new dynamic towns of Anglo-Scandinavian England, which exerted a centrifugal pull on specialist artisans and international trade from the tenth century—provisioning goods and services to their rural hinterlands in a manner that would become characteristic of the High Middle Ages.

Conclusions and Prospects

The touchstones and themes of the Cædmon narrative highlight several fundamentally important avenues of research where interdisciplinary perspectives can contribute in the interpretation of settlement archaeology and lifestyles in both England and Continental western Europe, between the seventh and late ninth centuries. Three such avenues have been pursued within this contribution. Firstly, the Cædmon story provides a window into the complexities of the inter-relationship between the secular and ecclesiastical elements of society, especially interaction between those members of the aristocratic elite playing secular and religious roles.

In the archaeological record, this interaction is expressed in both burial evidence and, to a certain extent, in evidence for provisioning, artisan activity, and exchange. Perhaps the most notable manifestation of interaction is the evidence for procurement of burial spaces, presumably for secular aristocratic families, at monastic cemeteries, such as that at Church Walk,

Hartlepool. Others include the likelihood of limited provisioning of certain monastic centers with a poor resource base, such as Iona; and also the potential provision of clerics/priests for residence at aristocratic estate centers.

The second principal avenue pursued concerns the attempt to identify particular lifestyles and social practices that can be associated with secular and ecclesiastical centers respectively. The two social settings for the Cædmon story, namely the secular center with its reeve, a hall, ancillary buildings, and animals, and Hild's monastery of Whitby, are the two principal types of settlement which have been the focus of archaeological study. Through the integrated analysis of the structural, artifactual, and biological remains from a range of settlements, it has been possible to identify a range of lifestyles—especially in terms of provisioning and consumption practices—that appear to be typical of the spectrum of activities undertaken by particular groups of people at secular estate centers and monasteries, in turn. This is especially the case with consumption practices associated with the secular aristocracy, with the conspicuous consumption of domestic (principally cattle) and wild animal resources (especially wildfowl), and exotic, imported feasting-kits used for ostentatious eating and drinking—features of secular, or what we might call lordly, identity. Textual and iconographic sources show their especial value in corroborating the importance of practices such as falconry, and the targeting of particular feast species, such as cranes and dolphins. Major monastic centers provide evidence of a series of lifestyles and physical remains that show a distinct contrast with secular centers—the concentration of specialist artisan activities, the presence of sculpture and inscribed stone monuments, their very limited evidence for the exploitation of wild resources, and having their major display buildings in stone.

The most important research theme to have been pursued, however, is the phenomenon of the transformation of social identities, which could and did occur between the seventh and ninth centuries. The tale of Cædmon demonstrates such a transformation at the individual level, just as other passages in Bede's *Ecclesiastical History* and Continental written sources of the seventh and eighth century demonstrate the transformation of secular estates and their principal settlements into monasteries or monastic estate centers. Surprisingly, despite the textual indications of settlement and estate transformation, archaeologists (and historians) have rarely sought indications of such change in the material remains of Middle Anglo-Saxon rural settlements. The exceptional occupation sequence from the rural settlement at Flixborough provides, for the first time, a material history of changing social practices through time, which probably represent a transformation from secular estate center to small monastery, and back to a secular estate center, within the period from the seventh to tenth centuries. Furthermore, the lifestyles deemed characteristic of secular and monastic identity within the occupation sequence correlate with the data from other settlements interpreted as secular centers or monasteries.

This phenomenon of transformation of social and settlement identity is key to understanding the dynamism and complexity of the seventh to ninth centuries, not just for Middle Anglo-Saxon England but also for Carolingian Europe, where the dynamic settlement transformation at Staffelsee may be very similar to that at Flixborough.[48] Indeed, such dynamic change of settlement character is also a feature of the tenth and eleventh centuries, in England and on the Continent, with secular estate centers becoming priories of major monasteries: for example, the excavated aristocratic settlement of Distré (Maine-et-Loire) becoming a priory of the abbey of Saint-Florent de Saumur in 1040.[49] The Cædmon story opens our eyes to the regularity of

48 See Brigitte Haas-Gebhard, *Die Insel Wörth im Staffelsee*, pp. 57–81.
49 See Delphine Pelaprat, "Un exemple de vie monastique en Anjou aux XIe et XIIe siècles: Le réseau des prieurés angevins de Saint-Florent de Saumur," *Fontevraud Histoire-Archéologie*, No. 1 (1992), 53–71; and A. Valais, *Distré "Les Murailles" 49 123 008 AH (Maine-et-Loire)*, Série Fouilles, Tome 1 (Nantes, 1997).

such transformation. A greater challenge for archaeologists is a consequence of the close interaction between secular and ecclesiastical elites, also evident in the Cædmon narrative. It is possible that only parts of some secular estate centers were given over as monasteries, with the secular elite still resident in an enceinte and undertaking secular pastimes within the context of a settlement, which may have been perceived from outside as purely ecclesiastical in nature, and have operated as such. The known appointment of secular aristocratic abbots in the early Carolingian period, who continued to indulge in secular pastimes, is another factor complicating "either-or" settlement and social definitions. Ultimately, it is perhaps from an appreciation of the complexities of life evident in the textual sources by archaeologists, and vice versa on the part of historians, that the true potential of interdisciplinary perspectives will be realized for our understanding of northwest European societies in the Early Middle Ages.[50]

---

50 Sincere thanks are extended to English Heritage for funding the Flixborough research, and to all colleagues who have worked on the project. I am also very grateful to the British Academy for providing the financial backing and institutional support to enable the comparative research on Continental European sites partly presented in this chapter; and thanks are also due to David Taylor, Bill Marsden and Humber Field Archaeology for production of the Figures. Finally, I would like to express my gratitude to Allen Frantzen and John Hines for providing such a stimulating forum for interdisciplinary perspectives at Kalamazoo in 2005, which has provided the foundation for this volume.

Changes and Exchanges in Bede's and Cædmon's World

JOHN HINES

THE NINE LINES OF VERSE first appended to texts of Bede's *Ecclesiastical History of the English People* in the mid-eighth century, and reproduced in various forms in many other Anglo-Saxon manuscripts, have been known as Cædmon's hymn since at least the nineteenth century.[1] Bede was careful and consistent in the terminology he used when referring to poetry, and indeed had his own clear concept of the *hymnus*: a term he used for Latin verse works in contemporary circulation in England, including some composed by himself. This discrepancy between modern custom and Bede's taxonomy is not suggested to be a crucial error in our perception of Cædmon's hymn—far from it. However, it does make the question of how Bede conceived of and regarded the composition of Cædmon's hymn both an intriguing and valid point of departure. Consideration of the whole Cædmon story in Book 4, chapter 24 of the *Ecclesiastical History* reveals the miracle that produced these verses to be the focal point—*only* the focal point, we might say—

---

1   The earliest use of the term "hymn" for these verses of which I am aware is that of John J. Conybeare, *Illustrations of Anglo-Saxon Poetry* (London, 1826), pp. 3–8: "Hymn of Cædmon." This term was not used by Rev. John Lingard, *The Antiquities of the Anglo-Saxon Church*, 2 vols. (Newcastle, 1806), to whom Conybeare refers. Lingard printed one version of the text in an appendix as "a short specimen of Anglo-Saxon poetry" (2:373–75). Nor have I found any occurrence of the term in the writings of the seventeenth-century scholars Junius, Hickes, and Wanley on Cædmon.

in a significantly more extensive story concerned with discourse, form, style, and linguistic function. It is, in effect, an exemplary narrative unified by a concern with what modern linguistics calls discourse analysis.[2] The broad and uncomplicated concerns of that field of study with the relationship between speech-acts and their circumstances, and their practical effects in social situations, are applied in this essay to both the poem and its literary, historical, and material contexts. Close reading with these matters in mind reveals a consistent thematic pattern in Bede's handling of the story that manifests the pattern of historically representative changes and exchanges referred to in my title.

Terminology and the Topic of Discourse

The strict control of vocabulary exercised by Bede involves both the nouns used to refer to verses and song and the verbs of composition and performance. This can be attributed to Bede's care to inculcate what would have been considered the right attitude towards the matter of the story in the reader. Book 4, chapter 24 opens by stating that the brother in question, Cædmon, "used to compose godly and religious songs" ("carmina religioni et pietati apta facere solebat"); *carmen* remains without exception the noun used for Cædmon's compositions, both the extant text we know of as Cædmon's hymn and the other works made up of verses ("versus") referred to in this chapter.[3] An

---

[2] For an introduction to discourse analysis, see J. L. Austin, *How to Do Things with Words*, 2nd ed. (Cambridge, Mass., 1975).

[3] All quotations are taken from the edited text of Bertram Colgrave and R. A. B. Mynors, ed., *Bede's Ecclesiastical History of the English People* (Oxford, 1969). In most cases, Colgrave and Mynors's translation is also quoted; however, Colgrave and Mynors varied the diction to produce a fluent and attractive style in their modern English version rather than adhering strictly to Bede's consistencies of terminology. In one case, it is consequently necessary for me to offer my own translation: this is duly noted in the relevant place.

alternative noun Bede might have used is *poema*, but this consistently represents a contrastive category. Other Englishmen tried to compose "religious poems" ("religiosa poemata"), but none could match Cædmon. Cædmon himself "could never compose any foolish or trivial poem" ("nil umquam friuoli et superuacui poematis facere potuit"). The term *hymnus* is also different. In the *Ecclesiastical History*, Bede uses it several times in his own verses on virginity, which he put into Book 4, chapter 20 of the work, as well as in another collection ("liber hymnorum") he had composed.[4]

Besides using the verb *facere* for the act of composition, the verbs most relevant to the presentation of what Cædmon did on the night in question and became accustomed to do, are *cantare* and *canere*, both essentially meaning "to sing." Bede's preference for the former in the infinitive and imperative forms, especially in the section in which the angelic figure ("quidam") instructs Cædmon to sing, alongside "canebat" from the latter, which occurs twice, in the imperfect tense, is no more than an idiosyncratic stylistic characteristic. This is proven when we find "quae dormiens ille canebat" ("which he sang as he slept") and "cuncta quae dormiens cantaverat" ("all that he had sung while asleep") close together immediately following this section.[5] The major point that emerges from reflection upon those two near-identical verbal units is that they embody a simple but significant transgression of normality, one that emphasizes the exceptional nature of

---

4   Bede's *liber hymnorum* is listed in the author's catalog of his own writings in Bede, *Ecclesiastical History*, 5.24., pp. 570–71; see also Putnam Fennell Jones, *A Concordance to the Historia Ecclesiastica* of Bede (Cambridge Mass, 1929), s.v. HYMNUS; Michael Lapidge, "Bede the Poet," The Jarrow Lecture (Jarrow, 1993), repr. in Michael Lapidge, *Anglo-Latin Literature 600–899* (London, 1996), pp. 313–38; see esp. pp. 320–32.

5   The characteristic nature of this stylistic idiosyncrasy is confirmed by the instances recorded in Jones, *Concordance*, svv. CANEO and CANTO.

John Hines

Cædmon's story. His was not a wide-awake experience in which he suddenly discovered that he could sing after all—it occurred in his sleep, during a dream. Such close attention to the verbs of singing at the beginning of the chapter draws our notice further to an absolutely crucial distinction Bede wished to make:

> For this man did not learn *the art of singing* from men or as instructed by man; but divinely aided he received *the gift of singing*. (my translation and emphases)

> Namque ipse non ab hominibus neque per hominem institutus canendi artem didicit, sed diuinitus adiutus gratis canendi donum accepit. (4.24, pp. 414-15)

Despite his rigorous consistency in separating the nouns *carmen* and *poema* within this chapter, and *hymnus* in the wider work, this narrowly focused analysis unsurprisingly reveals that Bede was a great deal more interested in the process of Cædmon's transformation and its consequences than he was in the generic classification of his work. At the very start of the chapter, our attention is drawn to a nexus of fundamental cultural exchanges and transformations. The normal process of human tradition and training has failed in Cædmon's case; he never learned any songs. God, as any lord of early medieval society, was expected to be a gift-giver to Cædmon. But this gift is gratis, and the counter-gift required is Cædmon's transformation into another order where he could promote Christianity in his own special way. Secular or ecclesiastic landlords of Anglo-Saxon England may indeed have supported favored clients in a comparable way, but none were likely to have been dispensing gifts of any significance to one of his or her cowherds. The lordly emancipation of slaves—not an especially generous or charitable action, as they then became the tied serfs of what tended to be a more efficient mode of production—was a rarity at this date.[6]

---

6 Bede, *Ecclesiastical History*, 4.13; David A. E. Pelteret, *Slavery in*

Changes and Exchanges in Bede's and Cædmon's World

That Bede considered it appropriate to paraphrase what he believed to be Cædmon's first song into Latin, but neither to translate it nor to quote it in the vernacular, has received considerable attention. What merits emphasis, in this respect, is how this can be seen as one of a series of positive and active transformations of texts within the story. It is all too tempting to become preoccupied with what Bede did *not* do—and maybe felt he *could* not do. Instances of textual transmission and change lie at the heart of this story. Cædmon had performed for him orally (this being the key semantic feature of the noun *sermo*, "speech," used here) a passage of sacred history or doctrine, which would have been translated into English as well as read from the page, so that he could *transferre* this, "carry it over," into the mode of song. His subsequent career involved listening to the literate in this way, and everything he heard, "he turned it into the most melodious song" ("in carmen dulcissimum conuertebat"). This process was not just a matter of formal and linguistic change, but also a simultaneous spiritual and intellectual transformation: "and it sounded so sweet as he recited it that his teachers became in turn his audience" ("Suauiusque resonando doctores suos uicissim auditores sui faciebat"). He infused many, we are told, with contempt for the world and a yearning for the heavenly life; he would try to draw men from the love of sin to a desire and zeal for good work. It is not over-reading to imagine, when we are told of his hostility to those "qui aliter *facere* uolebant" ("who wished to act otherwise"; my emphasis), that the use of the verb *facere* suggests corruption in the musical composition of an exemplary, harmonious Christian life.

The final section of the chapter, portraying Cædmon's final days and his last night, absolutely confirms that the speech-act, its circumstances, and its practical effects supply Bede with both the general motif and the consistent theme of Cædmon's life

---

Early Medieval England (Woodbridge, 1995), pp. 60 and 137–40; Chris Wickham, *Framing the Early Middle Ages: Europe and the Mediterranean, 400–800* (Oxford, 2005), pp. 259–65 and 533–47.

from the miracle to his death. Cædmon's still-healthy faculties are represented by the fact that he is able to speak and walk ("loqui . . . et ingredi"). Significantly then, the place he requests as a place of rest is denoted "locum quiescendi": "a place where he could rest," in Colgrave and Mynors' translation. More literally, it is "a place to grow quiet." Using different verbs of expression from the rest of this passage, those within the hospital "were talking and joking" ("loquerentur ac iocarentur"). Thereafter, much of the scene is portrayed through direct speech, using the verbs *rogare*, "to ask," *respondere*, "to answer," and, with the mentally and spiritually intense Cædmon as subject, *interrogare*, "to ask earnestly, interrogate." The conceit is summarized strikingly to conclude the chapter:

> Thus it came about that, as he had served the Lord with a simple and pure mind and with quiet devotion, so he departed into His presence and left the world by a quiet death; and his tongue which had uttered so many good words in praise of the Creator also uttered its last words in His praise, as he signed himself with the sign of the Cross and committed his spirit into God's hands.[7]

Cædmon's total transformation from cowherd to monk is epitomized here. His death scene unfolds as a perfect liturgical ritual. At his own insistence, he takes the Eucharist and expresses his own personal praise, *laus*, of God just when the brothers were to sing the regular office of Lauds.[8]

---

7 Sicque factum est ut, quomodo simplici ac pura mente tranquillaque deuotione Domino seruiente, ita etiam tranquilla morte mundum relinquens ad eius uisionem ueniret, illaque lingua, quae tot salutoria uerba in laudem Conditoris conposuerat, ultima quoque uerba in laudem ipsius, signendo sese et spiritum suum in manus eius commendando, clauderet. Colgrave and Mynors, *Bede's Ecclesiastical History*, 4.24, pp. 420–21.

8 Bonnie Effros, *Caring for Body and Soul: Burial and the Afterlife in the*

Changes and Exchanges in Bede's and Cædmon's World

Early medieval monastic hymnody consisted of sung or chanted metrical elements incorporated within the Divine Office in precisely this way.[9] Thus, even though Bede conspicuously does not use the term Cædmon's hymn, the shaping of the story fully demonstrates his belief that the hymn was the consummate type of creative poetic composition: a form of literary art that was liturgically valid, and to be placed alongside the Psalms and Canticles. Parallels and analogues for Cædmon's hymn have been found in many different sources, of several different textual types, including those categories of Biblical verse.[10] No wider discussion of those suggestions is needed here; however, comparison of the hymn with the Psalms on one specific point reveals a key matter. Although it is not cited by Daniel O'Donnell as a suggested parallel, Psalm 8 has much in common with Cædmon's hymn: the call to praise God; acknowledgement of God's heavenliness; adoration of God as Creator of the universe; thankful recognition of Man's special place on Earth, protected by God and given dominion over the world:

PSALM 8
O LORD our Lord, how excellent is thy name in all the earth!
who hast set thy glory above the heavens.
Out of the mouth of babes and sucklings hast thou ordained

Merovingian World (University Park, Penn., 2002), pp. 169–77; cf. Victoria Thompson, *Dying and Death in Later Anglo-Saxon England*, Anglo-Saxon Studies 4 (Woodbridge, 2004), pp. 57–91.

9 A. S. Walpole and A. J. Mason, *Early Latin Hymns* (Cambridge, 1922); Helmut Gneuss, *Hymnar und Hymnen im englischen Mittelalter: Studien zur Überlieferung, Glossierung und Übersetzung lateinischer Hymnen in England* (Tübingen, 1968). The worship of God as Creator is quite a familiar topic of early medieval hymnody.

10 For a recent survey, see Daniel O'Donnell, *Cædmon's Hymn: A Multimedia Study, Archive and Edition* (Woodbridge, Suffolk, 2005), pp. 29–59, and his essay in this volume, pp. 15–50.

> strength because of thine enemies, that thou mightest still the enemy and the avenger.
> When I consider thy heavens, the work of thy fingers, the moon and the stars, which thou hast ordained;
> What is man, that thou art mindful of him? and the son of man, that thou visitest him?
> For thou has made him a little lower than the angels, and hast crowned him with glory and honour.
> Thou madest him to have dominion over the works of thy hands; thou has put all things under his feet:
> All sheep and oxen, yea, and the beasts of the field;
> The fowl of the air, and the fish of the sea, and whatsoever passeth through the paths of the seas.
> O LORD our Lord, how excellent is thy name in all the earth!

A highly typical feature of the Psalms is that they culminate in the evocation and assertion of a spiritually positive conclusion. Many of them may start by expressing a state of doubt, fear or exhortation, but at the end, the message is not of the exhortatory, prospective kind represented by the subjunctive of the Lord's Prayer—"Hallowed *be* Thy name." The mood of the verb is rather the indicative, announcing and celebrating a situation that is already as it should be: "O LORD our Lord, how excellent *is* thy name in all the earth."[11] That is not how Cædmon's hymn ends. Bede presents Cædmon's life and work as a poet as

---

11 Vulgate: "Domine Dominus noster, quem admirabile est nomen tuum in universa terra!" (I quote the Latin that would have been the most familiar form in seventh- and eighth-century England. The translation reproduced in the text here is that of the Authorized Version.) There is a copious scholarly and critical literature on the Psalms, but much of this, unsurprisingly, is focused upon the religious thought of the texts and their history in Jewish and Christian ritual, not on their poetic structure. See, however, E. Jenni, "Zu den doxologischen Schlußformeln des Psalters," *Theologische Zeitschrift*, 40 (1984), 114–20.

something more genuinely dramatic—participating in changes and exchanges in the course of time—and so growing towards the positive spiritual closure consummated at his earthly death and entry into glory.

The story of Cædmon is thus considerably more than the showcase for another of the miracles of Book 4 of the *Ecclesiastical History*. The thematic emphasis of Bede's account does not lie so much on the extraordinary and positive power of the divine made manifest in Cædmon's reception of the gift of song as it does on teaching: how Cædmon played a unique historical part in the broad flow of mission—the Christian work of expanding and consolidating Christendom, the people and kingdom of God on Earth. That Bede saw both the art of literature and the vernacular medium as fully adaptable to this end is a matter of interest and importance in itself.[12] The *Ecclesiastical History* as a whole is an exemplary missionary hand-book. As we see in its accounts of Egbert, Wihtberht, Willibrord, and others, it tells of the conversion of the English, and the establishment of the Church among them, and looks forward to the ultimate conversion of their Germanic kindred on the Continent and even in Scandinavia (5.9–11, pp. 474–87).

---

12 Martin Irvine, *The Making of Textual Culture: "Grammatica" and Literary Theory 350–1100*, Cambridge Studies in Medieval Literature 19 (Cambridge, 1994), pp. 272–98 and esp. pp. 431–35. In the latter section, Irvine stresses the implications of the already established literate culture into which Cædmon was fitted. His portrayal of Cædmon as commentator, though, neglects Bede's representation of Cædmon as preacher: "By his songs, the minds of many were often inspired to despise the world and to long for the heavenly life" ("Cuius carminibus multorum saepe animi ad contemtum saeculi et appetitum sunt uitae caelestis accensi"); "he sought to turn his hearers away from delight in sin and arouse in them the love and practice of good works" ("homines ab amore scelerum abstrahere, ad dilectionem vero et sollentiam bonae actionis excitare curabat").

This, then, was for Bede the most profound aspect of Cædmon's assimilation to a larger, Godly scheme. It is indeed remarkable how many instances of transgression are endorsed within this text, the most sensitive of which are breaches of the normal order of social relationships. Cædmon is not just an aged layman who unexpectedly becomes a monk; the idea of a cowherd fulfilling the functions of the *clericus*, attended to by his own teachers, is really quite shocking. Thus, we should also be alert to the social implications of the reference to acquired competence in cultural traditions and the gift of song, as well as to the potentially troubling acceptance that this man's visionary experience in sleep and dream was entirely valid in the pragmatic circumstances of wakeful reality. Although Cædmon gave their society a new and valent form of Old English verse, it still seemed inappropriate—one barrier he could not transgress—for Bede to commit those works to writing on his parchments.

As a result, we have all the justification we need for examining the circumstances, the origins, the early transmission, and the recording of the story of Cædmon, and the text of his hymn as widely as we can, in order to recognize and appreciate the contextualized function that was so critical to Bede. We understand perfectly well that *historia*, to Bede and his intellectual circles, meant something very different from the objective recording of fact.[13] Bede would not endorse the suppression or falsification of information provided to him by his sources, of course. On the contrary, he was assiduous in trying to synthesize the given information into a coherent account. Coherency meant having a meaning relevant to his present as well as consistency with the ideological imperative of the recognition of and respect for God's purpose. In the same way as, according to Martin Irvine (above, note 12), Bede's story of Cædmon converts the reality of illiteracy and orality by inscribing it as a fiction of written history, socially and materially. Chapter 24 of Book 4 reaches out from

---

13 Ruth Morse, *Truth and Convention in the Middle Ages: Rhetoric, Representation, and Reality* (Cambridge, 1991), esp. pp. 1–13.

the cloister to the cowshed, bringing Cædmon within the former, yet leaving an awareness of the crossing of the threshold between the two clear in the reader's mind. In that sense, the story creates a portal between two otherwise rigidly controlled and bounded social settings; and it leaves the doorway open.

Archaeology and Social Context

For historical information on the monasteries of Northumbria in the seventh and earlier eighth centuries, we remain largely dependent upon Bede. Contemporary and complementary sources, such as the anonymous versions of the *History of the Abbots* with the *Life of Ceolfrith* and of the *Life of Cuthbert*, substantiate the fact that he wrote not in complete isolation but within a school of literati.[14] There is also a considerable volume of archaeological evidence from several of these sites, including the three of immediate relevance to Cædmon and Bede: Whitby, Jarrow, and Wearmouth. The analysis and publication of the results of archaeological excavations at those sites have unfortunately been slow and incomplete; nevertheless, as we shall see, there are useful insights to be drawn from this evidence.

The limits to the real and practical range of Bede's direct knowledge of what was, to him, the only recent history of Northumbrian monasteries, is sharply brought home by the fact that he offers precise detail on the physical development of the monasteries only at Lindisfarne, Jarrow, and Wearmouth. He has much less to say about Hartlepool, Melrose, or Whitby. In the case of Lindisfarne, Bede records the rebuilding and enlargement of the church, and the leading of a thatched, timber structure originally built by Finan under the episcopacy of Eadberht (3.17, 3.25; pp. 262–67, 294–309). Considerable attention is given to

---

14 *Historia Abbatum auctore anonymo* [*HAA*], ed. by Charles Plummer, *Venerabilis Baedae Opera Historica*, 2 vols. (Oxford, 1896), 1:388–404; *Two Lives of Saint Cuthbert: A Life by an Anonymous Monk and Bede's Prose Life*, ed. and trans. Bertram Colgrave (Cambridge, 1985).

John Hines

Cuthbert's colonization of one of the Farne Islands, with details on the structures raised there and how he sought to cultivate the soil despite the apparent barrenness of the island.[15] The *Ecclesiastical History* assures us that his occupancy of the island was continued successfully for twelve years by Oethelwald (5.1, pp. 454–57). There is a close association in Bede's history between information on buildings and the housing of saints' relics—themselves, like Aidan's bones, subject to exhumation, translation, and division (3.17, 3.26, 4.3, 4.30; pp. 262–67, 308–11, 336–47, 442–45). Such relics were *memoria* in a substantive and tangible form, but they were by no means inert remnants of the past, dust gathering dust. The monastic museums were markedly dynamic.

It is Bede's *Historia Abbatum* that yields similar detail concerning the foundation and building of the twin monastery of Jarrow and Wearmouth. This includes the story of how Benedict Biscop brought stone masons from Gaul to build a church "in the Roman manner," followed by glaziers who made glass windows for the church itself, its porticus, and the monastic chambers. He also imported special accessories for the church: sacred vessels and vestments, books, and images.[16] The account of the foundation of Jarrow as twin to Wearmouth is followed immediately in this source by an intriguing description of Eosterwine, the former nobleman and military retainer of King Ecgfrith, who had become a monk and deputized for Benedict Biscop during his absences. In a mirror image of Cædmon's social transformation, this man showed such humility that he would work with the other monks at winnowing, threshing, milking, ploughing, and smithing, and in a series of named special service places: the mill or bakery, the garden, and the kitchen.[17] Again, like

---

15 In addition to comments in the *Ecclesiastical History*, 4.28 (pp. 434–39), see Bede, *Vita sancti Cudbercti*, chs. 17–21, in Colgrave, *Two Lives*, pp. 214–27.

16 Bede, *Historia Abbatum* [*HAB*], ch. 9, in Plummer, ed., *Opera Historica*, I, 364–87.

17 "Et quidem cum fuisset minister Æcgfridi regis, relictis semel

Cædmon, Eosterwine had specific foreknowledge of his time of death and spent his last five days in some sort of secluded building ("in secretiore se aede locabat").

The principal archaeological excavations at the site of the Whitby monastery were conducted in the early 1920s and published in 1943.[18] These excavations revealed and mapped a complex set of stone buildings, the sequencing, absolute dating, and functions of which cannot now be determined in any great detail, although we know that the complex is essentially Anglo-Saxon. There is evidence for a wall or bank that may have enclosed the whole site, and a lane or broad pathway flanked by buildings within the enclosed area. A matter of considerable interest is that many fragments of dressed, carved, and inscribed stones of the Middle Anglo-Saxon period (seventh to ninth centuries) were found in the course of excavations here.[19] Some of this collection seems to be architectural masonry, but most pieces are sculpted crosses or grave-covers, all of which seem to be funerary memorials. The commemoration of the dead was

---

negotiis saecularibus, depositis armis, assumpta militia spiritali, tantum mansit humilis, fratrumque simillimus aliorum, ut uentilare cum eis et triturare, oues uitulasque mulgere, in pistrino, in orto, in coquina, in cunctis monasterii operibus iocundus et obediens gauderet exerceri": *HAB*, ch. 8, in Plummer, ed., *Opera Historica*, I, pp. 371-2.

18 C. R. Peers and C. A. Ralegh Radford, "The Saxon Monastery of Whitby," *Archaeologia*, 89 (1943), 27–88; Rosemary J. Cramp, "Monastic Sites," and "Analysis of the Finds Register and Location Plan of Whitby Abbey," in David M. Wilson, ed., *The Archaeology of Anglo-Saxon England* (Cambridge, 1967), pp. 201–52, esp. pp. 223–39, and 453–57; Philip Rahtz, "The Building Plan of the Anglo-Saxon Monastery of Whitby Abbey," in Wilson, ed., *The Archaeology of Anglo-Saxon England*, pp. 459–62.

19 Including limited further excavation in 2001. James Lang, *The British Academy Corpus of Anglo-Saxon Stone Sculpture. Vol. VI: Northern Yorkshire* (Oxford, 2001), pp. 231–66 and 302–3.

physically very prominent within the monastery. Although contemporary secular settlements had adjacent cemeteries, for the monks literally to be living among and around the graves would have been very unusual. The scope for dating and tracing the influences on the epigraphy of these stones shows that Whitby was an especially early center of Christian stone sculpture in England, probably from the later seventh century onwards. We must look, once more, to late Merovingian Gaul for the source of models and the relevant technical expertise adopted here.[20] The smaller artifacts found in the excavations at Whitby include querns for grinding grain, styli for writing, and tools for making and working cloth in the form of loomweights, spindle-whorls, shears, and needles. One large hearth was identified as a possible forge, but none of the waste-products normally associated with ironworking were recorded in the vicinity. There are a large number of coins known to be from the Anglo-Saxon monastic phase of the site: 42 from the eighth century and 115 from the ninth, but none from the tenth century.[21]

The post-war excavations at Wearmouth and at Jarrow, directed by Rosemary Cramp, have produced a richer range of artifactual finds; unfortunately, these have only been published in summary form as yet.[22] The range is fundamentally similar to that listed for Whitby, and the inclusion of styli and coins corroborates the diversity of special activities found at these

---

20 Lang, *Corpus: Northern Yorkshire*, pp. 39–40, and 51–52 (John Higgitt, "The Inscriptions").

21 These figures are derived from the online record of early medieval coins found in England maintained at the Fitzwilliam Museum, Cambridge, combining data from the *Early Medieval Corpus of Coin Finds* and *Sylloge of Coins of the British Isles:* http://www.fitzmuseum.cam.ac.uk/dept/coins/emc/ (accessed 14 July 2006).

22 Cramp, "Monastic Life," 229–41; Rosemary Cramp, *Wearmouth and Jarrow Monastic Sites, Vol. 1* (Swindon, 2006). The detailed reports on the finds appeared in Volume 2 of this definitive excavation report (2006).

sites. Most striking among the activities represented by material found at Jarrow is the particularly strong evidence for craft production. Using this, it has proven possible to identify dedicated craft areas and workshops within the site. The latter were closest to the bank of the River Don, which flows into the Tyne at Jarrow. The river was used for the supply of water and for waste removal, and this location would also have been convenient for the unloading of raw materials from boats. It would also have been where most visiting traders would arrive; and from the corner of the site, finished products would have been transported away (see Figure d). It has been suggested that the principal building in this zone, Building D, might have functioned as a dedicated guest-house before being given over to craft-use, but this is speculative and perhaps unnecessary.[23] The crafts represented here include glassworking for jewelry and ornament, and some iron- and bronzeworking. Lead was also worked in the area at some stage, but, like a mortar mixer identified at Wearmouth, could have been entirely for construction work within the monastery.

A conspicuous aspect of the evidence published in detail from Wearmouth and Jarrow so far is the frequency of structural development at the sites—especially in their earliest phases—which would include the time when Bede knew them. This should be compared with Chris Loveluck's discussion of the phases and changes at Flixborough in this volume, and no less with Faith Wallis's discussion of the image of the building as a figure of stability. At Lindisfarne, unfortunately, no *in situ* archaeology has yet been discovered or identified relating to the monastery in its earliest phase before the Viking raid of 793, although there is a considerable collection of carved and inscribed stones dating from this period.[24] A building oriented on

23 Cramp, *Wearmouth and Jarrow*, pp. 212–41.
24 Dierdre O'Sullivan and Robert Young, *English Heritage Book of Lindisfarne Holy Island* (London, 1995); Rosemary Cramp, *The British Academy Corpus of Anglo-Saxon Stone Sculpture. Vol. I: County*

an East–West alignment and surrounded by graves at Yeavering, however, has plausibly been identified as a seventh-century timber church, similar to the kind referred to by Bede.[25] Bede also referred to a monastery at Tynemouth on the northern side of the Tyne from Jarrow; excavations here have revealed a number of rectangular timber buildings of Anglo-Saxon date—but unfortunately not more precisely dated, nor with any clearly identifiable functions.[26]

The Construction of Wearmouth and Jarrow

Partial and scattered though they are, the historical records of Lindisfarne and the archaeological evidence from Yeavering and Tynemouth together usefully highlight just how remarkably distinctive the construction of the monasteries at Wearmouth and Jarrow was. Rosemary Cramp plausibly reconstructs these twin monasteries as having very similar core layouts, with a pair of stone buildings—standing end-to-end and parallel to the church itself—for the monks to occupy for their lives and activities apart from acts of worship, with an open area some 15–20 meters wide between the buildings and the church. In what appear to be three principal phases of building at Wearmouth, this yard was first crossed by a stone-walled porticus. It was then successively enclosed with walls on the three sides south of the church, after which the two buildings were constructed. In the third phase, the yard was extended to the west (Figures a, b, and c). This whole sequence appears to have been quite a rapid

Durham and Northumberland, 2 parts (Oxford, 1984), pp. 194–208.

25 Brian Hope-Taylor, *Yeavering: An Anglo-British Centre of Early Northumbria*, Department of the Environment Archaeology Report 7 (London, 1977), pp. 73–78 and 164–69.

26 Bede, *Ecclesiastical History*, 5.6, pp. 464–69. See G. Jobey, "Excavations at Tynemouth Priory and Castle," *Archaeologia Aeliana*, 4 ser. 45 (1967), 33–104 at pp. 42–49; Cramp, "Monastic Sites," pp. 217–20.

process. The evidence for rebuilding at Jarrow takes the form of modification—both extension and subdivision—of the two main buildings south of the church, Buildings A and B. Building A was divided into two unequal chambers, one twice the size of the other, apparently *ab initio*; there was also a tantalizing column base on the central axis, but not quite in the absolute middle of the larger room. This could well have served to support an upper floor. At a later stage, an annex was added to the south side of the building forming a T-shape (Figure d). Building B, meanwhile, was partitioned into one large chamber and two small chambers at the eastern end: looking very much like the private cells that we know, *inter alios*, Bede, Cuthbert, and Eostorwine used.

Altogether, we can form quite a detailed impression of the diverse and substantial economic functions of the earlier Northumbrian monasteries, quite apart from their readily recognized and widely appreciated spiritual, intellectual, and artistic importance.[27] The monasteries were centers of rich, specialized craftwork, and were physically organized and structured in order to accommodate that. Besides the riverside craft zone identified at Jarrow, we should note the suggestion, based on the reportedly unusual animal-bone assemblage uncovered at the Green Shiels settlement on Holy Island, that this farmstead may have specialized in producing the calf-skin required for vellum manuscripts at Lindisfarne.[28] Although immediate local use and consumption of the products was apparently the prime motive

---

27 John Blair, *The Church in Anglo-Saxon Society* (Oxford, 2005), esp. pp. 251–61; Peter Sawyer, "Early Fairs and Markets in England and Scandinavia," in B. L. Anderson and A. J. H. Latham (eds.), *The Market in History* (London, 1986), pp. 59–77.

28 Dierdre O'Sullivan, "Space, Silence and Shortage on Lindisfarne: The Archaeology of Asceticism," in Helena Hamerow and Arthur MacGregor, eds., *Image and Power in the Archaeology of Early Medieval Britain* (Oxford, 2001), pp. 33–52. Once more, O'Sullivan discusses the implications of data that are yet to be fully published.

John Hines

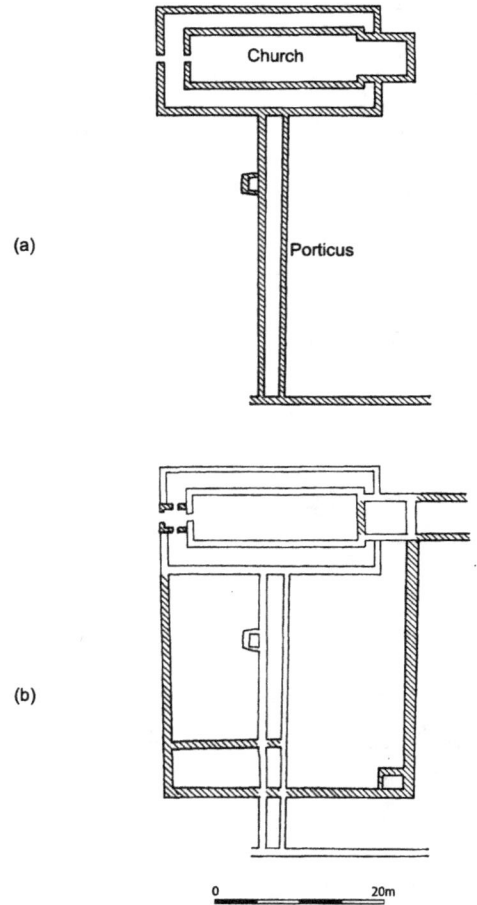

Figures a, b (above), and c (opposite, top): Wearmouth: Cramp's Phases 1–3. New walling of the phase shaded. North to the top; for scale bar, see (b). It should be noted that because of the limits of excavation, it is not known if there were further buildings or features at the southern edge of the site.

Changes and Exchanges in Bede's and Cædmon's World

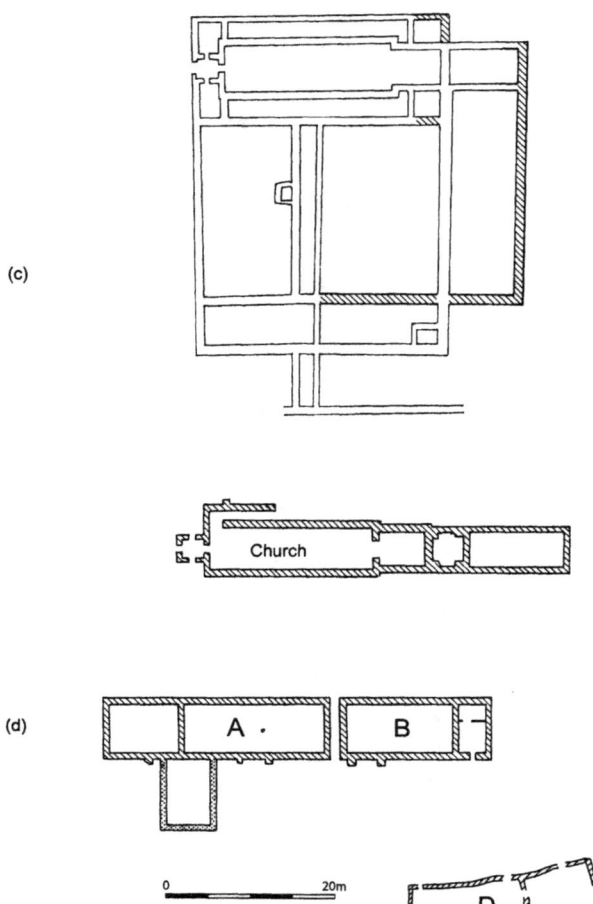

Figure d (above): Jarrow, with the Church, and Buildings A, B, and D marked. Redrawn by the author after Cramp, *Wearmouth and Jarrow*.

for the development of these economic functions, the sites grew into regional centers of exchange. This is evidenced by the diversity of coinage brought to the sites and sporadically dropped there. The late eighth-century Northumbrian Latin poem *De Abbatibus* describes precisely how a monastery could stockpile tradable produce from its landed endowments.[29]

There was probably more driving this development than the fortuitous and favorable coincidence of proto-urban communities of men freed from the constant labour required in the fundamental subsistence economy at coastal or riverine locations, which evolved to function as colonies of specialist workers at nodes where trade could take place. Outside the Christian world, it has been noted that "central places" with special trading functions emerged in Scandinavia, in a gradual process from the third century through to the Viking Period, at or around which there is frequently evidence for some strong cult and sacral character.[30] There is a cogent case to be made that it was

29 Eorpuinus hunc sequitur commissi pastor ouilis,/ presbyter egregius, uitae studiosus amator,/ sensibus et prudens et cuncto strenuus actu. / diuitias tribuit laxato mentis opimo / iam gremio monachis, quos lurida inedia pressit,/ inque modum mirum dispersae ad premia certa diuitiae crescent (Eorpwine followed him [Eanmund] as shepherd of the fold, and to him it was entrusted. He was an excellent priest, a zealous lover of (monastic) life, both instinctively prudent and vigorous in all his activities. He brought riches to the monks, whom terrible hunger had afflicted, by opening the splendid treasury of his mind, and wealth grew to a marvellous extent, when put out for reliable returns.) Æthelwulf, *De Abbatibus*. Ed. & trans. by A. Campbell (Oxford, 1967), lines 403–9.

30 Dagfinn Skre, ed., *Kaupang in Skiringssal*, Kaupang Excavation Project Publication Series I (Aarhus, 2007), pp. 385-459; Birgitta Hårdh and Lars Larsson (eds.), *Central Places in the Migration and Merovingian Periods*. Acta Archaeologica Lundensia Ser. in 8°, Uppåkrastudier 6 (Stockholm, 2002); Lars Jørgensen, "Manor

Changes and Exchanges in Bede's and Cædmon's World

not just the pragmatic existence of a focal point where people would gather that stimulated the growth of regular trade there, but, more importantly, the shared understanding that the sanctity of the site would protect strangers with its special taboos and sanctuary—and consequently, people could safely seek to negotiate trades there in the usual competitive manner. Anglo-Saxon charter evidence, particularly from the seventh and eighth centuries, makes it quite clear not only that monasteries were established as the equivalent of major, self-sufficient multiple estate centers—to collect produce from the hides under their control—but also that major churchmen and houses were

enjoying the benefit of others' tolls.[31]

These facts illuminate Bede's much-cited complaint about the secularization of what he regarded as purely nominal or even false monasteries in his letter to Ecgbert, Archbishop of York.[32] Although there is an undertone of concern about material worldliness throughout Bede's letter, his major concern was the lack of celibacy and the continued sexual indulgence of those in these new monasteries. Such behavior would presumably encourage any scandalous rumors about the regular double monasteries. If Rosemary Cramp is right to draw attention

---

and Market at Lake Tissø in the Sixth to Eleventh Centuries: The Danish 'Productive' Sites," in Tim Pestell and Katharina Ulmschneider (eds.), *Markets in Early Medieval Europe: Trading and "Productive" Sites, 650–850* (Macclesfield, 2003), pp. 175–207; Torun Zachrisson, "The Holiness of Helgö," in Bo Gyllensvärd et al., *Excavations at Helgö XVI: Exotic and Sacral Finds from Helgö.* Kungl. Vitterhets Historie och Antikvitets Akademien (Stockholm, 2004), pp. 143–75.

31 Susan E. Kelly, "Eighth-Century Trading Privileges from Anglo-Saxon England," *Early Medieval Europe*, 1 (1992), 3–28.

32 *Epistola ad Ecgbertum Episcopum*: Plummer (ed.), *Opera Historica*, I, 405–423; trans. by Dorothy Whitelock, *English Historical Documents. Vol. I, c. 500–1042* (London, 1955), pp. 735–45, no. 170.

to the way in which the layout of the monasteries of Wearmouth and Jarrow reproduced that of the Roman villa—and Jarrow was close to Roman sites at the eastern end of Hadrian's Wall, and much Roman material was physically re-used at the site—it is far from over-fanciful to think of Bede's position, and the attitudes implicit in his complaint, as representing a new version of the Roman senatorial ideal of *otium*. That is, he saw a world of productive, civilized leisure taking shape and offering freedom from worldly business.[33] The early medieval transformation that *otium* had gone through had, in this case, little to do with a lofty disdain for politics and commerce. Rather, the new preserves of civilized, Christian *romanitas* were determinedly exempt from warfare and from begetting and raising fighting men. As Bede tells Ecgbert, this was precisely what the secular, lordly class—not the learned—should be doing.

Cædmon's place in society was originally quite different from both of these. Everything indicates that he was unfree. Bede tells us only what duties were imposed upon him: both that night-time care of the cattle was assigned to him—possibly a practical task for an older man—and that he was subject to the *uilicus*, the steward or reeve. It is not actually stated that this steward was an official of the monastic estate, although that seems to be implied by the man's immediate and ready access to Hild, the abbess. With 10 hides of land, Whitby did not have a very large estate (compared with the 150 hides ultimately claimed for Wearmouth and Jarrow), but this is enough for us to realize that we should not assume Cædmon was physically in a close relationship with the monastery before the miracle.[34] Certainly, Cædmon's subjection is consistently and solidly reflected in the narrative: he has to be introduced to the abbess by

33 Cramp, *Wearmouth and Jarrow*, pp. 356–359; Wickham, *Early Middle Ages*, pp. 157–58 and 200–2.
34 Bede, *Ecclesiastical History*, 3.24, pp. 288–95; *HAA*, chapters 7 and 11, pp. 367-8, and *HAB*, chapters 4, 9 and 15, pp. 379-80; see Cramp, *Wearmouth and Jarrow*, p. 37.

a higher ranking man; he is commanded ("iussus est") to relate his dream; and the teachers order him ("praecipientes eum") to produce more poetry, a job he takes ("suscepto negotio").

Reading with a consciousness of Cædmon's social position, it is of particular interest that only one chapter of Book 4 of the *Ecclesiastical History,* chapter 23—which outlines the life and career of Hild, daughter of Hereric who was a nephew of King Edwin of Northumbria, perhaps a sister's son as we know of no brothers that king had—separates the story of Cædmon from the tale of a Northumbrian nobleman, Imma, captured after the battle with the Mercians near the River Trent and sold into slavery. Although Imma tried to pass himself off as a poor peasant ("rusticus et pauper"), his true social position was eventually recognized because of his appearance, his clothes, and his speech ("ex uultu et habitu et sermonibus eius"). In the sequence of Book 4, the story of Imma is an excursus from the death of Ælfwine of Deira (679) and falls in an appropriate place, immediately before the death and retrospective biography of Hild in A.D. 680. We cannot suggest that Bede has juxtaposed the stories solely to highlight their thematic parallels; all the same, we might even say all the more, both *do* portray the development of Northumbrian Christianity in a society with a sharp hierarchy where, *inter alia,* accent and discourse were considered characteristic of rank. There is a secular, social anxiety at the heart of Bede's remonstrances in his letter to Ecgbert as much as a moral concern for the purity of the Church. That anxiety was, in essence, a fear of social and economic inertia, which would leave the king no longer able to strike deals with and to reward his military followers in the way necessary to ensure the security of the kingdom. In very different ways, the stories of Imma, Hild, and Cædmon are all stories of social mobility—changing, even exchanging, places, but all eventually achieving both a respectable and a spiritually exemplary position. For Imma and Hild, the rewards for these Christian qualities were innately bound with their kinship and noble descent.

John Hines

For Cædmon, his social liberation and ascent and his spiritual transformation are indistinguishable; all are equally implicit in those events of his life Bede narrates.

No less than in the letter to Ecgbert, we may claim that Bede's account of Cædmon reveals a full if perhaps subconcious—even in some ways resisted—appreciation on its author's part of the practical role of the monastic community and its central place in the material culture of his world. We have referred—perhaps rather cursorily, but sufficiently—to the swiftly developing, widespread, and significant character of the monastic sites of the seventh and eighth centuries as centers of production, distribution, exchange, and trade. They were not the only sites that served this economic development. By the early eighth century the four earliest towns—which Bede refers to as *emporia*, although the Old English term *wic* is now preferred in archaeology and history—had been established: two immediately alongside the sees of London and York, and two as new port sites at Ipswich and Southampton.[35] There were undoubtedly many more small landing places and production sites around the coasts and major river-systems, some at religious houses such as Jarrow, others of an entirely utilitarian and secular character, as a site excavated at West Hythe, Kent.[36] It seems highly likely that the recently emergent, much-discussed archaeological phenomenon of the "productive site," a hot-spot of rich metalwork finds, mostly of the late seventh to early ninth centuries, represents more than anything else a widespread network of market sites, functioning at fixed dates. Some of these sites have clear connections with

---

35 C. J. Scull, "Urban centres in pre-Viking England?," in John Hines, ed., *The Anglo-Saxons from the Migration Period to the Eighth Century: An Ethnographic Perspective* (Woodbridge, 1997), pp. 269–310; David Hill and Robert Cowie (eds.), *Wics: The Early Medieval Trading Centres of Northern Europe* (Sheffield, 2001).

36 Mark Gardiner et al., "Continental Trade and Non-Urban Ports in Mid-Anglo-Saxon England: Excavations at *Sandtun*, West Hythe, Kent," *The Archaeological Journal*, 158 (2001), 161–290.

Changes and Exchanges in Bede's and Cædmon's World

what are subsequently known to be minster centers, although the overall interdependency of ecclesiastical and commercial economic structures remains a matter of keen debate.[37]

This new economic system and the relative economic boom that went with it was not just an Anglo-Saxon historical phenomenon. Essentially the same developments are widely found in northern and north-western Europe: contemporary emporia, landing sites, and productive sites are equally familiar around the North Sea and Baltic coasts, in Merovingian and Carolingian Francia, pre-Christian and converted Frisia and Saxony, in Denmark, and further afield in Slavonic lands.[38] One of the key rules of conduct at a trading site of any kind had to be that it was a place to do business. That is, it was a place where transactions were subject to negotiation and were not just ritualized exchanges performed according to a pre-existing set of rules.[39] What we may recognize, then, is that the free gift Cædmon miraculously received was something that—with access granted to the proper forum by the steward—he could sell as his own special product and thus bargain his way into a new and more favorable social position: not that of a burgess or a gildsman, for those desirable urban conditions were not yet available, but that of a brother within the monastic community.

---

37 Pestell and Ulmschneider (eds.), *Markets*, represents the evidence and the debate over how it may be interpreted very well.

38 Helen Clarke and Björn Ambrosiani, *Towns in the Viking Age*, rev. ed. (London:, 1995), esp. pp. 5–45; Jens Ulriksen, "Danish Sites and Settlements with a Maritime Context, 200–1200," *Antiquity*, 68 (1994), 797–811; Jens Ulriksen, *Anløbspladser: Besejling og Bebyggesle i Danmark mellem 200 og 1100 e.Kr.* (Roskilde, 1998).

39 John Hines, "Trading Places: Royalty and Urbanism in Norse Literature," in *Sagas and the Norwegian Experience*. 10th International Saga Conference Preprints (Trondheim, 1997), pp. 263–70; John Hines, "North Sea trade and the Proto-Urban Sequence," *Archaeologia Polona*, 32 (1994), 7–26; Skre (ed.), *Kaupang*, pp. 445-69.

Anglo-Saxon literary discourse—particularly Old English literary discourse—was participating in these social transactions and transformations both widely and dynamically. The story of Cædmon, and not least the transmission of the tale itself and the text of the hymn, is a drama played out on the cusp between orality and literacy. It is a telling example of the sensitivity and importance of the distinction between those two. Bede was acutely conscious that Cædmon's hymn could not truly be translated from English into Latin. He himself had, on many occasions, provided priests who lacked sufficient Latin with English versions of the Creed and Paternoster.[40] But there is no sign that he thought the English text of the song could be written in a Latin manuscript with his *Ecclesiastical History*, although it was added in scriptoria very soon after his death.[41] In this, he was typical of his time. There is a striking consistency in the fact that all of our earliest instances of written Old English verse take the form of quotations from poems or brief verse epitomes that form part of some much larger and generically more complex, even multimedia, artistic work. Verse appears in this way on the Franks Casket and the Ruthwell Cross in runes, and here in eighth-century manuscripts of the *Ecclesiastical History*.

The Hymn and a Welsh Analogue

Another analogue to the story of Cædmon may help us to define a key process involved here. There is a striking parallelism, not merely in the elements of the story, but in the spirit of Bede's attitude to Cædmon's song and that of the seventeenth-century Anglo-Welsh poet Henry Vaughan in a comparable situation, recorded in one of Vaughan's very few extant autograph letters, which he wrote to his cousin, the famous diarist and antiquarian John Aubrey, providing information on Welsh traditional poetry:

---

40 Plummer (ed.), *Opera Historica*, I, at pp. 408–9.
41 O'Donnell, *Cædmon's Hymn*, pp. 78–118.

Changes and Exchanges in Bede's and Cædmon's World

... for the antient Bards (though by the testimonie of their Enemies, the Romans;) a very learned societie: yet (like the Druids) they communicated nothing of their knowledge, butt by way of tradition: wch I suppose to be the reason that we have no account left vs: nor any sort of remains, or other monuments of their learning, or way of living.

As to the later Bards, who were no such men, butt had a societie & some rules & orders among themselves: & several sorts of measures & a kind of Lyric poetrie: wch are all sett down exactly In the learned John David Rhees, or Rhesus his Welch, or British grammer: you shall have there (in the later end of his book) a most curious Account of them. This vein of poetry they called Awen, which in their language signifies as much as Raptus, or a poetic furor; & (in truth) as many of them as I have conversed with are (as I may say) gifted or inspired with it. I was told by a very sober & knowing person (now dead) that in his time, there was a young lad father & motherless, & soe very poor that he was forced to beg; butt att last was taken vp by a rich man, that kept a great stock of sheep vpon the mountains not far from the place where I now dwell. who cloathed him & sent him into the mountains to keep his sheep. There in Summer time following the sheep & looking to their lambs, he fell into a deep sleep; In wch he dreamt, that he saw a beautifull young man with a garland of green leafs vpon his head, & an hawk vpon his fist: with a quiver full of Arrows att his back, coming towards him (whistling several measures or tunes all the way) & att last lett the hawk fly att him, w^{ch} (he dreamt) gott into his mouth & inward parts, & suddenly awaked in a great fear & consternation: butt possessed with such a vein, or gift of poetrie, that he left the sheep & went about the Countrey, making songs vpon all occasions, and came to be the most famous Bard in all the Countrey in his time.[42]

---

42 *The Works of Henry Vaughan*, ed. by L. C. Martin, 2nd ed. (Oxford, 1957), pp. 696–97.

John Hines

When Vaughan uses the expression "their language" here, he does so in the idiom of one gentleman schooled in English letters corresponding with another; in fact, there is every reason to believe that Vaughan's familiarity with the meaning of *awen*, and his ability to converse with Welsh poets, was because he spoke Welsh since childhood.[43]

It is of considerable interest, then, to reflect upon the idea that Bede, writing in Latin for both a national and an international, clerical readership, was concerned to, in effect, construct a sense of "us" and "them" in respect to native identity and literary tradition, as was Vaughan. Cædmon's gift of song may have been his key to social emancipation, but it was not—unlike Imma's speeches—something that revealed an innate nobility of social rank that had somehow become hidden. Perhaps the most significant implication of Cædmon's story, in relation to Old English literary history, is that it has often been denied that the Old English *scop* may have been a *þeow*, that is, one who was a servant, a slave, or unfree. The patrician Oxonian Professor C. L. Wrenn could imagine no such state of affairs; he consequently assigned to Cædmon's original social peers a tradition of "popular or 'folk' poetry," which must have contrasted with the aristocratic, cultured, and technically demanding tradition preserved by the "aristocratic warrior."[44] Certainly, when a "cyninges þegn" ("king's thane") composes verses celebrating Beowulf's victory over Grendel and juxtaposes that narrative with a tale from the historic legend of the Burgundian *Wælsingas*, we have to regard the performer-composer as one of the nobility, as was Imma.[45] But it is both reasonable and constructive to point out that the anxieties of Deor and the bragging of Widsith take

---

43 F. E. Hutchinson, *Henry Vaughan: A Life and Interpretation* (Oxford, 1947), pp. 156–64.

44 C. L. Wrenn, *A Study of Old English Literature* (London, 1967), pp. 36–37 and 74–80.

45 *Beowulf*, ed. Bruce Mitchell and Fred C. Robinson (Oxford, 1998), lines 867–900.

Changes and Exchanges in Bede's and Cædmon's World

on a thoroughly new force and credibility if we postulate that those rootless dependants owed their place and fortunes in the hall-society far more to the favor their skill found them than to their innate social rank and the expectations that went with that. It is true, too, that the image of King David playing the lyre in the Durham Cassiodorus manuscript, and the presence of lyres in seventh-century princely graves such as Sutton Hoo mound 1, Taplow, and Prittlewell, reinforce an association of the lyre with the highest aristocratic and royal circles. In the burials, however, the musical instrument represents the entertainment that was part of life in the hall. The burials also contain exceptional cooking and feasting equipment, but we can safely assume that the lord of the hall provided the feasts without cooking or serving them himself. Lyres are also known from more ordinary burial contexts at Bergh Apton and Morningthorpe, Norfolk; Snape, Suffolk; and Abingdon, Oxon (formerly Berkshire).[46] Graeme Lawson rightly notes, as we do here, that a wide range

---

46 Barbara Green and Andrew Rogerson, *The Anglo-Saxon Cemetery at Bergh Apton, Norfolk*. East Anglian Archaeology 7 (Gressenhall, 1978), esp. pp. 87–98 (Graeme Lawson, "The Lyre from Grave 22"); Barbara Green, Andrew Rogerson, and Susan G. White, *The Anglo-Saxon Cemetery at Morning Thorpe, Norfolk*. East Anglian Archaeology 36, 2 vols. (Gressenhall, 1987), esp. pp. 166–71 (Graeme Lawson, "Report on the Lyre Remains from Grave 97"). The fragment from Abingdon (E. T. Leeds and D. B. Harden, *The Anglo-Saxon Cemetery at Abingdon, Berkshire* [Oxford, 1936], p. 39, and pl. IXb), was not recognized for what it was until after detailed study of the Sutton Hoo mound 1 finds began in the later 1940s. See Myrtle and Rupert Bruce-Mitford, "The Musical Instrument," in Rupert Bruce-Mitford, *The Sutton Hoo Ship-Burial*, vol. 3/II (London, 1983), pp. 611–731. See also Robert Boenig, "The Anglo-Saxon Harp," *Speculum*, 71 (1996), 290–320. See further William Filmer-Sankey and Tim Pestell, *Snape Anglo-Saxon Cemetery: Excavations and Surveys 1824–1992*, East Anglian Archaeology 95 (Ipswich, 2001), esp. pp. 215–23 (Lawson, "The Lyre Remains from Grave 32").

of Anglo-Saxon society is associated with the *hearp*—apparently in different proprietorial ways. This is not to plead a forced argument that musical skill in seventh-century England was typically a low-caste phenomenon, and thus a route to preferral for the lucky few with rare accomplishments of that nature. More significantly, this special form of discourse in the vernacular shared by all ranks not only unified the community across the boundaries between social grades but also provided a means for transgressive advances, as in Cædmon's case, or even falls, as for the unfortunate Deor.

As both this essay and this whole volume show, the story of Cædmon is a rich example of the powerful connective and interactive valency between language, literature, society, and material life as elements of the cultural whole. It is, therefore, a powerful demonstration of how philology, critical reading, the histories of literature and society, and the material history that is archaeology, can be combined to give us a deeper and richer understanding not only of Bede's objectives in telling this story, but of the context in which he was writing. That understanding is not the result of an unsympathetic deconstruction that looks beyond his conscious religious beliefs to the pragmatic social and material interests involved in how he transmitted the story. Indeed, we can appreciate Bede's spirituality all the more when we understand how it was rooted in a substantial and realistic appraisal of the world, a world which Cædmon praised as God's wonderful handiwork, and also a world which Bede sought both to convert and to transcend.

Bibliography

Primary Works

Æthelwulf. *De abbatibus.* Ed. and trans. A. Campbell. Oxford, 1967.

Aldhelm. *Aldhelmi opera.* Ed. R. Ehwald. MGH auctores antiquissimi 15. Berlin, 1919.

Aldhelm. *Aldhelm, the Poetic Works.* Ed. Michael Lapidge and J. L. Rosier. Cambridge, 1985.

Anon. *De computo dialogus.* Ed. Migne, *Patrologia Latina.* Paris, vol. 90, cols. 647–64. 1844–82.

Augustine. *De doctrina christiana.* Ed. Joseph Martin, CCSL 32. Turnhout, 1962.

———. *Enarrationes in Psalmos.* Ed. E. Dekkers and J. Fraipont. CCSL 38–40. Turnhout, 1966.

Bede. *Bedae opera de temporibus.* Ed. C. W. Jones. Cambridge, Mass., 1969.

———. *A Biblical Miscellany.* Trans. W. Trent Foley and Arthur G. Holder. TTH 28. Liverpool, 1999.

———. *De arte metrica et de schematibus et tropis.* Ed. Calvin Kendall, CCSL 123A. Turnhout, 1975.

———. *De die iudicii.* Ed. J. Fraipont, CCSL 122. Turnhout, 1955.

———. *De tabernaculo.* Ed. D. Hurst, CCSL 119B. Turnhout, 1969.

———. *De templo.* Ed. David Hurst, CCSL 119A. Turnhout, 1969.

———. *De temporum ratione.* Ed. C. W. Jones, CCSL123B. Turnhout, 1977.

———. *Epistola ad Ecgbertum Episcopum.* In *Venerabilis Baedae opera historia,* ed. Plummer, 405–23.

———. *Bede's Ecclesiastical History of the English People.* Ed. and trans. Bertram Colgrave and R. A. B. Mynors. Oxford, 1969.

———. *The Ecclesiastical History of the English People.* Trans. Judith McClure and Roger Collins. Oxford, 1999.

———. *Expositio apocalypseos.* Ed. Roger Gryson. CCSL121A. Turnhout, 2001.

———. *Historia Abbatum auctore anonymo.* In *Venerabilis Baedae Opera Historica,* ed. Plummer, 388–404.

———. *Homeliarum euangelii libri II,* ed. D. Hurst, CCSL 122. Turnhout, 1955.

———. *Homilies on the Gospels.* Trans. Lawrence T. Martin and David Hurst, 2 vols., Cistercian Studies Series, 110 and 111. Kalamazoo, 1991.

———. *In Ezram et Neemiam.* Ed. David Hurst, CCSL 119A. Turnhout, 1969.

———. *In Genesim.* Ed. C. W. Jones. CCSL118A. Turnhout, 1967.

———. *In Lucae euangelium exposition.* Ed. David Hurst, CCSL 120. Turnhout, 1960.

———. *In primam partem Samuhelis Libri III.* Ed. David Hurst, CCSL 119B. Turnhout, 1962.

———. In *Regum XXX Quaestiones.* Ed. David Hurst, CCSL 119B. Turnhout, 1962.

———. *Libri II De arte metrica et De schematibus et tropis. The Art of Poetry and Rhetoric.* Ed. Calvin B.Kendall. Bibliotheca Germania, Series Nova, vol. 2. Saarbrücken, 1991.

———. *Liber hymnorum,* ed. J. Fraipont, CCSL 122. Turnhout, 1955.

———. *On Ezra and Nehemiah.* Trans. Scott DeGregorio. TTH 47. Liverpool, 2006.

———. *On the Tabernacle.* Trans. Arthur G. Holder. TTH 18. Liverpool, 1994.

———. *On the Temple.* Trans. Seán Connolly. TTH 21. Liverpool, 1995.

———. *The Reckoning of Time.* Trans. Faith Wallis. TTH 29. rev. ed. Liverpool, 2004.

———. *Vita metrica S. Cuthberti.* Ed. Werner Jaeger. *Bedas metrische Vita sancti Cuthberti,* Palaestra 198. Leipzig, 1935.

Benedict of Nursia. *Le règle de Saint Benoit.* Ed. Jean Neufville, trans. with commentary by Adalbert de Vogüé. Sources chrétiennes 181–86. Paris, 1971–77.

Boniface. *Bonifatii et Lullii epistolae.* Ed. M. Tangl. MGH epistolae selectae 1. 1916. Reprint, Berlin, 1955.

———. *The Letters of Saint Boniface.* Trans. Ephraim Emerton. New York, 1940.

Bradley, S. A. J., ed. and trans. *Anglo-Saxon Poetry: An Anthology of Old English Poems in Prose Translations with Introduction and Headnotes.* London, 1982.

Calder, D. G. *Sources and Analogues of Old English Poetry 2: The Major Germanic and Celtic Texts in Translation.* Cambridge, 1983.

Cameron, Angus, Ashley Crandell Amos, and Antonette diPaolo Healey, eds. *Dictionary of Old English: A to F.* Toronto, 2003.

Carnicelli, Thomas A., ed. *King Alfred's Version of St. Augustine's "Soliloquies."* Cambridge, Mass., 1969.

Cassian. *Iohannis Cassiani Conlationes XXIIII.* Ed. Michael Petchenig. CCSL 13, pt. 2. Vienna, 1886.

Clark-Hall, J. R., and H. D. Merritt. *A Concise Anglo-Saxon Dictiary,* 4th ed. Toronto, 1984.

Colgrave, Bertram, ed. and trans. *Two Lives of Saint Cuthbert: A Life by an Anonymous Monk of Lindisfarne and Bede's Prose Life.* Cambridge, 1985.

Cuthbert, *Epistola de obitu Baedae.* In *Venerabilis Baedae opera historia,* ed. Plummer, clx-clxiv.

Dobbie, Elliott van Kirk, ed. *The Anglo-Saxon Minor Poems.* The Anglo-Saxon Poetic Records 6. 1942. Reprinted New York, 1968.

———. *Beowulf and Judith,* The Anglo-Saxon Poetic Records 4. New York, 1953.

———. *The Manuscripts of Cædmon's Hymn and Bede's Death Song with a Critical Text of the Epistola Cuthberti de obitu Bedu.* New York, 1937.

Gollancz, I., ed. *The Cædmon Manuscript of Anglo-Saxon Biblical Poetry: Junius XI in the Bodleian Library.* Oxford, 1927.

Grattan. J. H. G., and C. Singer. *Anglo-Saxon Magic and Medicine.* Publications of the Wellcome Historical Medical Museum, n.s. 3. London, 1952.

Gregory the Great. *Moralia in Iob.* Ed. M. Adriaen. CCSL 143–143B. 3 vols. Turnhout, 1979–85.

Haddan, A. W., and W. Stubbs, eds. *Councils and Ecclesiastical Documents* relating to Great Britain and Ireland. 3 vols. Oxford, 1869–78.

Healey, Antonette di Paolo, et al., eds. *The Complete Corpus of Old English in Machine-readable Form (TEI Compatible Version)*, 2nd TEI-conformant ed. Oxford, 1994.

Healey, Antonette di Paolo and Richard L. Venezky, eds. *A Microfiche Concordance to the Dictionary of Old English.* Toronto, 1980; reprinted. 1985

Isidore of Seville. *Traité de la nature [De natura rerum].* Ed. and trans. Jacques Fontaine. Bibliothèque de l'École des hautes études hispaniques 28. Bordeaux, 1960.

———. *Etymologiae.*

Jerome. *Epistulae I–LXX.* Ed. Isidore Hilberg, CSEL 53. Vienna, 1910.

Krapp, George Philip, ed. *The Junius Manuscript,* The Anglo-Saxon Poetic Records 1. New York, 1931.

Krapp, George Philip, and Elliott Van Kirk Dobbie, eds. *The Exeter Book.* The Anglo-Saxon Poetic Records 3. New York, 1936.

Martin, L. C., ed. *The Works of Henry Vaughan.* 2nd ed. Oxford, 1957.

Migne, J.-P., ed. *Patrologiae cursus completus*, series latina. 221 vols. Paris, 1844–00.

Miller, Thomas, ed., *The Old English Version of Bede's Ecclesiastical History of the English People.* Early English Text Society, Original Series 95, 96, 110, 111. 1890-1898. Reprinted London, 1959-1963.

Plummer, Charles, ed. *Venerabilis Baedae opera historia.* 2 vols. 1896. Reprint, 1 vol., Oxford, 1946.

Primasius of Hadrumentum. *Commentarius in apocalypsim.* Ed. A. W. Adams. CCSL 92. Turnhout, 1985.

Quodvultdeus. *Liber promissionum.* Ed. R. Braun. CCSL60. Turnhout, 1976.

Ramsey, Boniface. *John Cassian: The Conferences.* Ancient Christian Writers 57. New York, 1997.

Smith, A. H., ed. *Three Northumbrian Poems: Cædmon's Hymn, Bede's Death Song, and the Leiden Riddle,* rev. ed. Exeter Medieval Texts. Exeter, 1978.

Whitelock, Dorothy, ed., *English Historical Documents. Vol. 1, c. 500–1042.* London, 1955.

William of Malmesbury. *Willelmi Malmesbiriensis monachi de gestis pontificum Anglorum libri quinque.* Rerum britannicarum medii ævi scriptores, or, Chronicles and memorials of Great Britain and Ireland during the middle ages. Ed. N. E. S. A. Hamilton. London, 1870.

Allen J. Frantzen and John Hines

Secondary Works

Abraham, Leonore. "Cædmon's Hymn and the *Gepwærnysse* (Fitness) of Things." *American Benedictine Review* 43 (1992), 331–44.

Adkin, Neil. *Jerome on Virginity: A Commentary on the Libellus De Virginitate Servanda (Letter 22)*, ARCA Classical and Medieval Texts, Papers and Monographs 42. Cambridge, 2003.

Anderson, Sue. "The Human Population," in Daniels and Loveluck, eds., *Anglo-Saxon Hartlepool and the Foundations of English Christianity*.

Andrén, Anders. *Between Artifacts and Texts: Historical Archaeology in Global Perspective*. London, 2001.

Anon. Review of Thrupp, *The Anglo-Saxon Home*. In *The Gentlemen's Magazine*, July 1862. 555.

Anon. "No Small Fry in Saxon Fishing Industry." *British Archaeology* 41. February 1999. *http://www.britarch.ac.uk/BA/ba41/ba41news.html#fry* (July 2006).

Antin, Paul. "Autour du songe de S. Jérôme." In *Recueil sur saint Jérôme*. Collection Latomus 95. 71–100. Brussels, 1968.

Archibald, Marion. "The Anglo-Saxon and Medieval Coins from Flixborough." In *Life and Economy at Early Medieval Flixborough*, ed. Loveluck and Evans. Chapter 7, in press.

Armstrong, Karen. *Muhammad: A Biography of the Prophet*. San Francisco, 1992.

Atherton, Mark. "Saxon or Celt? Cædmon, 'The Seafarer' and the Irish Tradition." In *Celts and Christians: New Approaches to the Religious Traditions of Britain and Ireland*, ed. Mark Atherton, 79–99. Cardiff, 2002.

Aurner, Nellie S. "Bede and Pausanias." *Modern Language Notes* 41 (1926), 535–36.

Austin, J. L. *How to Do Things with Words*, 2nd ed. Cambridge, Mass., 1975.

Bailey, R. N. "Gold Plaque, Bamburgh, Northumberland." In *The Making of England—Anglo-Saxon Art and Culture A.D. 600–900*, ed. Leslie Webster and Janet Backhouse, 58–59. London, 1991.

Bailey, Richard. "Innocent from the Great Offence." In *Theorizing Anglo-Saxon Stone Sculpture*, ed. Karkov and Orton, 93–103.

Barbé, Hervé, Michel Barret, Jean-Claude Routier, and Eddy Roy. "Aménagement du réseau hydrographique et urbanisation aux bords de l'abbaye Saint-Bertin. Données récentes de l'archéologie à Saint-Omer." *Revue du Nord—Archéologie de la Picardie et du Nord de la France* 80 (1998), 7–50.

Barrett, James H., A. M. Locker, and C. M. Roberts. "'Dark Age Economics' Revisited: the English Fish Bone Evidence, A.D. 600-1600." *Antiquity* 78 [301] (2004), 618-36.

Bender, Thomas, and Carl E. Schorske, eds. *American Academic Culture in Transformation: Fifty Years, Four Disciplines*. Princeton, 1997.

Bessinger, J. B., Jr. "Homage to Cædmon and Others: A Beowulfian Praise Song." In *Old English Studies in Honour of John C. Pope*, ed. by R.B. Burlin and E.B. Irving Jr., 91–106. Toronto, 1974.

Bieler, Ludwig, ed. and trans. *The Irish Penitentials*. Scriptores Latini Hiberniae 5. Dublin, 1963.

Bintliff, John, and Helena Hamerow, eds. *Europe Between Late Antiquity and the Middle Ages*. BAR International Series 617 London, 1995.

Blair, John. "Anglo-Saxon Minsters: A Topographical Review." In *Pastoral Care before the Parish*, ed. Blair and Sharpe, 226–66.

———. "Churches in the Early English Landscape: Social and Cultural Contexts." In *Church Archaeology—Research directions for the Future*, ed. John Blair and C. Pyrah, 6–18. CBA Research Report 104. York, 1996.

———. "Palaces or Minsters?–Northampton and Cheddar reconsidered." *Anglo-Saxon England* 25 (1996), 97–121.

———. *The Church in Anglo-Saxon Society.* Oxford, 2005.

Blair, John, and Richard Sharpe, eds. *Pastoral Care before the Parish.* Leicester, 1992.

Blair, Peter Hunter. "Whitby as a Centre of Learning in the Seventh Century." In *Learning and Literature in Anglo-Saxon England: Studies Presented to Peter Clemoes on the Occasion of his Sixty-Fifth Birthday,* ed. Michael Lapidge and Helmut Gneuss, 3–32. Cambridge, 1985.

Blake, N. F. "Cædmon's Hymn." *Notes and Queries* 207 (1962), 243–46.

Bloch, R. Howard, and Stephen G. Nichols, eds. *Medievalism and the Modernist Temper.* Baltimore, 1996.

Bloustein, Gerry. "On Not Dancing Like a 'Try Hard.'" Musical Visions : Selected Conference Proceedings from 6th National Australian/New Zealand IASPM and Inaugural Arnhem Land Performance Conference. Kent Town, Australia, 1999.

Boenig, Robert. "The Anglo-Saxon Harp." *Speculum,* 71 (1996), 290–320.

———. "Musical Instruments as Iconographical Artifacts in Medieval Poetry." In Perry, ed., *Material Culture and Cultural Materialisms,* 1–16.

Bonner, Gerald, ed. *Famulus Christi: Essays in Commemoration of the Thirteenth Centenary of the Birth of the Venerable Bede.* London, 1976.

Bourdieu, Pierre. *Outline of a Theory of Practice,* trans. Richard Nice. Cambridge, 1977.

Bourdillon, J., "The Animal Provisioning of Saxon Southampton." In *Environment and Economy in Anglo-Saxon England,* ed. Rackham, 120–25.

Brooke, Christopher. *The Monastic World 1000–1300.* New York, 1974

Brown, A. K. "The English Compass Points." *Medium Aevum* 47 (1978), 221–46.

Brown, George Hardin. *Bede the Educator.* Jarrow Lecture, 1996

———. "Old English Verse as a Medium for Christian Theology." In *Modes of Interpretation in Old English Literature*, ed. Phyllis Rugg Brown, Georgia Ronan Crampton, and Fred C. Robinson, 15–28. Toronto, 1986.

———. "The Psalms as the Foundation of Anglo-Saxon Learning." In *The Place of the Psalms in the Intellectual Culture of the Middle Ages*, ed. Nancy Van Deusen, 1–24. Albany, 1999.

Brown, M. and Okasha, E., "Inscribed Objects." In *Life and Economy at Early Medieval Flixborough*, ed. Loveluck and Evans. Chapter 3, in press.

Bruce-Mitford, Rupert. *The Sutton Hoo Ship Burial*, 3 vols. London, 1975, 1978, 1982.

Bruce-Mitford, Myrtle and Rupert. "The Musical Instrument." In *The Sutton Hoo Ship-Burial*, ed. Rupert Bruce-Mitford, 611–731. vol. 3.2. London, 1983.

Bühler, Pierre. *Présence, sentiment et rhétorique de la nature dans la littérature latine de la France médiévale de la fin de l'antiquité au XIIe siècle*. 2 vols. Paris, 1995.

Bullough, Donald. "The Educational Tradition in England from Alfred to Ælfric: Teaching utriusque linguae." *Settimane di Studio del centro Italiano di studi sull'alto medioevo* 19 (1972), 453–93.

Campbell, James. *Essays in Anglo-Saxon History*. London, 1986.

Carruthers, Mary. *The Book of Memory: A Study of Memory in Medieval Culture*. Cambridge Studies in Medieval Literature 10. Cambridge, 1990.

———. *The Craft of Thought. Meditation, Rhetoric, and the Making of Images, 400–1200*. Cambridge, 1998.

Carr, Robert D., Andrew Tester, and Peter Murphy. "The Middle Saxon Settlement at Staunch Meadow, Brandon." *Antiquity* 62, No. 235 (1988), 371–77.

Carver, M. O. H., ed. *The Age of Sutton Hoo: The Seventh Century in North-Western Europe*. Woodbridge, Suffolk, 1992.

Carver, Martin, and Cecily Spall. "Excavating a Parchmenerie: Archaeological Correlates of Making Parchment at the Pictish Monastery at Portmahomack, Easter Ross." *Proceedings of the Society of Antiquaries of Scotland* 134 (2004), 183–200.

Cavill, Paul. "The Manuscripts of Cædmon's Hymn." *Anglia* 118 (2000), 499–530.

———. "Bede and Cædmon's Hymn." "*Lastworda betst*": *Essays in Memory of Christine E. Fell, with her Unpublished Writings*, ed. C. Hough and K. A. Lowe, 1–17. Donington, England, 2002.

Certeau, Michel de. *The Practice of Everyday Life*, trans. Steven Rendall. Berkeley, 1984.

Clarke, Helen, and Björn Ambrosiani, *Towns in the Viking Age*, rev. ed. London:, 1995.

Conybeare, J. J. *Illustrations of Anglo-Saxon Poetry*. London, 1826.

Crabtree, Pam J. "Animal Exploitation in East Anglian Villages." In *Environment and Economy in Anglo-Saxon England*, ed. Rackham, 40–54.

———. "Production and Consumption in an Early Complex Society: Animal Use in Middle Saxon East Anglia." *World Archaeology* 28.1 (1996), 58–75.

Cramp, Rosemary J. *The British Academy Corpus of Anglo-Saxon Stone Sculpture. Vol. I: County Durham and Northumberland*, 2 parts. Oxford, 1984.

———. "Excavations at the Saxon Monastic Sites of Wearmouth and Jarrow, Co. Durham: An Interim Report." *Medieval Archaeology* 13 (1969), 21–66.

———. "Monastic Sites," and "Analysis of the Finds Register and Location Plan of Whitby Abbey." In *The Archaeology of Anglo-Saxon England*, ed. D. M. Wilson., 201–52, Appendix B, Appendix C.

———. "Monkwearmouth and Jarrow in their Continental Context." In *Churches Built in Ancient Times: Recent Studies in Early Christian archaeology*, ed. K. Painter, 279–94. London, 1994.

———. "A Reconsideration of the Monastic Site of Whitby." In *The Age of Migrating Ideas. Early Medieval Art in Northern Britain and Ireland*, ed. R. Michael Spearman and J. Higgitt, 64–73. Edinburgh, 1993.

———. *Wearmouth and Jarrow: Monastic Sites, Vol. 1*. Swindon, 2006.

Crépin, André. "Bede and the Vernacular." In *Famulus Christi*, ed. Bonner, 170–92.

Cunliffe, B. *Excavations at Portchester Castle, Volume II: Saxon London.* Report of the Research Committee of the Society of Antiquaries. London, 1976.

Daniels, Robin. "The Anglo-Saxon Monastery at Church Close, Hartlepool, Cleveland." *Archaeological Journal* 145 (1988), 158–210.

Daniels, Robin, and Loveluck, C. P., eds. *Anglo-Saxon Hartlepool and the Foundations of English Christianity. An Archaeology of the Anglo-Saxon Monastery.* Durham, in press.

Day, Virginia. "The Influence of the Catechetical *Narratio* on Old English and Some Other Medieval Literature." *Anglo-Saxon England* 3 (1974), 51–62.

DeGregorio, Scott. "Bede's *In Ezram et Neemiam*: A Document in Church Reform?" In *Bède le Vénérable: entre tradition et postérite*, ed. Stéphane Lebecq, Michel Perrin, and Olivier Szerwiniack, 97–107. Lille, 2005.

———. "Bede's In *Ezram et Neemiam* and the Reform of the Northumbrian Church." *Speculum* 79.1 (2004), 1–25.

———. "Footsteps of His Own: Bede's Commentary on Ezra-Nehemiah." In *Innovation and Tradition in the Writings of the Venerable Bede*, ed. DeGregorio, 143–68.

———, ed. *Innovation and Tradition in the Writings of the Venerable Bede.* Medieval European Series 7. Morgantown, WV, 2006.

———. "*Nostrorum socordiam temporum*: The Reforming Impulse of Bede's Later Exegesis." *Early Medieval Europe* 11.2 (2002), 107–22.

de Nie, Giselle. *Views from a Many-Windowed Tower: Studies of Imagination in the Works of Gregory of Tours.* Amsterdam, 1987.

———. *Word, Image, Experience: Dynamics of Miracle and Self-Perception in Sixth-Century Gaul.* Aldershot, 2003.

Dobbie, E. V. K. *The Manuscripts of Cædmon's Hymn and Bede's Death Song, with A Critical Edition of the "Epistola Cuthberti de obitu Bedae."* Columbia University Studies in English and Comparative Literature. New York, 1937.

Dobney, Keith, and Deborah Jaques. "Avian Signatures for Identity and Status in Anglo-Saxon England." *Acta zoologica cracoviensia* 45 (2002), 7–21.

Dobney, Keith, Deborah Jaques, J. Barrett, and C. Johnstone, *Farmers, Monks and Aristocrats. The Environmental Archaeology of an Anglo-Saxon Estate Centre at Flixborough, North Lincolnshire.* Excavations at Flixborough, vol. 3. Ed. C.P. Loveluck. Oxford, in press.

Dumville, D. N. "'Beowulf' and the Celtic World: The Uses of Evidence." *Traditio* 37 (1981), 109–60.

Dyer, Christopher. *Everyday Life in Medieval England.* London, 1994.

Early Medieval Corpus of Coin Finds and *Sylloge of Coins of the British Isles.* Fitzwilliam Museum, Cambridge. http://www.fitzmuseum.cam.ac.uk/dept/coins/emc/ (July 2006).

Eckenrode, Thomas R. "The Venerable Bede and the Pastoral Affirmation of the Christian Message in Anglo-Saxon England." *The Downside Review* 99 (1981), 258–78.

Effros, Bonnie. *Caring for Body and Soul: Burial and the Afterlife in the Merovingian World.* University Park, Penn., 2002.

Ettel, Peter. "Karlburg—Entwicklung eines königlich-bischöflichen Zentralortes am Main mit Burg und Talsiedlung vom 7. Bis zum 13. Jahrhundert." *Château Gaillard* 18 (1998), 75–85.

Fletcher, Richard A. *The Barbarian Conversion.* Berkeley and Los Angeles, 1999.

Fontaine, Jacques. *Isidore de Séville et la culture classique dans l'Espagne wisigothique.* 2 vols. Paris, 1959.

Foot, Sarah. "Parochial Ministry in Early Anglo-Saxon England: The Role of the Monastic Communities." In *The Ministry: Clerical and Lay*, ed. W. J. Sheils and Diana Wood, 43–54. Studies in Church History 26. Oxford, 1989.

Förster, Max. "Beiträge zur mittelalterlichen Volkskunde VIII. *Archiv* 129 (1912), 16–49.

Foucray, Bruno, and François Gentili. "Le village du Haut Moyen Age de Serris (Seine-et-Marne), lieudit "Les Ruelles" (VIIe-Xe siècle)." In *L'Habitat Rural du Haut Moyen Age (France, Pays-Bas, Danemark et Grande-Bretagne)*, ed. Claude Lorren and Patrick Périn, pp. 139–43. Condé-sur-Noireau, 1995.

———. "Serris—Chapelle cimétériale des Ruelles." In *Les premiers monuments chrétiens de la France*, ed. Noel Duval, vol. 3, 198–200. Paris, 1998.

Frank, Roberta. "The Search for the Anglo-Saxon Oral Poet." T. Northcote Toller Memorial Lecture. *Bulletin of the John Rylands University Library* 75 (1993), 11–36.

Frankis, P. J. "The Thematic Significance of *enta geweorc* and Related Imagery in 'The Wanderer.'" *Anglo-Saxon England* 2 (1973), 253–69.

Frantzen, Allen J. *Before the Closet: Same-sex Love from "Beowulf" to "Angels in America."* Chicago, 1998.

———. *Desire for Origins: New Language, Old English and Teaching the Tradition*. New Brunswick, 1990.

———. *The Literature of Penance in Anglo-Saxon England*. New Brunswick, 1983.

Frantzen, Allen J., ed. *Speaking Two Languages: Traditional Disciplines and Contemporary Theory in Medieval Studies*. Albany, 1991.

Frantzen, Allen J., and John D. Niles, eds. *The Construction of Social Identity in Anglo-Saxon England*. Gainesville, 1997.

Friedman, John Block. "The Architect's Compass in Creation Miniatures of the Later Middle Ages." *Traditio* 30 (1974), 419–29.

Fritz, Donald W. "Cædmon: A Monastic Exegete." *American Benedictine Review* 25:3 (1974), 351–63.

———. "Cædmon: A Traditional Christian Poet." *Mediaeval Studies* 31 (1969), 334–37.

Fry, Donald K. "Cædmon as a Formulaic Poet." *Forum for Modern Language Studies* 10 (1974), 227–47. Reprinted in *Oral Literature: Seven Essays*, ed. J. J. Duggan, 41–61. Edinburgh, 1975.

———. "The Memory of Cædmon." In *Oral Traditional Literature: A Festschrift for Albert Bates Lord*, ed. John Miles Foley, 282–93. Columbus, 1981.

———. "Old English Formula Statistics." *In Geardagum* 3 (1979), 1–6.

Fulk, R. D. *A History of Old English Meter*. Philadelphia, 1992.

Galinié, H. "Tours from an Archaeological Standpoint." In *Spaces of the Living and the Dead: An Archaeological Dialogue*, ed. Catherine Karkov, Kelly Wickham-Crowley, and Bailey Young, 87–105. American Early Medieval Studies 3. Oxford, 1999.

Garde, Judith N. *Old English Poetry in Medieval Christian Perspective: a Doctrinal Approach*. Cambridge, 1991.

Gardiner, Mark. "Economy and Landscape Change in Post-Roman and Early Medieval Sussex, 450–1175." In *The Archaeology of Sussex to AD 2000*, ed. Rudling, 153–54.

———. "The Exploitation of Sea Mammals in Medieval England: Bones and their Social Context." *Archaeological Journal* 154 (1997), 173–95.

Gardiner, M., et al. "Continental Trade and Non-Urban Ports in Mid-Saxon England. Excavations at Sandtun, West Hythe, Kent." *Archaeological Journal* 158 (2001), 161–290.

Gatch, Milton McC. "King Alfred's Version of Augustine's *Soliloquia*: Some Suggestions on its Rationale and Unity." In *Studies in Earlier Old English Prose*, ed. Szarmach, 17–45.

Gates, Tim. "Yeavering and Air Photography: Discovery and Interpretation." In Paul Frodsham and Colm O'Brien, eds.

Yeavering: People, Power, Place. Stroud, Gloucestershire, 2005, 65-83.

Gates, Tim, and Colm O'Brien. "Cropmarks at Milfield and New Bewick and the recognition of Grubenhäuser in Northumberland." *Archaeologia Aeliana*, 5th Series, No. 16 (1988), 1–9.

Glass, Dorothy. "*In Principio*: The Creation in the Middle Ages." In *Approaches to Nature in the Middle Ages*, ed. Lawrence D. Roberts, 67–104. Binghamton, 1982.

Grant, Annie. "The Animal Bones." In *Excavations at Portchester Castle, Volume II*, ed. Cunliffe, 262–87.

Godden, Malcolm. "King Alfred's Preface and the Teaching of Latin in Anglo-Saxon England." *English Historical Review* 117 (2002), 596–604.

Goffart, Walter. *The Narrators of Barbarian History*. Princeton, 1988.

———. "The *Historia Ecclesiastica*: Bede's Agenda and Ours." *Haskin's Society Journal* 2 (1990), 29–45.

———. "Bede's History in a Harsher Climate." In *Innovation and Tradition in the Writings of the Venerable Bede*, ed. DeGregorio, 203–26.

Gneuss, Helmut. *Hymnar und Hymnen im englischen Mittelalter: Studien zur Überlieferung, Glossierung und Übersetzung lateinischer Hymnen in England*. Tübingen, 1968.

Grant, Annie. "The Animal Bones." In *Excavations at Portchester Castle, Volume II: Saxon*, ed. Cunliffe, 262–87.

Green, Barbara, and Andrew Rogerson. *The Anglo-Saxon Cemetery at Bergh Apton, Norfolk*. East Anglian Archaeology 7. Gressenhall, 1978.

Green, Barbara, Andrew Rogerson, and Susan G. White, *The Anglo-Saxon Cemetery at Morning Thorpe, Norfolk*. East Anglian Archaeology 36, 2 vols. Gressenhall, 1987.

Green, Donald H. *The Carolingian Lord: Semantic Studies on Four Old High German Words: Balder, Frô, Trahtin, Hêrro*. Cambridge, 1965.

Green, Francis J. "Cereals and Plant Food: A Reassessment of the Saxon Economic Evidence from Wessex." In *Environment and Economy in Anglo-Saxon England,* ed. Rackham, 83–88.
Greenfield, Stanley B., and Daniel G. Calder. *A New Critical History of Old English Literature.* New York, 1986.
Griffith, M. S. "Poetic Language and the Paris Psalter: The Decay of the Old English Tradition." *Anglo-Saxon England* 20 (1991), 167–86.
Gurevich, Aron. *Medieval Popular Culture: Problems of Belief and Perception,* trans. János M. Bak and Paul A. Hollingsworth. Cambridge, 1988.

Haas-Gebhard, B. *Die Insel Wörth im Staffelsee.* Stuttgart, 2000.
Hagen, Ann. *A Handbook of Anglo-Saxon Food and Drink: Processing and Consumption.* Norfolk, 1992.
———. *A Second Handbook of Anglo-Saxon Food and Drink: Production and Distribution.* Norfolk, 1995.
Hamerow, Helena. *Early Medieval Settlements: The Archaeology of Rural Communities in North-West Europe 400–900.* Oxford, 2002.
Hamerow, Helena, and Arthur MacGregor, eds. *Image and Power in the Archaeology of Early Medieval Britain—Essays in honour of Rosemary Cramp.* Oxford, 2001.
Hårdh, Birgitta, and Lars Larsson, eds. *Central Places in the Migration and Merovingian Periods.* Acta Archaeologica Lundensia Ser. in 8°, Uppåkrastudier 6. Stockholm, 2002.
Herlihy, David. *Medieval Households.* Cambridge, 1985.
Henderson, George. *Vision and Image in Early Christian England.* Cambridge, 1999.
Hieatt, C. B. "Cædmon in Context: Transforming the Formula." *Journal of English and Germanic Philology* 84 (1985), 485–97.
Higham, N. J. *The Kingdom of Northumbria A.D. 350–1100.* Stroud, Gloucestershire, 1993.
———. *(Re-)Reading Bede: The "Ecclesiastical History" in Context.* London, 2006.

Hill, David, and Robert Cowie, eds. *Wics: The Early Medieval Trading Centres of Northern Europe*. Sheffield, 2001.

Hill, Peter. *Whithorn and St Ninian—The Excavation of a Monastic Town 1984–91*. Stroud, Gloucestershire, 1997.

Hiller, Jonathan, Daved Petts, and Tim Allen. "Discussion of the Anglo-Saxon Archaeology." In *Gathering the People, Settling the Land—The Archaeology of a Middle Thames Landscape, Anglo-Saxon to Post-medieval*, ed. Stuart Foreman, Jonthan Hiller, and David Petts, 57–72. Oxford, 2002.

Hines, John. "Trading Places: Royalty and Urbanism in Norse Literature." In *Sagas and the Norwegian Experience*. Papers of the Tenth International Saga Conference, 263–70. Trondheim, 1997.

———. "North Sea Trade and the Proto-Urban Sequence." *Archaeologia Polona*, 32 (1994), 7–26.

Hines, John, ed. *The Anglo-Saxons: From the Migration Period to the Eighth Century, an Ethnographic Perspective*. Woodbridge, Suffolk, 1997.

Hines, John. *Voices in the Past: English Literature and Archaeology*. Cambridge, 2004.

Hinton, D. A. *Archaeology, Economy and Society: England from the Fifth to the Fifteenth Century*. London, 1990.

Holsinger, Bruce W. *Music, Body, and Desire of Medieval Culture*. Stanford, 2001.

Holt, B. F. *Joseph Williams and the Pioneer Mission to the South-Eastern Bantu*. The Lovedale Historical Series. Lovedale, Cape Province (South Africa), 1954.

Hope-Taylor, Brian. *Yeavering—An Anglo-British Centre of Early Northumbria*. Department of the Environment Archaeology Report 7. London, 1977.

Howlett, D.R. "The Theology of Cædmon's Hymn." *Leeds Studies in English* 7 (1973–1974), 1–12.

Hume, K. "The Concept of the Hall in Old English Poetry." *Anglo-Saxon England* 3 (1974), 63–74.

Huppé, B. F. "Cædmon's Hymn." In *Old English Literature: Twenty-two Analytical Essays*, ed. Martin Stevens and Jerome Mandel, 117–38. Lincoln, Neb., 1968.

Huppé, Bernard. *Doctrine and Poetry: Augustine's Influence on Old English Poetry*. Albany, 1959.

Hutchinson, F. E. *Henry Vaughan: A Life and Interpretation*. Oxford, 1947.

Illmer, Detlef. *Formen der Erziehung und Wissensvermittlung im frühen Mittelalter*. Münchener Beiträge zur Mediävistik und Renaissance-Forschung 7. Munich, 1971.

Inglebert, Hervé. *Interpretatio christiana. Les mutations des savoirs (cosmographie, géographie, ethnographie, histoire) dans l'antiquité chrétienne 30–630 après J.-C.* Paris, 2001.

Irvine, Martin. *The Making of Textual Culture: "Grammatica" and Literary Theory 350–1100*. Cambridge Studies in Medieval Literature 19. Cambridge, 1994.

Isaac, G. R. "The Date and Origin of Cædmon's Hymn." *Neuphilologische Mitteilungen* 98 (1997), 217–28.

Jenni, E. "Zu den doxologischen Schlußformeln des Psalters." *Theologische Zeitschrift* 40 (1984), 114–20.

Jobey, George. "Excavations at the native settlement at Huckhoe, Northumberland, 1955–7." *Archaeologia Aeliana*, 4th Series, No 37 (1959), 217–78.

———. "Excavations at Tynemouth Priory and Castle." *Archaeologia Aeliana*, 4 ser. 45 (1967), 33–104.

———. "A Radiocarbon Date for the Palisaded Settlement at Huckhoe." *Archaeolgia Aeliana*, 4th Series, No 46 (1968), 293–95.

Jolly, Karen. "Father God and Mother Earth: Nature Mysticism in the Anglo-Saxon World." In *The Medieval World of Nature: a Book of Essays*, ed. Joyce E. Salisbury, 221–52. New York and London, 1993.

Jones, Putnam Fennell. *A Concordance to the Historia Ecclesiastica of Bede.* Cambridge, Mass., 1929.

Jordan, A. C. *Towards an African Literature: The Emergence of Literary Form in Xhosa.* Perspectives on Southern Africa, 6. Berkeley, 1973.

Jørgensen, Lars. "Manor and Market at Lake Tissø in the Sixth to Eleventh Centuries: The Danish 'Productive' Sites." In *Markets in Early Medieval Europe: Trading and "Productive" Sites, 650–850,* ed. Pestell and Ulmschneider, 175–207

Kane, George. "The Poetry of Cædmon," review of "The Poetry of Cædmon," by C. L. Wrenn. *Modern Language Review* 43 (1948), 250–52.

Karkov, Catherine E., and Fred Orton, eds. *Theorizing Anglo-Saxon Stone Sculpture.* Medieval European Studies 4. Morgantown, 2003.

Kelly, Susan E. "Eighth-Century Trading Privileges from Anglo-Saxon England." *Early Medieval Europe,* 1 (1992), 3–28.

Ker, N. R. *Catalogue of Manuscripts containing Anglo-Saxon.* Oxford, 1957.

Kieckhefer, Richard. *Magic in the Middle Ages.* Cambridge, 1988.

Kiernan, Kevin S. "Reading Cædmon's Hymn with Someone Else's Glosses." *Representations* 32 (1990), 157–74. Reprinted in *Old English Literature: Critical Essays,* ed. Liuzza, 102–24.

———, ed. 1999. *The Electronic Beowulf.* London, 1999.

Kirby, David. "Northumbria in the Time of Wilfrid." In *Saint Wilfrid at Hexham,* ed. D. P. Kirby, 1–34. Newcastle upon Tyne, 1974.

Klaeber, Fr. "Die christlichen Elemente im Beowulf." *Anglia* 35 (1911), 111–36.

———. "Analogues of the Story of Cædmon." *Modern Language Notes* 42 (1927), 390.

Klein, Julie Thompson. *Crossing Boundaries: Knowledge, Disciplinarities, and Interdisciplinarities.* Charlottesville, 1996.

———. *Mapping Interdisciplinary Studies.* New York, 1999.

Kleiner, Yu. "The Singer and the Interpreter: Cædmon and Bede." *Germanic Notes* 19 (1988), 2–6.

Kraus, Henry. *The Living Theatre of Medieval Art.* Bloomington, 1967.

Lang, James. *The British Academy Corpus of Anglo-Saxon Stone Sculpture. Vol. VI: Northern Yorkshire.* Oxford, 2001.

Lapidge, Michael. "The Anglo-Latin Background." In *A New Critical History of Old English Literature,* ed. Greenfield and Calder, 6–37. Reprinted in *Anglo-Latin Literature: 600–899.* London, 1996.

Lapidge, Michael. *Bede the Poet.* Jarrow Lecture, 1993. Reprinted in *Bede and His World: The Jarrow Lectures,* 2: 929–56. 2 vols. Aldershot, 1994.

———. "Ideas of Natural Order in Early Medieval Latin Poetry." PhD diss., University of Toronto, 1971.

Latour, Bruno. *We Have Never Been Modern.* Cambridge, Mass., 1993.

Lattuca, Lisa. *Creating Interdisciplinarity: Interdisciplinary Research and Teaching Among College and University Faculty.* Nashville, 2001.

Lavezzo, Kathy. "Chaucer and Everyday Death: *The Clerk's Tale,* Burial, and the Subject of Poverty." *Studies in the Age of Chaucer* 23 (2001), 255–87.

Leahy, Kevin. "Middle Anglo-Saxon Lincolnshire: An Emerging Picture." In *Markets in Early Medieval Europe,* ed. Pestell and Ulmschneider, 138–54.

Leclercq, Jean. *The Love of Learning and the Desire for God.* Trans. Catherine Misrahi. 3rd. ed. New York, 1982.

Lee, Alvin A. *The Guest-Hall of Eden: Four Essays on the Design of Old English Poetry.* New Haven and London, 1972.

Leeds, E. T., and D. B. Harden. *The Anglo-Saxon Cemetery at Abingdon, Berkshire.* Oxford, 1936.

Lees, Clare A., and Gillian R. Overing. "Birthing Bishops and Fathering Poets: Bede, Hild, and the Relations of Cultural

Production." *Exemplaria* 6 (1994), 35–65. Reprinted in *Old English Literature: Critical Essays*, ed. Liuzza, 124–56.

Lefebvre, Henri. *Everyday Life in the Modern World*, trans. Allen Lane. 1968; New York, 1971.

Lehman, W. P. *The Development of Germanic Verse Form.* New York, 1971.

Lerer, Seth. *Literacy and Power in Anglo-Saxon Literature.* Lincoln, 1991.

Lester, G. A. "The Cædmon Story and its Analogues." *Neophilologus* 58 (1974), 225–37.

Lingard, John. *The Antiquities of the Anglo-Saxon Church*, 2 vols. Newcastle, 1806.

Lings, M. *Muhammad: His Life Based on the Earliest Sources.* New York, 1983.

W. P. Lehman, *The Development of Germanic Verse Form.* New York, 1971.

Liuzza, Roy M. "The Tower of Babel: The Wanderer and The Ruins of History." *Studies in the Literary Imagination* 36 (2003), 1–35.

———, ed. *Old English Literature: Critical Essays.* New Haven and London, 2002.

Lord, A. B. *The Singer of Tales.* Ed. S. A. Mitchell and G. Nagy, 2nd ed. Cambridge, Mass., 2000.

Louis, E. "Archéologie des bâtiments monastiques, VIIème—IXème siècles: Le cas de Hamage (France, Département du Nord)." In *Religion and Belief in Medieval Europe*, Papers of the Medieval Europe Brugge 1997 Conference, vol. 4, ed. G. De Boe and F. Verhaeghe, 55–63. Zellik, 1997.

Loveluck, C. P. "Anglo-Saxon Hartlepool and the Foundations of English Christian Identity: the Wider Context and Importance of the Monastery." In Daniels and Loveluck, *Anglo-Saxon Hartlepool*, chapter 10 (in press).

———. "L'habitat anglo-saxon de Flixborough: dynamiques sociales et styles de vie (VIIe-XIe siècle)." *Les Nouvelles de l'Archéologie* 92, 2e trimestre, (2003), 16–20.

———. "A High-status Anglo-Saxon Settlement at Flixborough, Lincolnshire." *Antiquity* 72, No. 275 (1998), 146–61.

———. "The Romano-British to Anglo-Saxon Transition: Social Transformations from the Late Roman to Early Medieval Period in Northern England, A.D. 400–700." In *Past, Present and Future—The Archaeology of Northern England*, ed. C. Brooks, R. Daniels and A. Harding, 127–48. Architectural and Archaeological Society of Durham and Northumberland Research Report 5. Durham, 2002.

———. "Rural Settlement Hierarchy in the Age of Charlemagne." In *Charlemagne: Empire and Society*, ed. J. Story, 230–58. Manchester, 2005.

———, ed. *Rural Settlement, Lifestyles and Social Change in the later First Millennium AD*. Excavations at Flixborough, vol. 4. Oxford, forthcoming.

———. "*Terres Noires* and Early Medieval Rural Settlement Sequences: Conceptual Problems, Descriptive Limitations and Deposit Diversity." In *Terres Noires-Dark Earth. Collection D'Archéologie Jospeh Mertens* 14, ed. Laurent Verslype and Raymond Brulet, 86–96. Louvain-la-Neuve, 2004.

———. "Wealth, Waste and Conspicuous Consumption: Flixborough and its Importance for Middle and Late Saxon Rural Settlement Studies." In *Image and Power in the Archaeology of Early Medieval Britain*, ed. Hamerow and MacGregor, 78–130.

Loveluck, C. P., and Daniel Atkinson. *The Early Medieval Settlement Remains from Flixborough, Lincolnshire: The Occupation Sequence, c. A.D. 600–1000*. Excavations at Flixborough, vol. 1. Oxford, in press.

Loveluck, C. P., and David H. Evans, eds. *Life and Economy at Early Medieval Flixborough: The Artefact Evidence*. Excavations at Flixborough, vol. 2. Oxford, in press.

Lubac, H. de. *Exégèse médiévale: Les quatre sens de l'Écriture*. Paris, 1964.

Lucas, P.J. "Loyalty and Obedience in the Old English Genesis and the Interpolation of Genesis B into Genesis A." *Neophilologus* 76 (1992), 121–35.

Magennis, Hugh. *Images of Community in Old English Poetry.* Cambridge Studies in Anglo-Saxon England 18. Cambridge, 1993.

Magoun, Francis P. "Bede's Story of Cædmon: The Case History of an Anglo-Saxon Singer." *Speculum* 30 (1955), 49–63.

Manby, Terry. *Excavations at Thwing, East Yorkshire.* London, forthcoming.

May, Herbert G., and Bruce M. Metzger, ed. and trans., *The Oxford Annotated Bible* New York, 1962.

McCormick, F., "The Animal Bones from Ditch 1," in John Barber, "Excavations on Iona, 1979," *Proceedings of the Society of Antiquaries of Scotland* 111 (1981), 313–18.

McCormick, F. and Murphy, E. "The Animal Bones." In *Whithorn and St Ninian. The Excavation of a Monastic Town 1984–91*, ed. Peter Hill, 605–13. Stroud, 1997.

McCready, William D. "Bede, Isidore, and the *Epistola Cuthberti.*" *Traditio* 50 (1995), 75–94.

McKitterick, Rosamund. *The Carolingians and the Written Word.* Cambridge, 1989.

Meyvaert, Paul. "Bede the Scholar," in *Famulus Christi*, ed. Bonner, 40–69.

———. "The Date of Bede's *In Ezram* and His Image of Ezra in the Codex Amiatinus." *Speculum* 80 (2005), 1087–1133.

Miletich, John S. "The Quest for 'The Formula': A Comparative Reappraisal" *Modern Philology* 74 (1976–77), 111–23.

Mitchell, Bruce, and Fred C. Robinson, eds. *Beowulf.* Oxford, 1998.

———. *A Guide to Old English*, 6th ed. Oxford, 2001.

Morland, L. "Cædmon and the Germanic Tradition." In *De gustibus: Essays for Alain Renoir*, eds. J. M. Foley, J. C. Womack, and W. A. Womack, 324–58. Garland Reference Library of the Humanities, 1482. New York, 1992.

Morris, Richard. *Churches in the Landscape*. London, 1989.

———. *The Church In British Archaeology*. CBA Report no. 47. London, 1983.

Morrish, Jennifer. "King Alfred's Letter as a Source on Learning in England in the Ninth Century." In *Studies in Earlier Old English Prose*, ed. Szarmach, 87–107.

Morse, Ruth. *Truth and Convention in the Middle Ages: Rhetoric, Representation, and Reality*. Cambridge, 1991.

Naylor, John. *An Archaeology of Trade in Middle Saxon England*. BAR British Series 376. Oxford: 2004.

Neville, Jennifer. *Representations of the Natural World in Old English Poetry*. Cambridge Studies in Anglo-Saxon England 27. Cambridge, 1999.

Niles, John D. "Bede's Cædmon, 'The Man Who Had No Story' (Irish Tale-Type 2412B)." *Folklore* 117 (2006), 141–55.

———, ed. *Old English Literature in Context: Ten Essays*. Cambridge and Totowa, 1980.

O'Brien, Colm, and Roger Miket. "The Early Medieval Settlement of Thirlings, Northumberland." *Durham Archaeological Journal* 7 (1991), 57–91.

Obrist, Barbara. "La représentation carolingienne du zodiaque. À propos du manuscrit de Bâle, Universitätsbibliothek, F III 15a." *Cahiers de civilisation médievalé* 44 (2001), 3–33.

O'Connor, Terry P. "Bones from 46–54 Fishergate." *The Archaeology of York*, vol. 15: *The Animal Bones*, fasc. 4. London, 1991.

O'Connor, T.P. "8th-11th century economy and environment in York." In *Environment and Economy in Anglo-Saxon England*, ed. Rackham, 136–47.

O'Donnell, Daniel Paul. *Cædmon's Hymn: A Multi-Media Study, Edition and Archive*. SEENET Series A, vol. 7. Woodbridge, Suffolk, 2005.

O'Keeffe, Katherine O'Brien. "Orality and the Developing Text of Cædmon's Hymn." In *Old English Literature: Critical Essays*, ed. Liuzza, 79–101.

———. *Visible Song. Transitional Literacy in Old English Verse.* Cambridge Studies in Anglo-Saxon England 4. Cambridge, 1990.

Olsen, Bjørnar. "Material Culture after Text: Re-Membering Things." *Norwegian Archaeological Review* 36 (2003), 87–104.

Opland, Jeff. *Anglo-Saxon Oral Poetry: A Study of the Tradition.* New Haven, 1980.

———. "Cædmon and Ntsikana: Anglo-Saxon and Xhosa Traditional Poets." *Annals of the Grahamstown Historical Society* 2 (1977), 56–65.

———. "From Horseback to Monastic Cell: The Impact on English Literature of the Introduction of Writing." In *Old English Literature in Context: Ten Essays*, ed. Niles, 30–43.

Orchard, Andy. *The Poetic Art of Aldhelm.* Cambridge Studies in Anglo-Saxon England, 8. Cambridge, 1994.

Orton, Fred. "Rethinking the Ruthwell and Bewcastle Monuments: Some Strictures on Similarity; Some Questions of History." In *Theorizing Anglo-Saxon Stone Sculpture*, ed. Karkov and Orton, 65–92.

Orton, P. R. "Cædmon and Christian Poetry." *Neuphilologische Mitteilungen* 84 (1983), 163–70.

O'Sullivan, D., "Space, Silence and Shortage on Lindisfarne: the Archaeology of Asceticism." In *Image and Power in the Archaeology of Early Medieval Britain*, ed. Hamerow and MacGregor, 33–52.

O'Sullivan, Dierdre, and Robert Young. *English Heritage Book of Lindisfarne Holy Island.* London, 1995.

Palgrave, Francis. *History of England: Anglo-Saxon Period.* London, 1831.

Panovsky, Erwin, and Gerda Panofsky-Soergel, eds., *Abbot Suger: On the Abbey Church of St. Denis and Its Art Treasures*, 2nd ed. Princeton, 1979.

Peers, C. R. and C.A. Ralegh Radford, "The Saxon Monastery of Whitby." *Archaeologia* 89 (1943), 27–88.

Pelaprat, Delphine. "Un exemple de vie monastique en Anjou aux XIe et XIIe siècles: Le réseau des prieurés angevins de Saint-Florent de Saumur." *Fontevraud Histoire-Archéologie* 1 (1992), 53–71.

Pelteret, David A. E. *Slavery in Early Medieval England.* Woodbridge, 1995.

Perry, D. R., *Castle Park, Dunbar—Two Thousand Years on a Fortified Headland.* Society of Antiquaries of Scotland Monograph 16. Edinburgh 2000.

Perry, Curtis, ed. *Material Culture and Cultural Materialisms.* Turnhout, 2001.

Pestell, Tim. "The Afterlife of 'Productive' Sites in East Anglia." In *Markets in Early Medieval Europe*, ed. Pestell and Ulmschneider, 122–37.

———. *Landscapes of Monastic Foundation: The Establishment of Religious Houses in East Anglia, c.650–1200.* Woodbridge, 2004.

Pestell, Tim, and Katharina Ulmschneider, eds., *Markets in Early Medieval Europe: Trading and "Productive" Sites, 650–850.* Macclesfield, 2003.

Pope, John C., ed. *Seven Old English Poems.* Indianapolis, 1966.

Pound, Louise. "Cædmon's Dream Song." In *Studies in English Philology: A Miscellany in Honor of Frederick Klaeber*, ed. Kempe Malone and M. B. Ruud, 232–39. Minneapolis, 1929.

Rackham, James, ed. *Environment and Economy in Anglo-Saxon England: A Review of Recent Work on the Environmental Archaeology of Rural and Urban Anglo-Saxon Settlements in England.* CBA Research Report 89. York, 1994.

Rahtz, Philip. "The Building Plan of the Anglo-Saxon Monastery of Whitby Abbey." In *The Archaeology of Anglo-Saxon England*, ed. Wilson, 459–62.

———. *The Saxon and Medieval Palaces at Cheddar.* Ed. S. M. Hirst. BAR British Series 65. Oxford, 1979.

———. *Glastonbury*. London, 1993.
Ray, Roger. "Bede's *Vera Lex Historiae*." *Speculum* 55 (1980), 1–21.
———. "Bede and Cicero." *Anglo-Saxon England* 16 (1986), 1–15.
———. *Bede, Rhetoric, and the Creation of Christian Latin Culture*. Jarrow Lecture, 1997
———. "Who Did Bede Think He Was?" In *Innovation and Tradition in the Writings of the Venerable Bede*, ed. DeGregorio, 11–35.
Riché, Pierre. *Education and Culture in the Barbarian West from the Sixth through the Eighth Century*. Trans. John J. Contreni. Columbia, 1978.
Remley, Paul G. *Old English Biblical Verse: Studies in Genesis, Exodus and Daniel*. Cambridge Studies in Anglo-Saxon England 16. Cambridge, 1996.
Roberts, Jane. "Anglo-Saxon Vocabulary as a Reflection of Material Culture." In *The Age of Sutton Hoo: The Seventh Century in North-Western Europe*, ed. M. O. H. Carver, 185–202. Woodbridge, Suffolk, 1992.
Robinson, Fred. *Beowulf and the Appositive Style*. The Hodges Lectures. Knoxville, 1985.
———. "'Bede's' Envoi to the Old English *History*: An Experiment in Editing." *Studies in Philology* 78 (1981), 4-19, also published in *Anglo-Saxon Studies*, ed. Joseph S. Wittig. Chapel Hill, 1981.
———. "Old English Literature in its Most Immediate Context." In *Old English Literature in Context*, ed. Niles, 11–29.
Rogerson, Andrew. "Six Middle Anglo-Saxon Sites in West Norfolk." In *Markets in Early Medieval Europe. Trading and "Productive" Sites, 650–850*, ed. Pestell and Ulmschneider, 110–21.
Rudling, David, ed. *The Archaeology of Sussex to AD 2000*. Norfolk, 2003.
Ruffing, John. "The Labor Structure of Ælfric's *Colloquy*." In *The Work of Work: Servitude, Slavery, and Labor in Medieval England*,

ed. Allen J. Frantzen and Douglas Moffat, 55–70. Glasgow, 1994.

Russell, James C. *The Germanization of Early Medieval Christianity.* New York and Oxford, 1994.

Savage, Anne. "The Old English *Exodus* and the Colonization of the Promised Land." *New Medieval Literatures* 4 (2001), 39–60.

Sawyer, Peter. "Early Fairs and Markets in England and Scandinavia." In *The Market in History,* ed. B. L. Anderson and A. J. H. Latham, 59–77. London, 1986.

Schiffer, Michael B. *Formation Processes of the Archaeological Record.* Albuquerque, 1987.

Schrader, R. J. "Cædmon and the Monks: The Beowulf-Poet and Literary Continuity in the Early Middle Ages." *American Benedictine Review* 31 (1980), 39–69.

Schwab, Ute. "The Miracles of Cædmon." *English Studies* 64 (1983), 1–17.

Shepherd, G. "The Prophetic Cædmon." *Review of English Studies,* n.s. 5 (1954), 113–22.

Scull, Christopher J. "Approaches to Material Culture and Social Dynamics of the Migrration Period in Eastern England." In *Europe Between Late Antiquity and the Middle Ages,* ed. Bintliff and Hamerow, pp. 71–83.

———. "Urban Centres in pre-Viking England?" In *The Anglo-Saxons from the Migration Period to the Eighth Century,* ed. Hines, 269–310.

See, Klaus von. "Cædmon und Muhammed," *Zeitschrift für deutsches Altertum und deutsche Literatur* 112 (1983), 225–33.

Shippey, T. A. *Old English Verse.* London, 1972.

Sims-Williams, Patrick. *Religion and Literature in Western England 600–800.* Cambridge Studies in Anglo-Saxon England 3. Cambridge, 1990.

Skre, Dagfinn, ed. *Kaupang in Skiringssal.* Kaupang Excavation Project Publication Series I. Aarhus, 2007.

Smith, Ian M., "Patterns of Settlement and Land Use of the Late Anglian Period in the Tweed Basin." In *Studies in Late Anglo-Saxon Settlement*, ed. M.L. Faull, 177–96. Oxford, 1984.

Smyth, Marina. *Understanding the Universe in Seventh-Century Ireland*. Studies in Celtic History 15. Woodbridge, 1996.

Souter, Alexander. *A Glossary of Later Latin to 600 A.D.* Oxford, 1949.

Stanley, E. G. "New Formulas for Old: Cædmon's Hymn." In *Pagans and Christians: The Interplay between Christian Latin and Traditional Germanic Cultures in Early Medieval Europe*, ed. T. Hofstra, L. A. R. J. Houwen, and A. A. McDonald, 131–48. Groningen, 1995.

———. "St Cædmon." *Notes and Queries* 243 (1998), 4–5.

Stenton, Sir Frank. *Anglo-Saxon England*, 3rd ed. Oxford, 1971.

Story, Joanne. *Carolingian Connections. Anglo-Saxon England and Carolingian Francia, c. 750–870*. Aldershot, 2003.

Sweet, Henry, ed. *King Alfred's West-Saxon Version of Gregory's Pastoral Care*. Early English Text Society, O. S. 45, 50. London, 1871; repr. New York, 1973.

Szarmach, Paul E., ed. *Studies in Earlier Old English Prose: Sixteen Original Contributions*. Albany, 1986.

Taylor, Paul Beekman. "Heorot, Earth and Asgard: Christian Poetry and Pagan Myth." *Tennessee Studies in Literature* 11 (1966), 119–43.

Taylor, H.M. "The Architectural Interest of Æthelwulf's *De Abbatibus*." *Anglo-Saxon England* 3 (1974), 164–73.

Thacker, Alan. "Bede's Ideal of Reform." In *Ideal and Reality in Frankish and Anglo-Saxon Society: Studies Presented to J. M. Wallace-Hadrill*, ed. Patrick Wormald et al., 130–53. Oxford, 1983.

———. "Monks, Preaching and Pastoral Care." In *Pastoral Care Before the Parish*, ed. Blair and Sharpe. 137–70.

Thompson, Victoria. *Dying and Death in Later Anglo-Saxon England*. Anglo-Saxon Studies 4. Woodbridge, 2004.

Thrupp, John. *The Anglo-Saxon Home: A History of the Domestic Institutions and Customs of England from the Fifth to the Eleventh Century*. London, 1862.

Thundy, Zacharias P. "The Qur'ān: Source or Analogue of Bede's Cædmon Story?" *Islamic Culture* 63 (989), 105–10.

Tinniswood, Alision, and Anthony Harding, "Anglo-Saxon Occupation and Industrial Features in the Henge Monument at Yeavering, Northumberland." *Durham Archaeological Journal* 7 (1991), 93–108.

Ulmschneider, Katharina. "History, Archaeology, and the Isle of Wight in the Middle Saxon Period." *Medieval Archaeology* 43 (1999), 19–44.

———. "Settlement, Economy and the "Productive Site" in Anglo-Saxon Lincolnshire, A.D. 650–780." *Medieval Archaeology* 44 (2000), 53–79.

———. *Markets, Minsters and Metal-Detectors: The Archaeology of Middle Saxon Lincolnshire and Hampshire Compared*. BAR British Series 307 Oxford, 2000.

Ulriksen, Jens. "Danish Sites and Settlements with a Maritime Context, 200–1200." *Antiquity*, 68 (1994), 797–811.

———. *Anløbspladser: Besejling og Bebyggesle i Danmark mellem 200 og 1100 e.Kr.* Roskilde, 1998.

Valais, A. *Distré "Les Murailles" 49 123 008 AH (Maine-et-Loire)*. Série Fouilles, Tome 1. Nantes, 1997.

Van Der Walt, A. G. P. "The Homiliary of the Venerable Bede and Early Medieval Preaching" Ph.D. thesis, University of London, 1980.

Van Fleteren, Frederick. "St. Augustine, Neoplatonism, and the Liberal Arts: The Background to *De doctrina christiana*." In *De doctrina christiana: A Classic of Western Culture*, ed. Duane W. H. Arnold and Pamela Bright, 14–24. Christianity and Judaism in Antiquity 9. Notre Dame, 1995.

Wade, Keith. "A Settlement at Bonhunt Farm, Wicken Bonhunt, Essex." In *Archaeology in Essex to A.D. 1500*, ed. D. G. Buckley, 96–102. CBA Research Report 34. London, 1980.

Wallis, Faith. "Images of Order in the Medieval Computus." In *Ideas of Order in the Middle Ages*, ed. Warren Ginsberg, 45–67. Acta 15. Binghamton, 1990.

———. "'Number Mystique' in Early Medieval Computus Texts." In *Mathematics and the Divine: a Historical Study*, ed. Tuen Koetsier and L. Bergmans, 181–99. Amsterdam, 2005.

———. "*Si naturam quaeras*: Reframing Bede's 'Science.'" In *Innovation and Tradition in the Writings of the Venerable Bede*, ed. DeGregorio, 65–99.

Walpole, A. S., and A. J. Mason, *Early Latin Hymns*. Cambridge, 1922.

Ward, Benedicta. *Bede and the Psalter*. Jarrow Lecture, 1991. Reprinted in *Bede and His World: The Jarrow Lectures*, 2: 869–902. 2 vols. Aldershot, 1994.

———. "Miracles and History: A Reconsideration of the Miracle Stories Used by Bede." In *Famulus Christi*, ed. Bonner, 70–76.

———. *The Venerable Bede*. Cistercian Studies Series 169. Kalamazoo, 1998.

Wehlau, Ruth. *The Riddle of Creation: Metaphorical Structures in Old English Poetry*. New York, 1997.

———. "Rumination and Re-creation: Poetic Instruction in *The Order of the World*." *Florilegium* 13 (1994), 65–77.

West, Philip J. "Rumination in Bede's Account of Cædmon," *Monastic Studies* 12 (1976), 217–26.

Whitwell, Ben. "Flixborough," *Current Archaeology* 126, vol. 11, no. 6 (1991), 244–47.

Wickham, Chris. *Framing the Early Middle Ages: Europe and the Mediterranean, 400–800*. Oxford, 2005.

Wieland, Gernot. "Chewing the Cud over Cædmon." *Old English Newsletter* 14 (1981), 39–40.

———. "Cædmon, the Clean Animal," *American Benedictine Review* 35 (1984), 194–203.

Williams, Raymond. *Marxism and Literature.* Oxford, 1977.
Wilson, David M., ed. *The Archaeology of Anglo-Saxon England.* Cambridge, 1967.
Winden, J. C. M. van. "The Early Christian Exegesis of 'Heaven and Earth' in Genesis 1,1." In *Romanitas et Christianitas. Studia Iano Henrico Waszink . . . oblata,* ed. W. den Boer, P.G. van der Nat, C.M.J. Sicking and J.C.M. van Winden, 371–82. Amsterdam, 1973.
Wood, Ian. "How Popular Was Medieval Devotion?" *Essays in Medieval Studies* 14 (1997), 1–14.
Wormald, Patrick. "Bede, Beowulf and the Conversion of the Anglo-Saxon Aristocracy." In *Bede and Anglo-Saxon England: Papers in Honour of the 1300th Anniversary of the Birth of Bede,* ed. Robert T. Farrell, 32–95. BAR 46. London, 1978.
———. Review of *Image and Power in the Archaeology of Early Medieval Britain,* ed. Hamerow and MacGregor. *English Historical Review* 119 (2004), 159–61.
Wrenn, C. L. "The Poetry of Cædmon." Sir Israel Gollancz Memorial Lecture, *Proceedings of the British Academy* 32 (1946), 277–95.
———. *A Study of Old English Literature.* London, 1967.
Wright, Neil. "Bede and Vergil." *Romano barbarica* 6 (1981–82), 361–79.
Wyss, M. "Saint-Denis (France), Du mausolée hypothetique du Bas-Empire à l'ensemble basilical carolingien." In *Death and Burial in Medieval Europe,* ed. Guy De Boe and Frans Verhaeghe, 111–14. Papers of the Medieval Europe Brugge 1997 conference, vol 2. Zellik, 1997.

Yorke, Barbara. "Lindsey: The Lost Kingdom Found?" In *Pre-Viking Lindsey,* ed. Alan Vince, 141–50. Lincoln, 1993.

Zachrisson, Torun. "The Holiness of Helgö." In *Excavations at Helgö XVI: Exotic and Sacral Finds from Helgö,* ed. Bo Gyllensvärd et al., 143–75. Kungl. Vitterhets Historie och Antikvitets Akademien. Stockholm, 2004.

Zaluckyj, Sarah, with Marge Feryok and John Zaluckyj. *Mercia: The Anglo-Saxon Kingdom of Central England.* Woonton, Herefordshire, 2001.

Zupitza, J. "Über den Hymnus Cädmons," *Zeitschrift für deutsches Altertum und deutswche Literatur,* 22 (1878), 210–23.

Index

Only notes containing references not in the text are indexed.

Abingdon (Oxon), 219
Adam (Genesis 2), 117-18
Adamnan (Irish monk), 128-29, vision of, 130-31, 136
Advent Lyrics (*Christ I*), 107-8n52
Ælfric, *Colloquy*, 142-43
Ælfwine (brother of Ecgfrith), 213
Æthelred (king), 136
Æthelthryth (queen), 75, 132, 136
Æthelwealh (king), 122
Æthelwulf, *De abbatibus* 98
Agriculture, 126-27, 143, 148
Aidan (bishop), 59n15, 73; bones of, 202
Aldhelm, as vernacular poet, 27-28, 60n21, vision of, 28, 31-32, 34-36, 49; *Enigmata*, 31
Alfred (king), 58, and poetry, 28; *Pastoral Care*, 144; *Soliloquies*, 148-49
Amulets, 116, 118, 125-26, 134; *see also* Magic
Animals,
 consumption of 170, 180-81, 183-85
 named by Adam, 117-18

Animal husbandry, 180-81, 183-85, 207; and magic, 134
Archaeology,
 changing methods of, 163-64
 expanding nature of, 145-46
 and textual evidence, 140-42, 153-57, 168-69
 interdisciplinary nature of, 141-42, 220
 and material culture, 114-16, 220
Architecture,
 biblical, 101
 and meditation, 101-2, 107
 as figure for creation, 91-92
 in Old English poems, 107-8
 see also Roof and Church
Aubrey, John (friend of Vaughan), 216
Auguries, 116; *see also* Magic.
Augustine of Hippo, St., 65-66, 68, 87, 99-100, 104

Bailey, Richard N., 8
Bamburgh (Northumberland), 158, 164
Baptism of South Saxons, 123-24
Barking (Essex), 111-12

Index

Barley, 126-27
Bawsey (Norfolk), 161
Bede
  death of, 56-57, 136
  descriptions of physical
    world by, 96-97
  education of, 60-61, 65
  goals as writer, 58
  Latin poetry of, 59-60
  rhetorical works, 61-62
  use of miracles by, 21, 83,
    112-13, 121-22, 139-40
  and Latin learning,
    61, 65-66, 68
  and monastic
    encyclopedia, 99-102
  and pagan literary
    culture, 62-68, 78
  and pastoral care in
    Northumbria, 53-55, 69-74
  and poetry, 56-68, 191-93
  and social mobility,
    213-14, 218, 220
  and song, 56-57, 62-63
  and the vernacular, 52-59, 68
  as reformer, 53-54, 68-
    79, 113, 128, 214
Works of:
  computistical works,
    83, 95-99, 106
  De arte metrica, 60, 62
  Historia Abbatum, 202
  Historia Ecclesiasticum
    (references to Cædmon's
    hymn or life are listed
    under those headings),
    Bede's rationale for
      composing, 74
    conversion, as theme in,
      42, 59, 89n16, 199
    everyday life in, 114,
      139-40, 146-47
    focus on Northumbrian
      Church reforms in,
      53-54, 68-71, 74, 77
    miracles in 112-15, 118;
      concentration of in Book
      4, 113. See also Adamnan,
      Barking, Chad, Cuthbert,
      Imma, Owine, Wilfrid.
    Old English translation
      of, 135, 147
    paganism seen in, 42,
      118-27, 134, 137-39
    revivalism in, 113
    as textual source for
      archaeologists, 153-54, 163
  De natura rerum liber, 83
  De schematibus et tropis, 61-62
  De tabernaculo, 105-6
  De templo, 72-74
  De temporibus, 83
  De temporum ratione,
    83, 97-98, 106-7
  Episistola ad Ecgbertum
    Episcopum, 52-56, 69-
    72, 74-75, 211-13
  Expositio Apocalypseos,
    101, 108-9
  Homily for Holy
    Saturday, 64-65
  In Ezram et Neemiam, 72, 74

Index

*In Lucae euangelium
    expositio*, 62-63
*In primum partem
    Samuhelis*, 63, 66-67
In principium Genesis 83,
    89-90, 96, 101-2
*In Regum librum XXX
    quaestiones*, 63n31
Vita sancti Cuthberti, 201
Benedict Biscop
    (abbot), 136, 202
Beowulf, creation themes in,
    81, 93-94; Grendel in, 218.
    see also Cædmon's hymn.
Bergh Apton (Norfolk) 219
Bessinger, J. B., 94
Bethel (1 Kings 16:34), 63
Blair, John, 70
Boniface, St. (bishop), 89n16
Bramford (Suffolk), 165
Brownlee, John (Scottish
    missionary), 30, 32
Buildings,
    archaeological evidence of,
        157, 160, 169, 173-74, 186-87
    monastic, 125-27 (Farne);
        129-30 (Coldingham); 186,
        203 (Whitby); 205 (Jarrow)
    figurative meaning of, 91, 93-
        99 (cosmos); 101-2, 205 (for
        community and stability);
        102, 148 (for God's work)
    and display, 157, 186
Burial customs, 164-66, 174-
    77, 187-88, 203-4, 219

Cædmon,
    death of, 32; 195-96, 199
    social standing of, 77-
        79, 200-1, 212-13
    education and training
        of, 23-24, 33-34
    social mobility of, 134,
        213-15; as transgressive,
        193-94, 199-200, 220
    his transformation, as
        Bede's theme, 194, 196
    and animals, 150-51
    and music, 135, 138
    and rumination, 78,
        83-84, 86, 91
    as "anti-guslar," 33
    as figure for settlement
        transformation, 150-52,
        166, 169, 175, 189-90
    as historical person, 17n8
    as teacher, 199-200
    as monk, 76-77, 83-
        84, 135, 150, 215
    as traditional poet, 17-
        20, 46, 48-50, 78
    as untraditional poet,
        33-34, 36, 42, 75
Cædmon's hymn,
    analogues to: 22-27
        (Mohammed's Call);
        197-98 (Psalm 8); 20-
        21 (St. Dunstan); 216-
        18 (Henry Vaughan)
    audience of, 25, 41, 46, 49, 81,
    Bede's paraphrase of,
        46-49, 86, 195

Index

building metaphor in, 91-92, 94-96, 98, 109-10
change and exchange as themes of, 192, 194
creation as theme in, 80-82
diction of and formulae in, 37-43, 192-94
general themes of, 88
hybridity of, 138-39
Northumbrian version of, 3, 38
orality and literacy in, 200, 216
sources of, 85-88
traditional poetic qualities of, 37, 40-42, 46, 49-50
translations of, 4-5
West Saxon version of, 3-4
and *Beowulf,* 43-44, 94
and Cædmon's identity as monk, 82-83
and *The Dream of the Rood,* 44-45;
and exchange, 192, 215
and labor, 135
and "monastic encyclopedia," 110
and monastic reform, 69, 78-79, 213
as literary criticism, 133
as origin of Anglo-Saxon poetry, 26, 41, 51 88n15
in context of Bede's other works, 52, 59, 68-69, 77-79
see also God, epithets for and Song, gift of.

Cædwalla (king), 122
Calder, Daniel G., 4
Carmen, describing Cædmon's compositions, 192; *see also Hymnus, Poema.*
Carruthers, Mary, 86
Cassian, John, *Conferences,* 102n42
Cedd (brother of Chad), 133-34
Cemeteries, 164-66, 174-75, 187-88, 203-5; *see also* Burial customs.
Chad. St. (abbot, bishop), 76, 132-34, 136
Christ and Satan, 102
Church, as image of universe, 98
Coifi (counselor), 120
Coins,
at Yeavering, 157
at Flixborough, 177, 183
at Whitby, 204, 210
Colloquy, The, 142-43
Coldingham (Berwick), destruction of, 78, 128-32, 136
Computus, 95, 97, 99,
and divine design, 102-4, 106
Convivium (*gebeorscip,* Anglo-Saxon feast), 32-33, 35, 135, 137, 177, 180-81, 186, 188
Cosmas Indicopleustes (Greek author), 93
Cosmos, in Anglo-Saxon thought, 95
Hellenic model of, 100
seen as church, 98

Index

in Bede, 96
in Bible and Mesopotamian texts, 93
Cramp, Rosemary, 153-54, 204, 211
Creation accounts, in Old English, 81; *see also Beowulf* and Cædmon's hymn.
Cultural studies, 114
Cuthbert, St. (bishop), 75, 125-27, 145, 201-2
Cuthbert (abbot), letter to Cuthwin, 56-58

Daniel (bishop), 89n16
David (king), 219
De computo dialogues (anon.), 103-5
Deor, 219-20
Discourse analysis, 192
Distré (Maine-et-Loire), 189
Dolphins, as feast food, 181
Dream of the Rood, The, 44-45
Dumfries (Scotland), 175
Dunbar (Lothian), 158, 164, 175
Dunstan, St., tale of, 20

Eadberht (bishop), 201
Easter, date of, 97
Ecgfrith (king), 202
Edwin (king), 120, 213
Egbert (archbishop), 52
Emporia (*wic*), 214-15; *see also* Trade.
Eorcenwold (bishop), 76
Eosterwine (retainer of Ecgfrith), 202-3
Eve (Genesis 2), 117; body of, 102

Fabula (pagan stories), 63, 78, 138
Falconry, 180-81, 186, 188
Faricius of Arezzo, *Vita S. Aldhelmi*, 28, 31, 60n21
Farne Islands, (Northumberland), 126-27, 201-2
Finan (archbishop), 201
Fishing, 123-25, 162-63
Flixborough (North Lincolnshire),
 animal consumption at, 180-81, 183-86
 archaeology of, 161, 165, 169-87, 205
 buildings at, 169, 173-74, 181, 186
 cemeteries at, 174-77
 coins at, 177, 183
 conspicuous consumption at, 177-81
 craft works at, 173, 181-84, 187-88
 dynamic character of, 171-74
 trade at, 177-78
 as "Conesby," 186
Food, and settlement archaeology, 143-45
 objects related to, 143-46, 169, 177, 219

Index

Franks Casket, 216

Galloway (Scotland), 175
Genesis A, 95
Gifts of Men, The, 107n52
Glassware, 169, 177-79, 182
God, epithets for (*frea, dryctin, uard*),
  in Cædmon's hymn,
    40-43, 45-49, 63
  in *The Dream of the Rood*, 45, 94
  as craft worker, 147
  as measurer, 102-3
Goffart, Walter, 74-75
Green Shiels (Holy Island), 207
Greenfield, Stanley B., 4
Gregory the Great, pope,
  letter to Mellitus, 59, 118-21
Moralia in Job, 103n42, 110
Gurevich, Aron, 116-18, 138

Hadrian (abbot), 75, 83
Hall, Anglo-Saxon "world hall,"
  as figure for church,
    98; for cosmos, 95;
    for stability, 107
  as theme in Cædmon's
    hymn, 92-95
  social meaning of, 93;
Hamage (Nord-Pas-de-Calais), 186
Hartlepool (Co. Durham),
  167, 175, 177-80, 184
  cemeteries at 164-65, 187
    (Cross Close, Church
    Walk, Gladstone Road)

Heliand (Old Saxon), 16
Heorot Hall (*Beowulf*), 93-94
Hereric (nephew of
  Edwin), 213
Herlihy, David, 145-46
Hiel (Bethelite in 1
  Kings 16:34), 63
Hild, abbess of Streanaeshalch
  and Whitby, 24-25, 31, 42,
  46, 152, 164, 167, 186
  death of, 114, 136, 213
  and monastic ideal, 75, 77
  at Hartlepool, 177-80, 212
Hines, John, 114-15, 148
Historia, Bede's concept of, 200
History of the Abbots (anon.), 201
Holsinger, Bruce W., 137
Hope-Taylor, Brian,
  119-20, 153-54
Hours, monastic (laudes), 82
Hrothgar (king in
  Beowulf), 93-94
Hunting, 180, 184, 186
Hymnus (Latin verse),
  191, 193, 194

Imma (thegn), 114, 140,
  218; as peasant, 213
Inscriptions, in metal or stone,
  157, 182, 185, 188, 203, 205
Interdisciplinarity, 7-9,
  192, 141-42, 220
Iona (Scotland), 184
Ipswich (Suffolk), trade at, 214
Ireland, Colin, 8
Irvine, Martin, 200

Index

James (deacon of Paulinus), 136
Jarrow (Tyne and Wear), 154, 184, 186, 201-2
 craft works and buildings at 205, 207
 site of, 204-5
Jerome, St., views on learning, 66
John (arch-chanter), 136

Kieckhefer, Richard, 138
Kiernan, Kevin, 80
Kobe, William, 29-30

Labor, manual, 148, 210
 in Eden, 117-18;
 monastic, 132-35
 representations of, 142-43, 147-48
Laity, education of, 54, 125, 133
Lamps, 97-98, 109, 112, 139
Lastingham (Yorkshire), 132
Latour, Bruno, 116
Lawson, Graeme, 219
Lester, G. A., 19
Life of Ceolfrith, 201
Lindisfarne (Northumbria),
 church at, 201
 scriptoria of, 207
 settlement at, 125-27, 167
 Viking raids on, 205
Literacy, 160, 163; and Cædmon, 200, 216
London, trade at, 214
Loveluck, Chris, 140-42, 205

Lyre, 219

Magic, 118, 125-26, 138; *see also* Amulets.
Market sites, 214-15; *see also* Emporia.
McCready, William, 139
Medical metaphor, 129
Meditation, monastic, 83-86, 87n11, 101; of Mohammed, 22-24; *see also Ruminatio*.
Metalwork, 159, 182, 187, 204-5, 214
Manuscripts:
 Cambridge, Corpus Christ College, MS 191, 145n57
 London, British Library, Cotton Tiberius C.vi, 103n; Cotton Tiberius B.v, 181
Mellitus (archbishop), 59, 118-19
Milfield (Northumberland), 158
Millstone (quernstone), 144-45, 204
Miracles, 1
 defined, 113
 distribution of in *Ecclesiastical History*, 113;
 of light, 111-12, 136, 139
 and popular consciousness, 118
 their power over objects, 113-14, 122
Mohammed (prophet), visions of, 22-23

Index

use of reveals gift, 24-26; *see also* Cædmon's hymn.
Monasteries,
  distinguished from secular estates, 156-57, 160, 162-64
  endowment of, 70, 167
  and trade, 157, 214-15
Monkwearmouth (Wearmouth) and Jarrow (Tyne and Wear), 154, 184
  archaeology of, 201, 204-5,
  coins at, 204
  construction of, 206-10
  economic functions of 207, 210-11
  founding of, 202
  and Roman villa, 211-12
Morningthorpe (Norfolk), 219
Musical instruments, 33, 219; *see also* Lyre and Harp
Music,
  Bede's language of, 192-93
  discourse of, 137
  secular, 136
  and the body, 137
  and medieval hymnody, 197-98
  as metaphor for Christian life, 195
  in *Historia Ecclesiastica*, Book 4, 135-37 147
  in Owine's vision, 132-35; s*ee also* Song

Natura, in Bede's works, 96-97

Natural world, and humans, 115-18, 121-23, 133-34
Neville, Jennifer, 91, 93-95
Noah's Ark, 101-2, 105
Ntsikana (Xhosa poet), 27
  and Cædmon, 31-32, 34-36, 49
  vision of, 29-30

Objects; *see* Things
Oethelwald (monk), 202
Offa (king), 182
Old English verse, as multimedia, 216.
Olsen, Bjornar, 114-16, 138, 142
Order of the World, The, 107
Orton, P. A., 5
Orton, Fred, 8
Oswald (king), 59n15
Oswiu (king), 167
Otium, Roman ideal, and Bede, 212
Owine (monk), 132-35, 147

Paganism; *see* Bede, Works of, *Historia Ecclesiasticum*
Palgrave, Francis, 16
Paulinus (bishop), 120, 136
Peers, C. R., 153-54
Penitentials, 128-29, 146
Pestell, Tom, 141
Plowing, 144-45
Poema (poem), 193-94
Popular culture, defined, 138
Portchester Castle (Hampshire), 160, 180-81

Index

Pottery, 177, 183
Principium creaturarum (theme of Cædmon's hymn), 88-92, 113, 147
Prophecy, Ntsikana's gift of, 29
Prosnostication, 144, 146
Psalm 8, as analogue for Cædmon's hymn, 197-98
Putta (bishop), 136

Quodvultdeus, *Liber promissionum*, 102
Qur'an, 22-26

Radford, C. Ralegh, 153-54, 186
Rædwald (king), 121
Rahtz, Philip, 153-54
Ramayana (Sanskrit epic), 20
Ray, Roger, 58
Recognitiones (pseudo-Clementine), 96
Relics, as memorials, 202
Revelation, Mohammed's gift of, 22-23, 25-26
River sytems, and craft zones, 163, 205, 207, 214
Roberts, Jane, 142
Roof, as figure, 95-96, 101 (for time and stability), 109-10 (for heaven); *see also* Architecture.
Ruffing, John, 142-43
Ruin, The, 10, 121n21
Ruminatio, 78, 83-84, 86, 91
Ruthwell Cross, 216

Saint-Florent de Saumur (Anjou), 189
Saul and Jonathan (1 Samuel 13-14), 66-68
Science, medieval, 80-81, 104
Scop, as slave (*þeow*), 218
Scopcræft, of Cædmon, 78
Secular estates,
 compared to monasteries, 155-57
 archaeological characteristics of, 157-59
Serris (France), 176
Settlement archaeology,
 and social status, 151-52
 history of, 153-63, 168-69
 interpretive problems in, 168-69
 use of textual labels in, 153-56, 162-64
Settlements, early medieval,
 archaeology of, 153-54
 dynamic nature of, 152-53, 163, 166-68, 188-90
 royal versus monastic, 140-41, 162-64, 166-67
 rural, 162-63
 in England, compared to France and Germany, 153, 160, 167-68, 175, 186, 189
 in Gaul, 204
 on the North Sea, 153, 157
Sexual sins, 128-29, 131, 211
Slaves, emancipation of, 194
Snape, Suffolk, 219

Index

Social identity, and archaeological evidence, 188-98
Song,
  gift of, 19-20, 25, 194, 199-200, 218
  pagan, 63, 136, 194
  Latin terms for, 192-93
South Saxons, 122-24
Southampton, trade at, 214
Speech acts, 192, 195
Sprouston (Borders), 11
St. Bertin (Nord-Pas-de-Calais), 167
Staffelsee (Germany), 167, 189
Stars, as candles, 99n34
Staunch Meadow (Suffolk), 161, 165, 175
Stenton, Sir Frank, 120
Stone sculpture, at monastic settlements, 157, 185-86, 203, 205
Streaneshalch; *see* Whitby
Stephen of Ripon (Eddius Stephanus), 136
Styli, at Flixborough, 157, 161-63; at Whitby, 204
Suger (abbot), 148
Sutton Hoo, 219
Synod of Whitby, 75

Textiles and clothmaking,
  at Coldingham, 130-31
  at Flixborough, 182, 184
  at Whitby, 204
  at Yeavering, 159
Theodore of Tarsus (archbishop), 75, 136
Things (ordinary objects),
  Christian views of, 116-19, 127, 133-34, 147-48
  superstitions about, 123-24
  and cultural memory, 114-15
  and miracles, 113-14, 139-40
  and words, 142, 145-47
  as symbols, 115-16, 121-22
Thwing (East Yorkshire), 165
Time, beginning of, 90-91, 97-101, 110; *see also Principium creaturarum.*
Torhtgyth (nun), 76
Trade networks, 144-45, 157, 159-61, 163, 205, 214-15
  and proto-urban communities, 210-11; *see also* Emporia.
Trumberht (monk), 133

Valmiki (*Ramayana*), 20
Vaughan, Henry (poet), 216-18
Vellum, production of, 185
Vézelay, France, 148
Vikings, and material objects, 115-16
Vita S. Aldhelmi, 28-28

Wallis, Faith, 205
Wanderer, The, 107, 120-21
Ward, Benedicta, 21, 112, 140
Wælsingas (Burgundian

legend), 218
Water, and firmament, 96
Waterways, and trade, 158-59
West Hythe (Kent), 214
Wearmouth; *see*
  Monkwearmouth
Wheat, 126-27
Whitby (Yorkshire; taken
  as Streaneshalch), 201
  excavations of, 203-4
  settlement of, 152, 167, 175
  size of estate at, 212
Whithorn (Scotland), 175, 184
Wicken Bonhunt
  (Essex), 160, 180-81
Widsith, 219
Wieland, Gernot, 32
Wilfrid (bishop), 75,
  122-23, 136
William of Malmesbury,
  Gesta Pontificum Anglorum,
  28, 31, 34-35, 60n21
Williams, Joseph
  (missionary), 32
Williams, Raymond, 117n12
Wormald, Patrick, 141
Wrenn, C. L., 1, 218
Writing, 182; *see also* Styli
  and Inscriptions.

Yeavering (Northumbria), 119-
  21, 154, 157-59, 165, 205-6
York, trade at, 177, 214

www.ingramcontent.com/pod-product-compliance
Lightning Source LLC
Chambersburg PA
CBHW061438300426
44114CB00014B/1732